IMAGES
of America

SOUTH BATON ROUGE

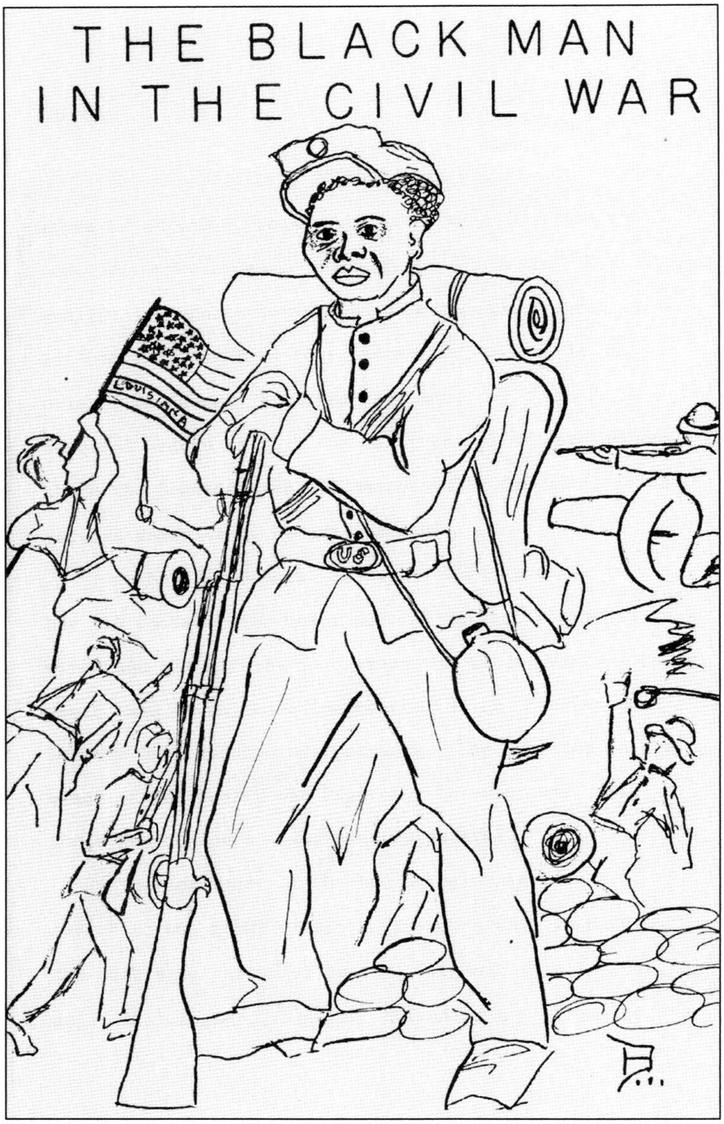

Black participation in military conflicts goes back many generations. People of African ancestry in America were on battlefields prior to and during the American Revolution. Black men played important roles in defeating the British and making an independent American a reality even when many people of color remained in bondage. Black men and women were also important participants in the Civil War. Blacks in Baton Rouge were among the many valiant participants. Baton Rouge was the site of important battles and also served as a refuge for former slaves as the Union army swept through the Deep South. Documentation of the horrors of slavery, including photographs of badly bruised slaves, were used to win over the hearts and minds of other Americans. (Courtesy of East Baton Rouge Parish Public Library Digital Archive.)

On the Cover: This c. 1910 photograph includes children in front of a school. It is part of a special collection on free people of color in Baton Rouge. This particular image is one of the artifacts related to the Turnbull family, who were among the free people of color in Baton Rouge. It appears to show African American male and female students and adults who likely served as teachers or in some other supportive role. Blacks in South Baton Rouge have a long history of creating their own educational opportunities when laws and social norms placed formal and informal restrictions on their access to predominately white educational institutions. The creation of schools in South Baton Rouge, which led to the founding of historic McKinley High School, is just one example. Members of the Turnbull family attended and graduated from McKinley High School. (Courtesy of Dudley Turnbull and Family Papers, MSS 2907, Free People of Color, LSU Libraries.)

IMAGES
of America

SOUTH BATON ROUGE

Lori Latrice Martin, PhD,
and Raymond A. Jetson

ARCADIA
PUBLISHING

ISBN 978-1-4671-2472-0

Published by Arcadia Publishing
Charleston, South Carolina

Printed in the United States of America

Library of Congress Control Number: 2016953890

For all general information, please contact Arcadia Publishing:
Telephone 843-853-2070
Fax 843-853-0044
E-mail sales@arcadiapublishing.com
For customer service and orders:
Toll-Free 1-888-313-2665

Visit us on the Internet at www.arcadiapublishing.com

To the participants of the historic 1953 Baton Rouge bus boycott, whose commitment to social justice forever transformed the community from within

Contents

ACKNOWLEDGMENTS

The authors wish to extend their deepest appreciation and gratitude to the following individuals and organizations for their contributions to *South Baton Rouge*: East Baton Rouge Parish Public Library, Main Library; Hill Memorial Library, Louisiana State University; the Toni Morrison Society; McKinley High School Alumni Center; Baton Rouge Commemoration Committee; Tat Yau; Jahaan Chandler; and Barbara and Elvin Dalcourt.

INTRODUCTION

Founded in 1699, Baton Rouge was the site of many historic events and home to many people, including many of African ancestry. South Baton Rouge is a historic African American community within Baton Rouge, the capital of Louisiana. South Baton Rouge was one of the first places African Americans could receive a high school education in the state. The community was also the site of the nation's first successful bus boycott. When laws restricted where African Americans could live, work, learn, and play, South Baton Rouge was a refuge. African American restaurants, theaters, gas stations, and other businesses populated the community, and change makers, including African American lawyers, judges, clergy, educators, and the city's first African American nurses, help to sustain the community through the end of legal segregation and beyond.

The city of Baton Rouge dates back nearly 200 years. Between 1817 and the early part of the 20th century, Baton Rouge was a relatively small town bound by the Spanish Town neighborhood, National Cemetery, the Mississippi River, and Beauregard Town. During the era of slavery, many blacks were enslaved, while some others were free. Regardless of their enslavement status, blacks in Baton Rouge in the early 1800s and beyond were treated as chattel or as second-class citizens. The Civil War had a tremendous impact on the city.

Race has always played an important part of the lives of Americans, and South Baton Rouge is no exception. A recent report, "How Did We Get Here: A Brief History of Black Baton Rouge," written by law professor Christopher Tyson in April 2016 as part of the Urban Congress, provides an overview of historic moments in African American history in Baton Rouge. The report provides the context and backdrop for understanding the experiences of African Americans, or blacks, (we use the terms interchangeably to refer to anyone of African ancestry) in South Baton Rouge in particular. The report focuses on the early years, the arrival of Standard Oil, the civil rights movement, and the battle to desegregate schools and concludes with the state of black Baton Rouge today.

According to "How Did We Get Here," Baton Rouge was under Union control by the spring of 1862. Blacks fought during the Civil War in Baton Rouge, and the city was also a haven for slaves seeking freedom. From the years leading up to the Civil War through the years immediately following the conflict, the black population in Baton Rouge almost doubled, and the black residents endured the promises and failures of Reconstruction. For example, while black males in Baton Rouge could vote after the adoption of the Fifteenth Amendment and black males held important elected positions, limitations were still placed on access to valued resources such as wealth, status, and power. Over 40 black representatives occupied seats in the Louisiana State Senate in 1868, but the compromise that ended Reconstruction in 1877 turned back the hands of progress, and by 1898, the report notes, "most blacks were totally disenfranchised by the new state constitution . . . and were excluded from politics for decades."

In *South Baton Rouge*, we examine many of these events, places, and people, documenting the rich and complex history of identified and unidentified men, women, and children; civic groups, associations, and volunteer organizations; and faith-based African American institutions that planted the seeds of hope and laid the foundation of faith that today benefits African Americans in South Baton Rouge and beyond.

We include notable families, churches, schools, and businesses in South Baton Rouge during the period under study, followed by a series of related images. The images include moments in time from descendants of the Turnbull family and historic houses of worship. *South Baton Rouge* also explores the role of blacks in South Baton Rouge in the fight to ensure that people of color received equal treatment under the law. The images reflect that struggle and include photographs related to school desegregation, the financing of Brooks Park, and the Baton Rouge bus boycott and other acts of civil disobedience.

A special honor was bestowed upon South Baton Rouge by the Toni Morrison Society on Saturday, February 6, 2016. South Baton Rouge was selected as a site for a commemorative bench. The society's Bench by the Road Project is an international outdoor memorial. The project was created as a way to remember the experiences of people of African ancestry across the globe. While there are many monuments and memorials devoted to many groups and events, noted author Toni Morrison lamented the absence of memorials to African slaves and their descendants. The Bench by the Road Project attempts to right this historic wrong. South Baton Rouge was selected as one of only 20 locations on the planet so honored for its role in the history of the African American experience. Photographs from the historic event are included in *South Baton Rouge*. The bench was placed at McKinley High School Alumni Center, which is the former site of McKinley High School, the first high school for African American boys and girls in southeastern Louisiana.

We conclude with yet another historic event for black South Baton Rouge. In January 2016, South Baton Rouge hosted the nation's first black president, Barack Obama, at McKinley High School. We also address the significance and implications of what is contained within these pages for the past, present, and future generations. Images captured during the historic visit are included in the final chapter.

It is our sincere hope the words and images presented give readers a greater appreciation for the struggles and triumphs of blacks in South Baton Rouge then and now. It is also out hope that our book serves as a catalyst for others to—in the words of an old proverb—share the tale of African Americans in South Baton Rouge from the perspective of the lion and not the hunter.

One

Historic South Baton Rouge Individuals and Families

South Baton Rouge is an important area of Louisiana's capital city. South Baton Rouge is home to many lifelong residents, historic businesses and buildings, cultural traditions, noted faith-based institutions and clergy, sports legends, precedent-setting protests, and important educational institutions. While much is written about the history of neighboring New Orleans and the section of the city to the north, less is written about the history of South Baton Rouge. The few works tend to focus on a wide variety of groups and fail to give each group under study due consideration. Additionally, the relatively few works on South Baton Rouge are narrow in focus and exclude the history and experiences of many people and places, restricting an understanding of the unique experiences of important groups and neighborhoods, while current books and articles about South Baton Rouge tend to focus on very limited historical periods. *South Baton Rouge* addresses these oversights through an examination of the experiences of people of African ancestry in the communities south of Florida Boulevard from the enslavement era through the 1970s. Over this time period, many of the social institutions in the city in general and South Baton Rouge in particular were both attempting to respond to and to push back against formal and informal mandates to desegregate many areas of public life, including in schools and sports.

Despite experiencing racial oppression, many blacks thrived. Evidence documenting the abilities of people of color to thrive during and after slavery in Baton Rouge can be found in the experiences of families. In most societies and within many groups, the family is one of the most significant social institutions of all. In the case of people of African ancestry who were involuntarily brought to the present-day United States to be exploited for labor and treated as chattel rather than human begins, the enslavement system thrived and depended on the dissolution of black families. Consequently, people of African ancestry with familial, clan, and ethnic ties were often purposefully separated. The threat of such separation was used by those in positions of authority to impose their will on the enslaved population. It was, unfortunately, not uncommon for infants to be torn from their mother's breasts or for siblings or fathers and sons to be sold to households, farms, and plantations miles apart from one another. Marriage among slaves was in many cases not recognized, and the status of children born to slaves followed that of the mother, regardless of the status of the biological father, which not only gave slaveholders an economic incentive to control black reproduction but also gave some an economic incentive to rape black women. There were no consequences under a legal system that could not fathom that raping a woman of African ancestry was even possible, because black women were not presumed to have the purity and virtuosity many assumed was inherent in white women; rather, black women were characterized as highly sexualized, as evidenced in the often-cited Jezebel caricature.

During the enslavement period, Louisiana, including South Baton Rouge, was home to free people of color. Despite recent efforts by a nationally known publishing company to describe slaves in a high school textbook for students in Texas as immigrant "workers" on agricultural plantations, scholarly research is very clear that the institution of slavery was both peculiar and brutal. The brutality and inhumanity of the race-based chattel slave system were also far-reaching; slavery impacted the lives of even free people of color, who were in Louisiana as early as the 1720s. Prior to the Civil War, Louisiana had the largest population of free people of color in the nation. Irrespective of their status as free people, people of color in the state did not enjoy the same rights and privileges as members of the dominant racial group. Free blacks during much of the 1700s were legally prohibited from cohabitating with slaves and from aiding fugitive slaves. In fact, it was not out of the ordinary for the dominant racial group to use free blacks to punish enslaved blacks. The passing of the Louisiana colony from the hands of the French to the Spanish, along with manumissions that followed the American Revolution, contributed to the growth of the free black population in the state. "Slaves, Free Blacks, and Race in the Legal Regimes of Cuba, Louisiana, and Virginia: A Comparison," an article in the *North Carolina Law Review* comparing the enslavement systems of Cuba, Virginia, and Louisiana, describes the ability of slaves to win their freedom in Louisiana during the 1800s as exceptionable. "Compared to other states in the United States, the lingering influence of civil law in Louisiana allowed greater rights of manumission, including the right to sue for freedom without a next friend or guardian ad litem. The Supreme Court of Louisiana confirmed in an 1816 ruling that self-purchase was still enforceable in the state. 266 Louisiana did follow the U.S. southern trend of increasing restrictions on manumission in the nineteenth century, passing laws requiring freed slaves to leave the state and new regulations on free people of color, culminating in re-enslavement laws in the 1850s." The free black population made important contributions to Louisiana and to the nation during the antebellum era and in the eras that followed. This chapter looks at the experiences of free people of color in South Baton Rouge through photographs and other artifacts belonging to the Dudley Turnbull family. The Turnbull family were members of the black Catholic community. Members of the family also and attended and graduated from the first high school for blacks in the state, McKinley High School, located in South Baton Rouge. Photographs of important events in the lives of the Turnbull family, such as religious rites of passage, are included in this chapter along with photographs of other residents from Civil War veterans and beyond.

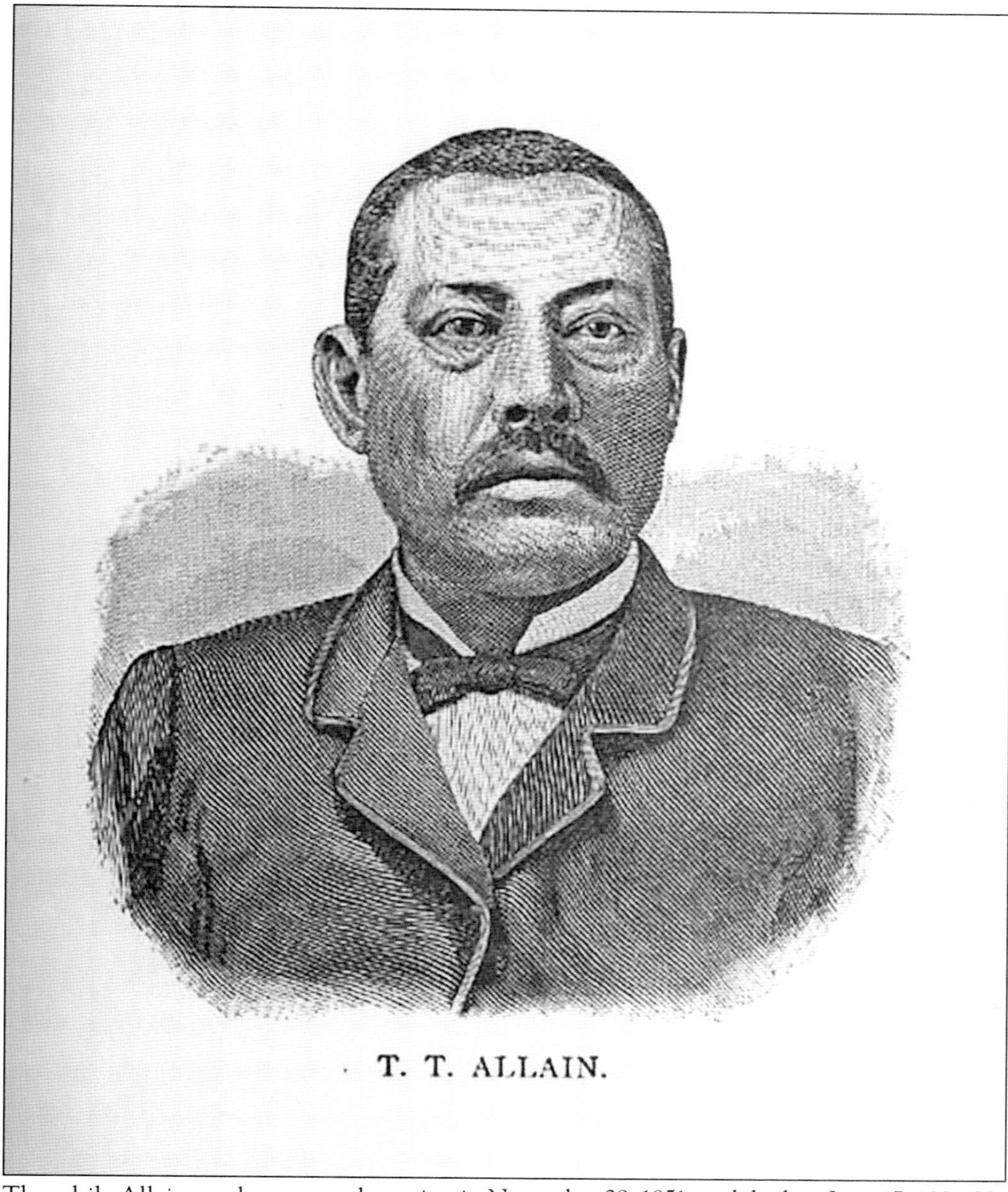

Theophile Allain was born on a plantation in November 29, 1851, and died on June 17, 1921. He is buried in the historic St. Joseph Catholic Cemetery in South Baton Rouge. Allain was born a slave. His mother was a slave, and his father was a slave owner who treated him as a free person. He traveled with his father to Europe and was educated in the North. Allain went on to become a black farmer, merchant, and politician. He was elected to the Louisiana State Legislature in 1870 but denied a seat due to balloting irregularities. Allain served as election supervisor in 1872, as a member of the Louisiana House of Representatives from 1872 through 1874, and in the Louisiana Senate from 1874 until 1880. He served in the Louisiana House again between 1881 and 1890. (Courtesy of Documenting the American South, University Library, University of North Carolina at Chapel Hill.)

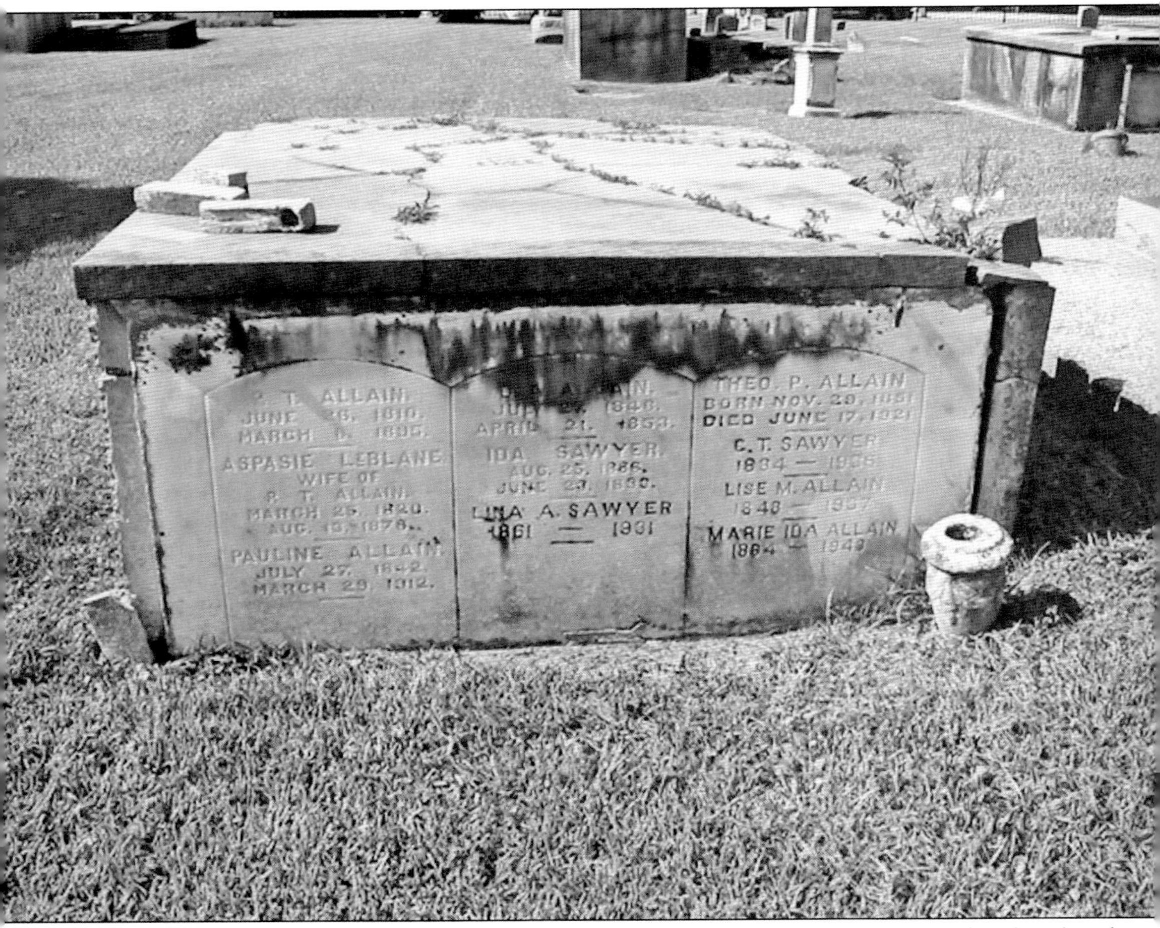

Theophile Allain was not only a successful business owner, farmer, and politician, he also played an integral role in establishing Southern University. Southern University is a historically black university in north Baton Rouge, and it was the only institution in the city for blacks pursuing postsecondary degrees until the 1960s. Louisiana State University is located in South Baton Rouge but prohibited blacks from enrolling in classes or even stepping foot on campus. Many college-educated residents of South Baton Rouge are graduates of Southern University. Theophile Allain, whose final resting place is shown here, supported a state-supported black institution even when some influential blacks believed the establishment of the institution of higher learning represented a concession to racial segregation. It was not uncommon for blacks to establish their own institutions when excluded from predominately white institutions, including colleges and universities. (Courtesy of Findagrave, burial: St. Joseph Catholic Cemetery.)

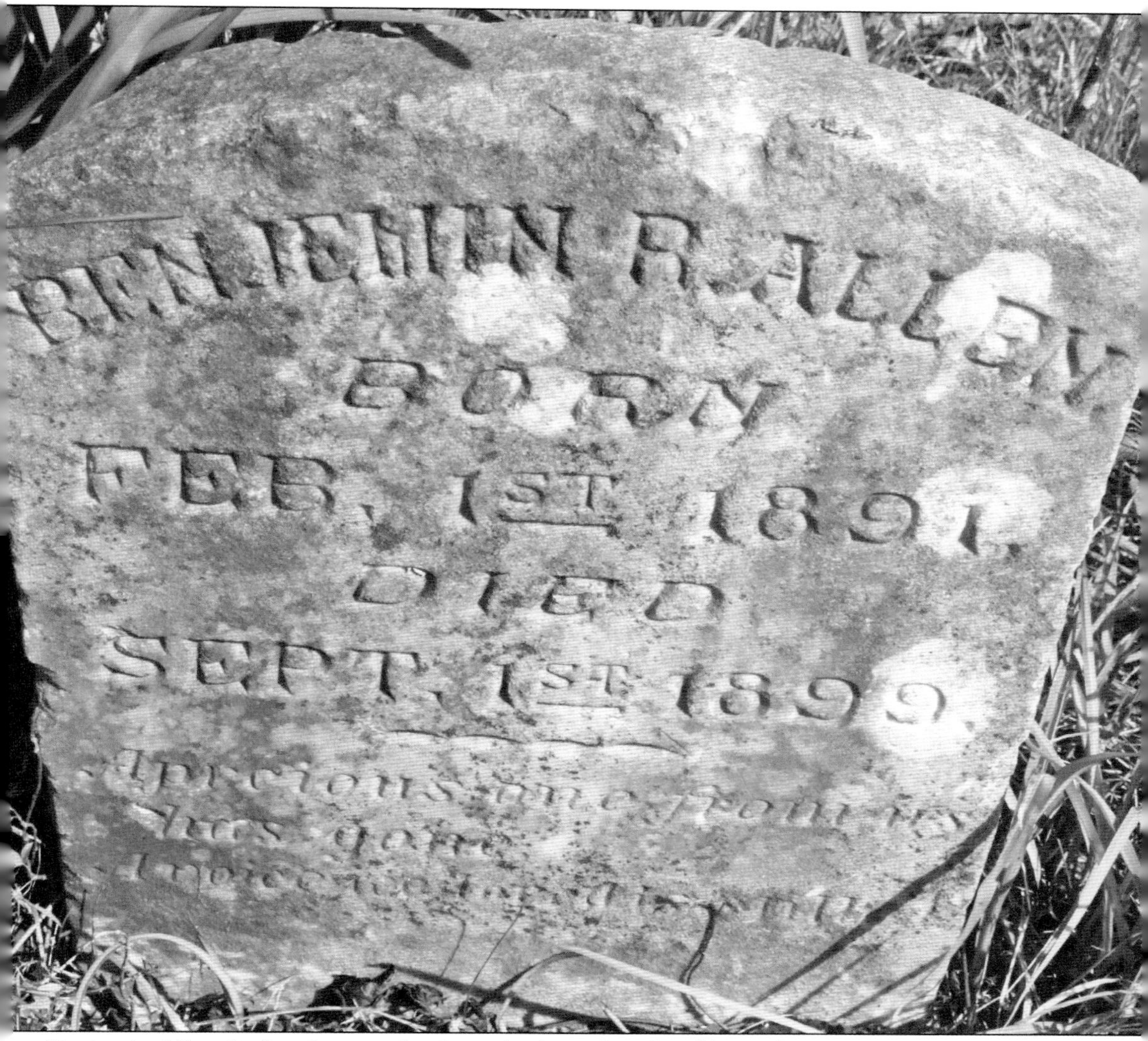

Benjamin Allen died at the age of eight and is buried in the oldest African American cemetery in Baton Rouge. Sweet Olive Cemetery was established in 1898 by a fraternal organization. It is believed the first burials took place prior to 1898. Allen is buried alongside many well-known former residents of Baton Rouge in the cemetery in South Baton Rouge. Mattie Caney is also buried in this historic cemetery. Carney was one of the best known seamstresses in Baton Rouge during her lifetime. She died in 1937 in Houston while visiting her husband, but she served the city of Baton Rouge as a seamstress for 25 of her 45 years. She was described as a leading woman in town. Women met in her South Thirteenth Street home regularly. Born on Bayou Sara Road, Carney made dresses for many black residents for their christening, their first day of school, and graduation. Carney's funeral was held at Wesley Chapel Methodist Episcopal Church, a black congregation, and both blacks and whites were in attendance. (Courtesy of Findagrave, burial: Sweet Olive Cemetery.)

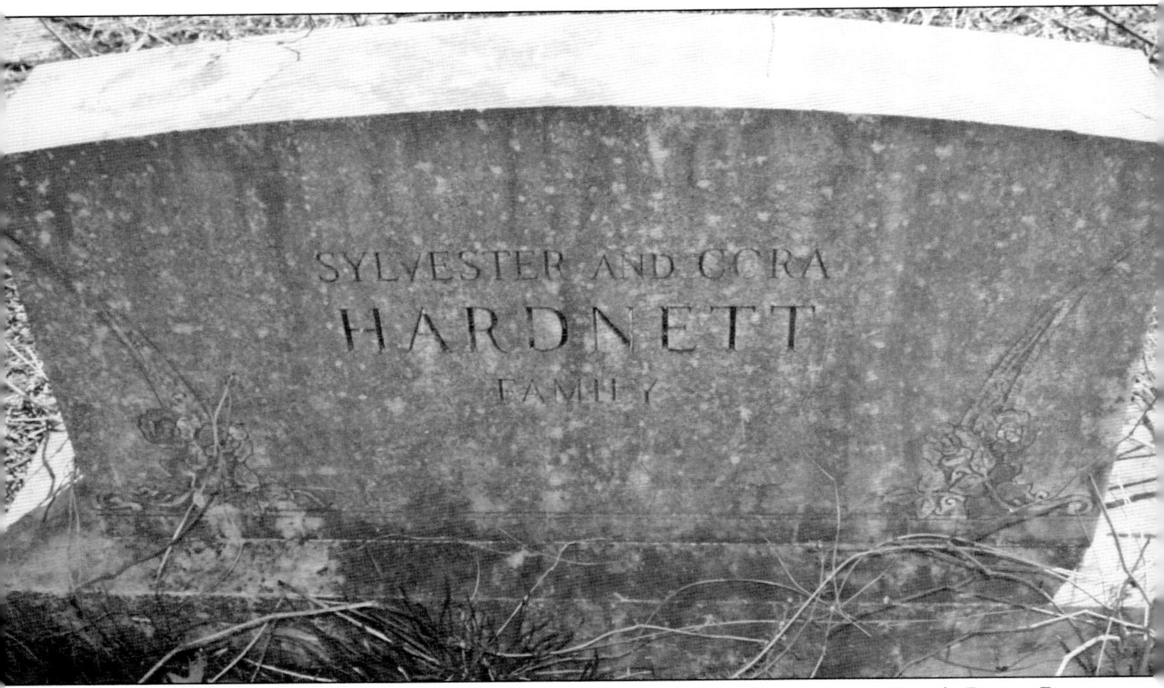

Sylvester Hardnett is interred at the historic Sweet Olive Cemetery in South Baton Rouge. Hardnett was born a slave and lived until the age of 90 in 1939. His funeral was held at St. Mark's Church and was attended by blacks and whites at a time when such race mixing even during religious services was not common. Prominent white residents even visited his house to pay their respects. Sylvester was a fixture in court. He sat on the front row bench listening to cases without fail for more than a decade before a heart attack made it physically impossible for him to attend. When asked why he attended court proceedings so faithfully, Hardnett reported that he liked to listen and learn. Hardnett is just one of the many interesting people buried in Baton Rouge's first cemetery for African Americans. (Courtesy of Findagrave, burial: Sweet Olive Cemetery.)

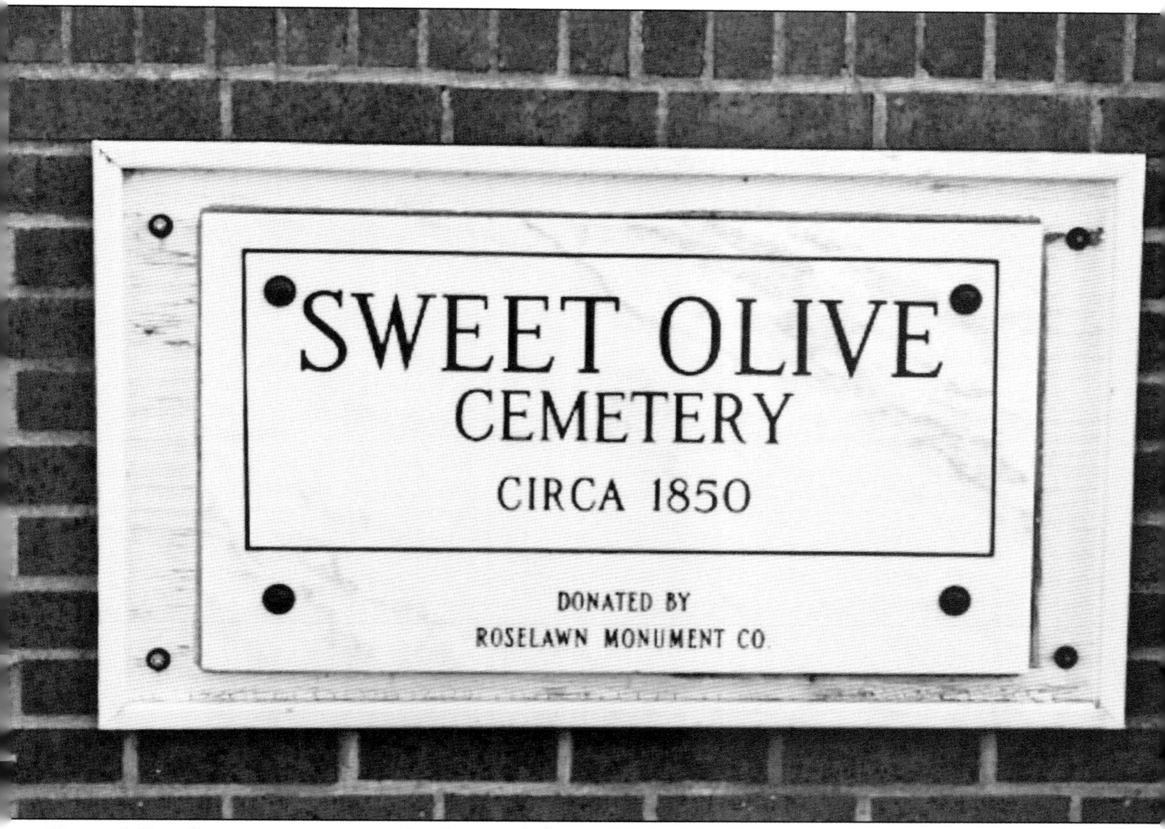

Sweet Olive Cemetery was one of only two African American cemeteries in Baton Rouge until 1926, and it was the closest to the center of 19th-century Baton Rouge. First African Baptist Benevolent Society and Sons and Daughters of Mount Pleasant Baptist Church were the official incorporators. The cemetery is bordered by Northern Boulevard, Delphine and Baxter Streets, Louisiana Avenue, and South Twenty-Second Street. Grave markers ranged from very elaborate designs to homemade markers. Ada Pollock-Bludon, founder of a black boardinghouse in South Baton Rouge, is one of the white people buried in the cemetery. The cemetery was closed due to overcrowding, financial problems, and legal disputes. Appeals for state support were rejected on the basis that blacks should fund their own cemeteries at the same time the state was funding Confederate cemeteries. (Courtesy of Findagrave, burial: Sweet Olive Cemetery.)

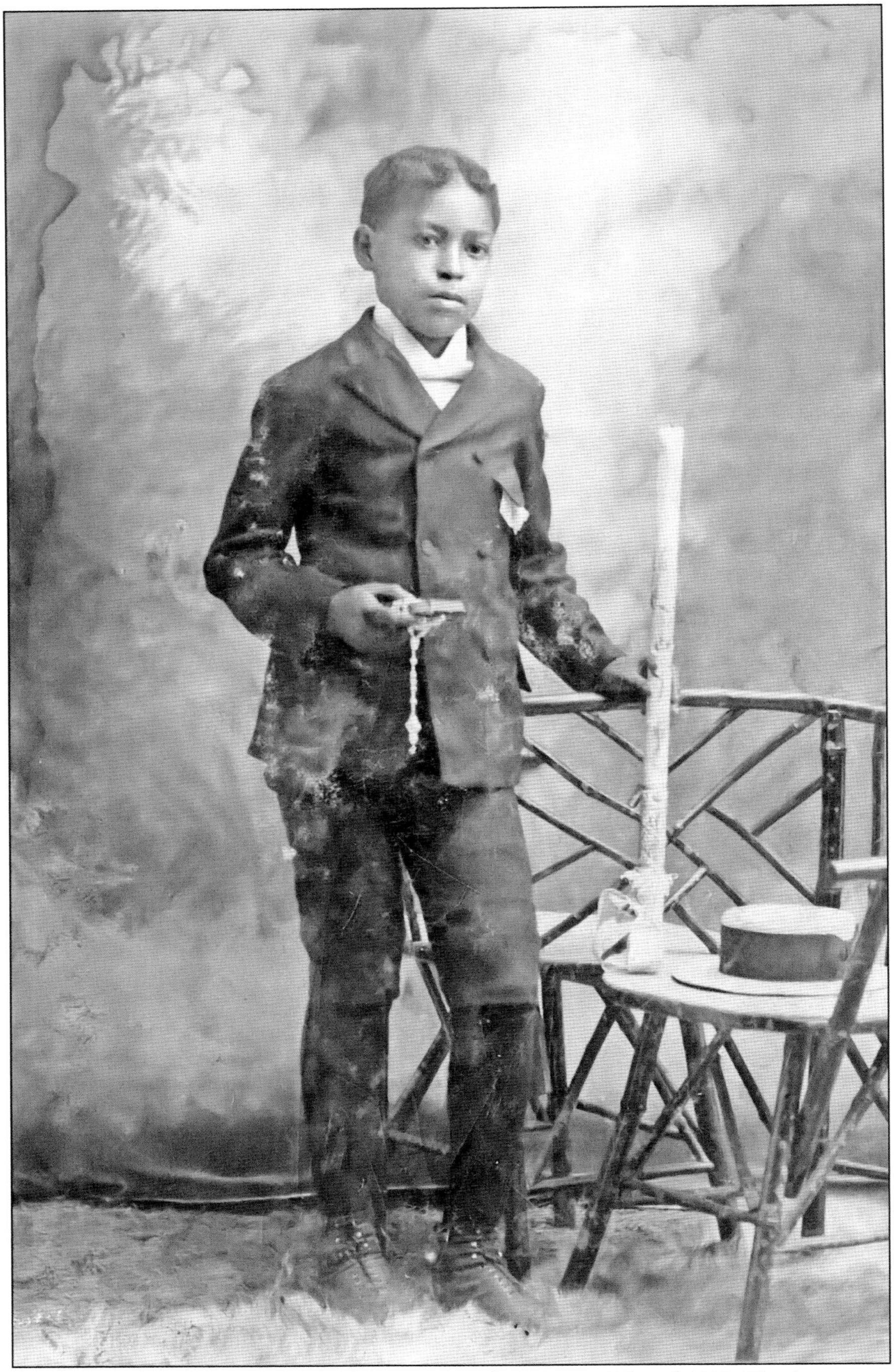

This photograph of a young boy was taken sometime between 1895 and 1910. The boy is a member of the Turnbull family. The Turnbulls were among the many free people of color who lived in Baton Rouge, attended what would become McKinley High School, and were devout Catholics. Note the rosary beads. The photograph commemorates the youngster's Holy Communion. (Courtesy of Dudley Turnbull and Family Papers, MSS 2907, Free People of Color, LSU Libraries.)

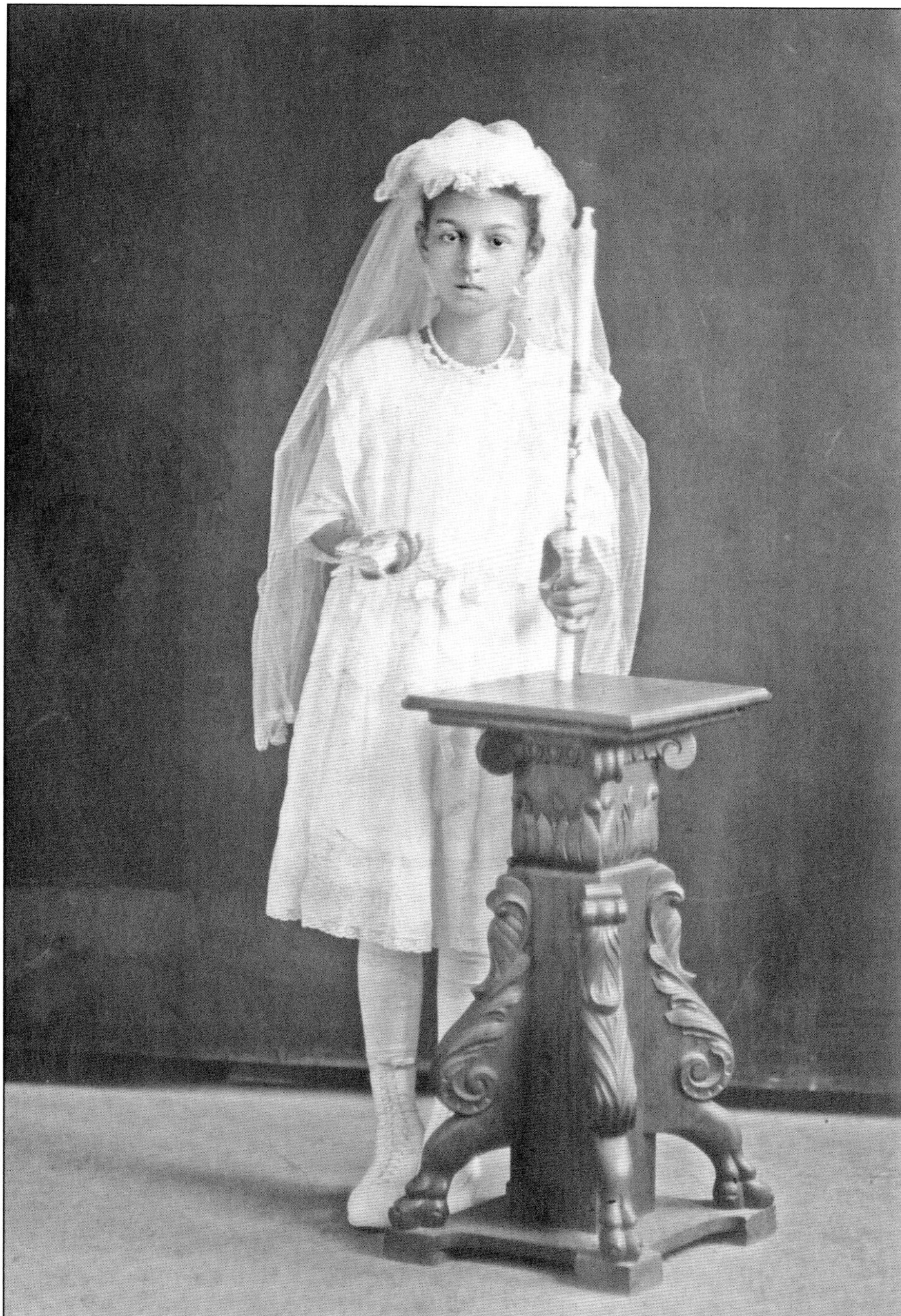

Catholicism plays an important role in the lives of many Americans across the nation, and this was the case in the latter part of the 19th century and the early part of the 20th century in Baton Rouge. A young female member of the Dudley Turnbull family is pictured here showing what young people of color wore on the occasion of their Holy Communion. (Courtesy of Dudley Turnbull and Family Papers, MSS 2907, Free People of Color, LSU Libraries.)

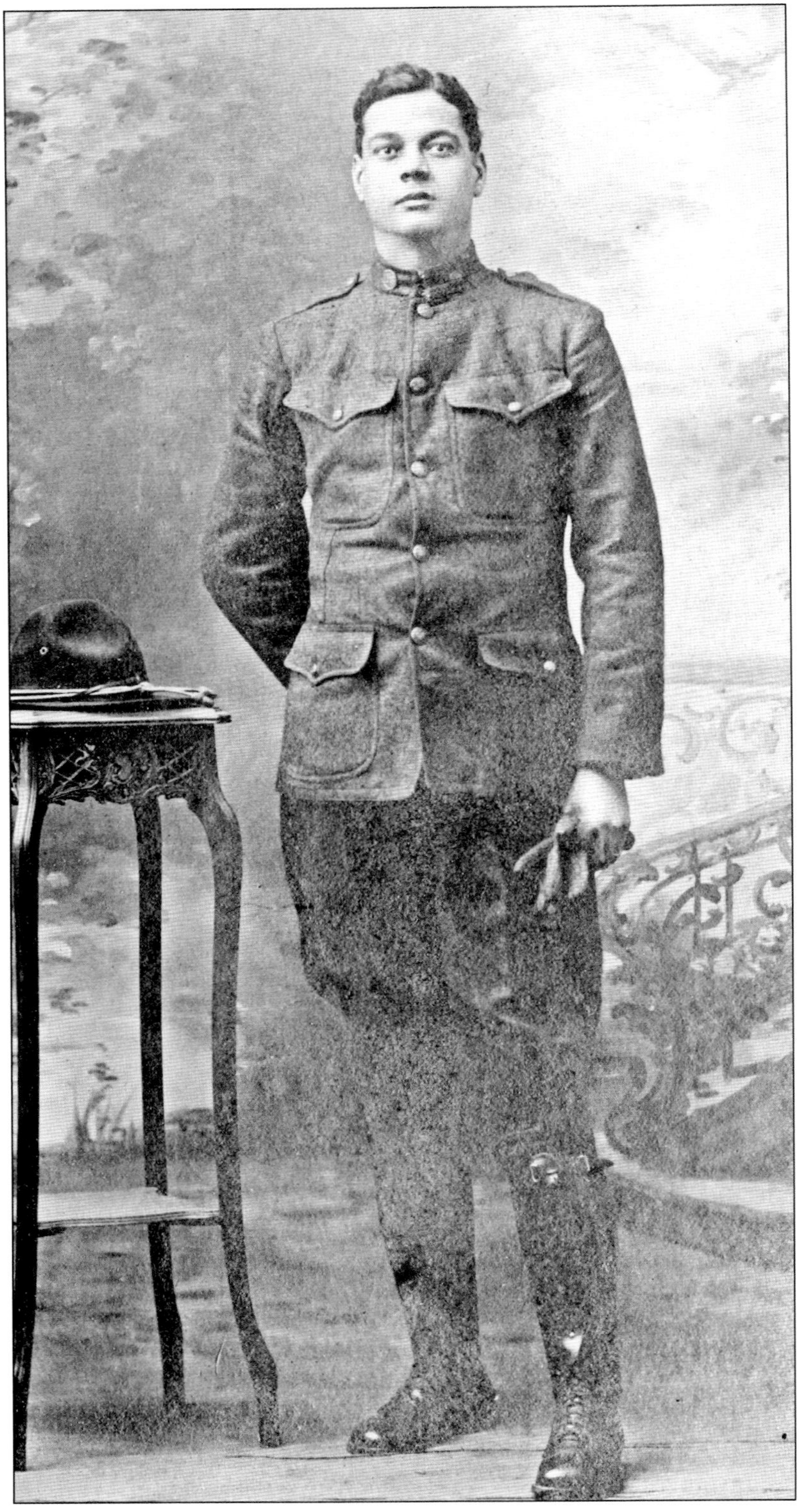

Alex Hebert was one of many to serve during World War I. He was the brother of Juanita Hebert Turnbull, and his ancestors were free people of color from Baton Rouge. Historians believe he lived in South Baton Rouge for a time. Hebert is buried in the historic St. Joseph Cemetery, where other members of the Turnbull family are buried. (Courtesy of Dudley Turnbull and Family Papers, MSS 2907, Free People of Color, LSU Libraries.)

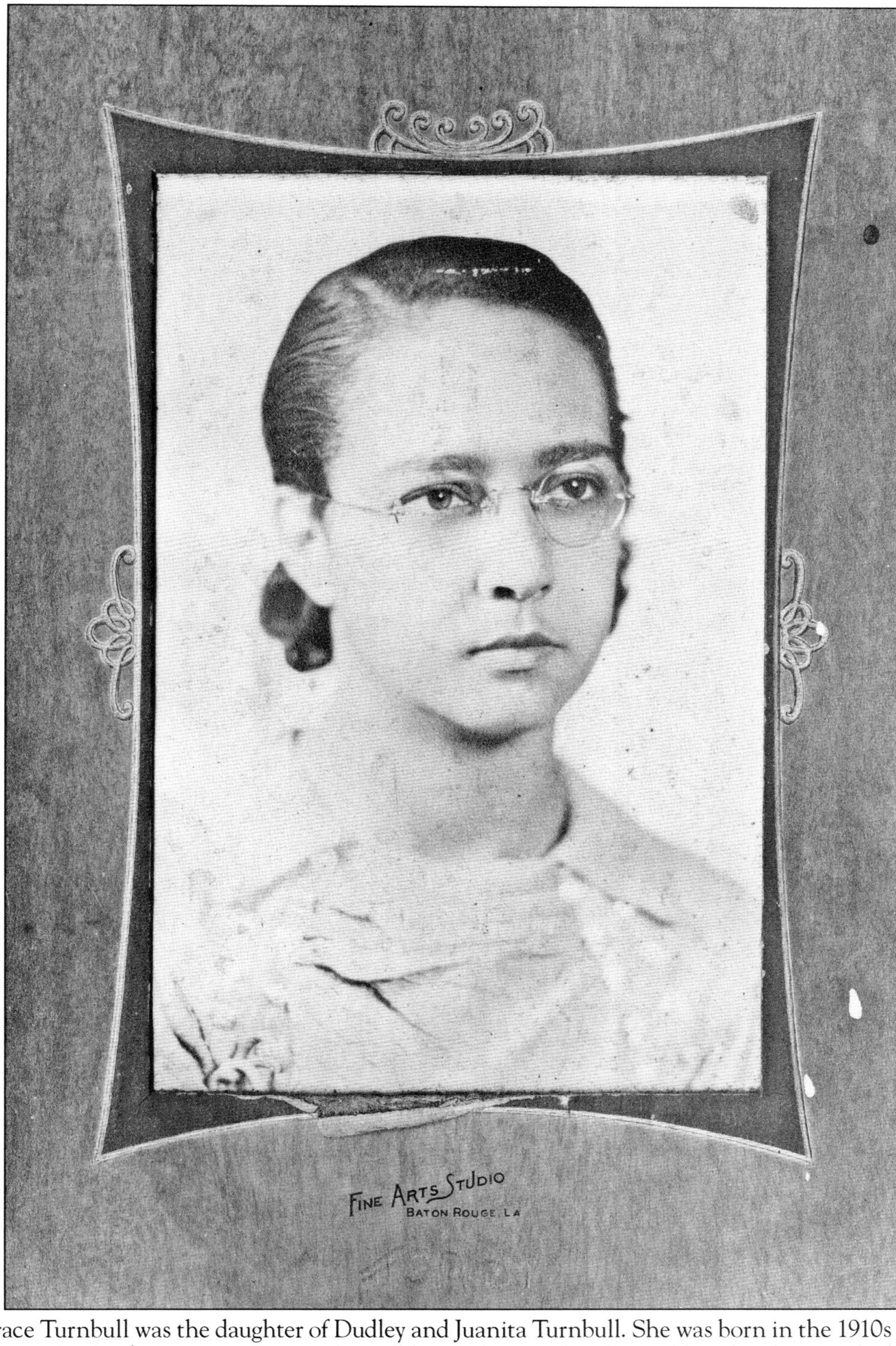

Grace Turnbull was the daughter of Dudley and Juanita Turnbull. She was born in the 1910s in a home valued at $3,500. Census records note that at the age of 17 she could read and write. She lived with her two sisters and three brothers. This photograph was taken in the early 1940s. (Courtesy of Dudley Turnbull and Family Papers, MSS 2907, Free People of Color, LSU Libraries.)

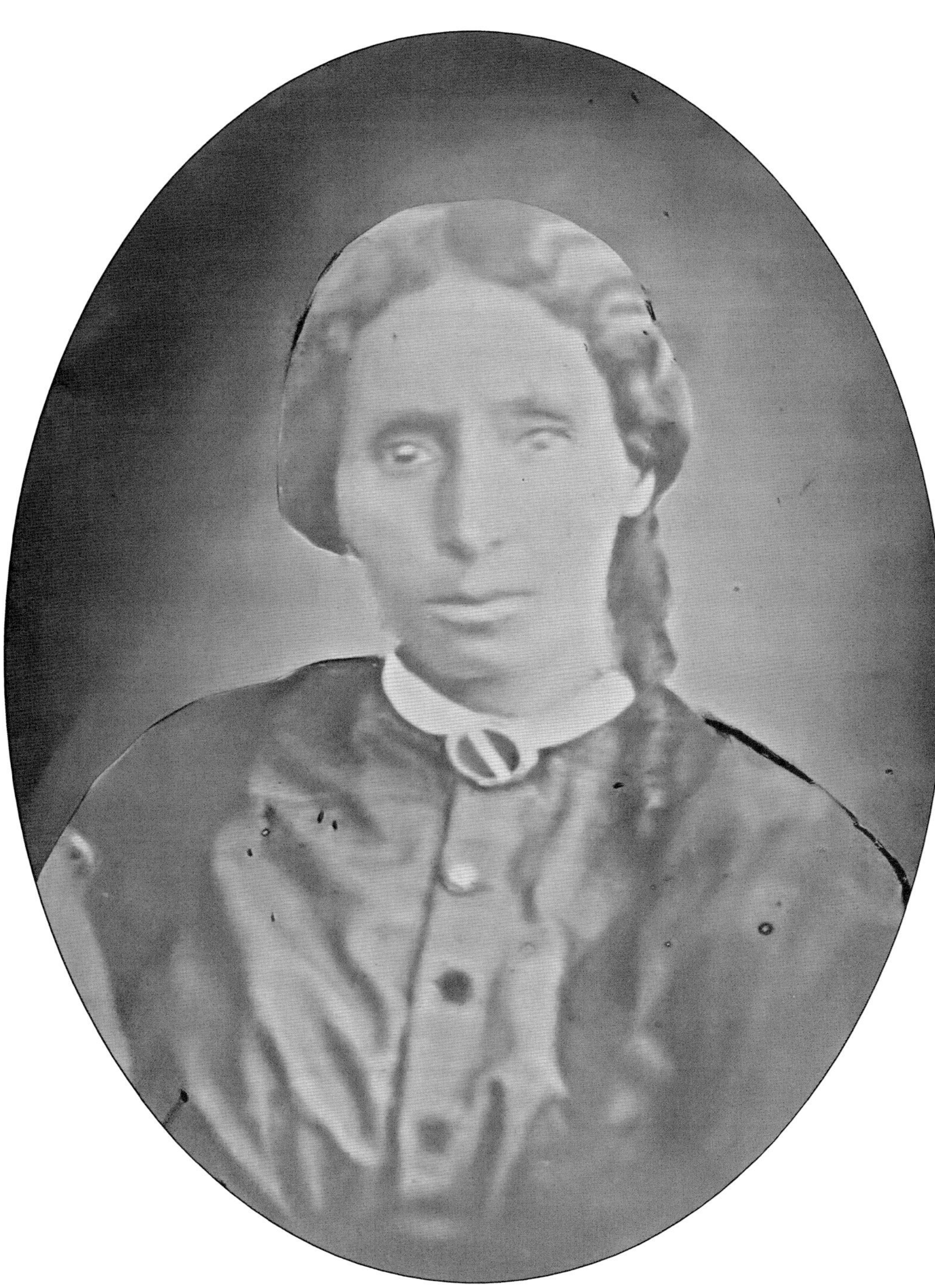

Taken at the end of the 19th century, this photograph shows Rosemarie Aldometer Mather Turnbull. She married Dudley Turnbull. Both were free people of color. She was the daughter of George Mather and Jane Giddings, who were also both free people of color. (Courtesy of Dudley Turnbull and Family Papers, MSS 2907, Free People of Color, LSU Libraries.)

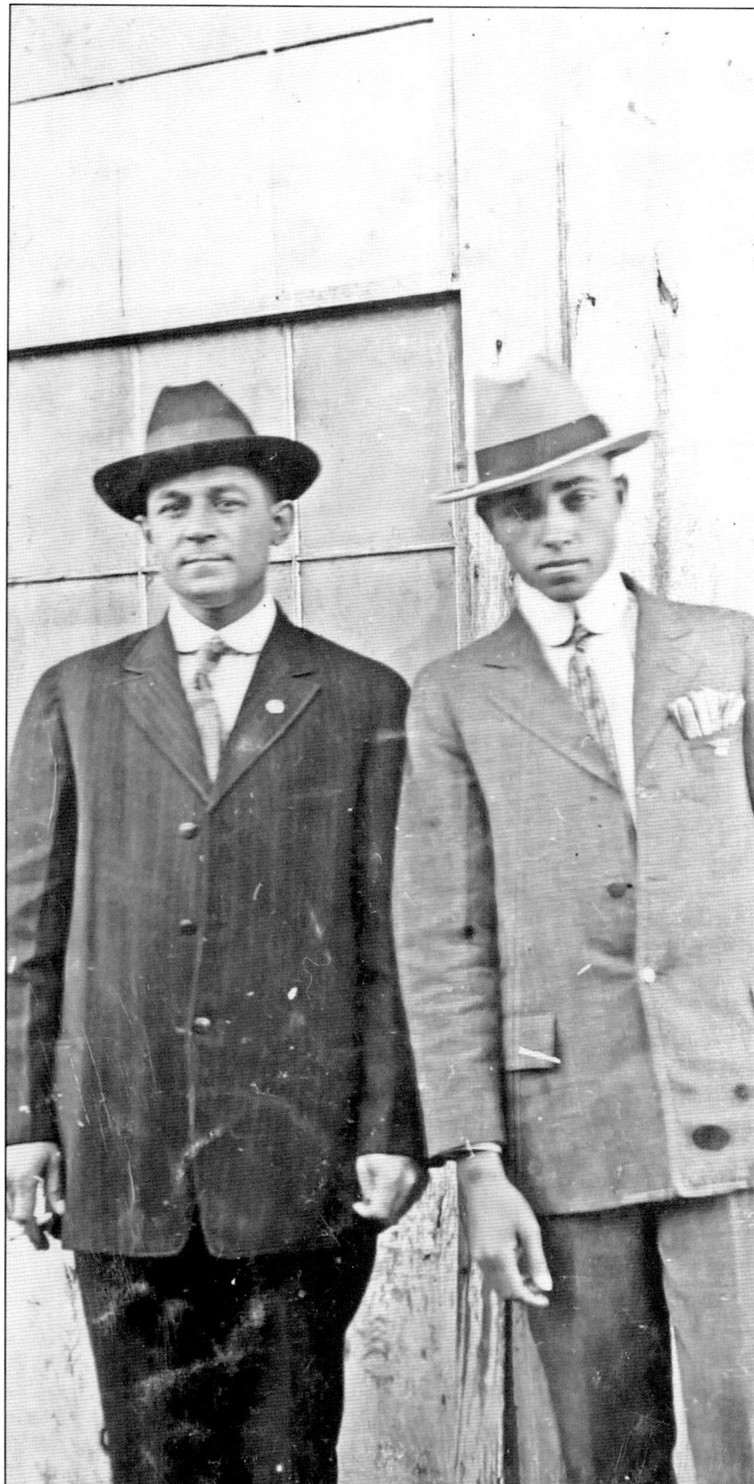

Dudley Turnbull Jr. (left) is pictured with an unidentified friend in 1937. Turnbull worked as plasterer. He was also a very active member of the African American Catholic community in Baton Rouge. Many African Americans were Catholic, and there remains a substantial African American Catholic community in Baton Rouge now. The son of Dudley Turnbull Sr. and Rosemarie Aldometer Mather Turnbull, Dudley Turnbull Jr. married Juanita Hebert, the daughter of Cora Hebert, a free woman of color. To Dudley Jr. and Juanita's union were born seven children. One of their children, daughter Naomi, worked as a maid. Her sister Grace graduated from East Baton Rouge Colored High School. Today, the school is known as McKinley Senior High School. (Courtesy of Dudley Turnbull and Family Papers, MSS 2907, Free People of Color, LSU Libraries.)

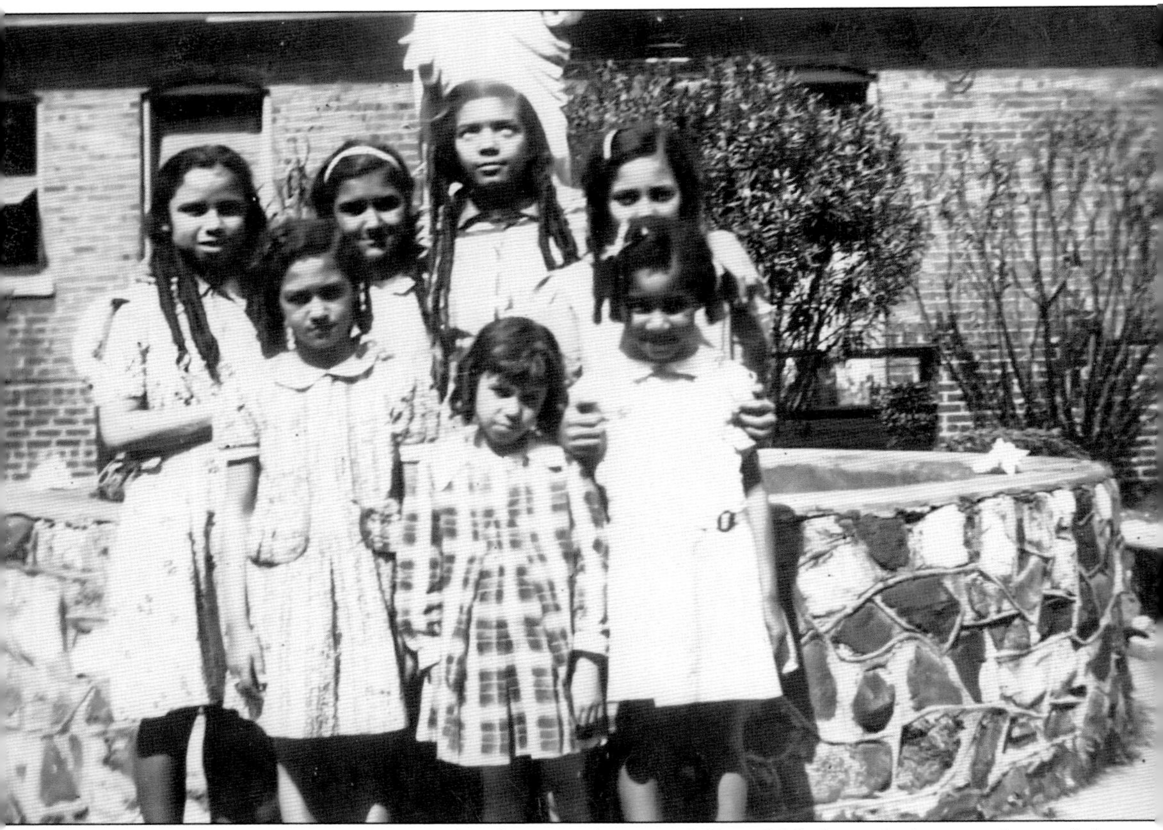

This photograph of unidentified girls was taken in 1952 and likely includes members of the Turnbull family, made up of many free people of color. Baton Rouge was home to many free people of color during the enslavement era, and many of their descendants remained in the area thereafter. While far more people of color lived in New Orleans than Baton Rouge, the latter, including South Baton Rogue, was important in the history of free people of color in Louisiana. Dudley Turnbull Sr., one of the earliest members of the Turnbull family for whom documents are available, was born around 1852. He worked as a steamboat watchman. He also worked in restaurants and eating houses. Members of the Turnbull family attended schools in South Baton Rouge, including McKinley High School and St. Francis Xavier. (Courtesy of Dudley Turnbull and Family Papers, MSS 2907, Free People of Color, LSU Libraries.)

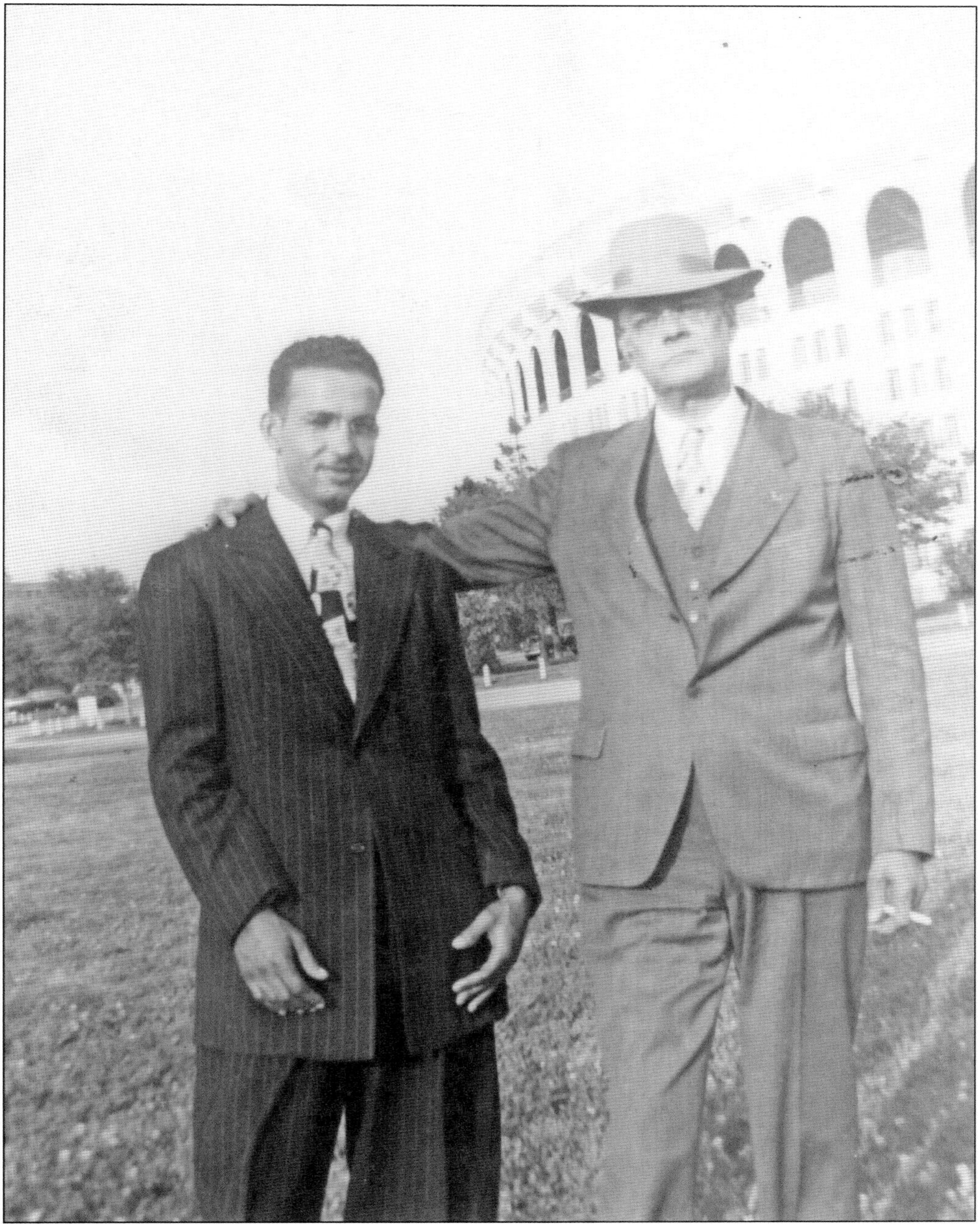

Bruce Turnbull (left) was one of seven children of Dudley Turnbull Jr. and Juanita Hebert Turnbull. Bruce and his brother Kenneth often penned letters to their father while he was working away from home. Bruce is pictured here in front of Tiger Stadium in 1946 with Alex Hebert. Louisiana State University, where Tiger Stadium is located, is in the southern portion of the capital city. The university was off-limits to blacks for many years. The first African American undergraduate student was not allowed to enroll until the 1960s, and African Americans did not wear LSU athletic uniforms until the 1970s. (Courtesy of Dudley Turnbull and Family Papers, MSS 2907, Free People of Color, LSU Libraries.)

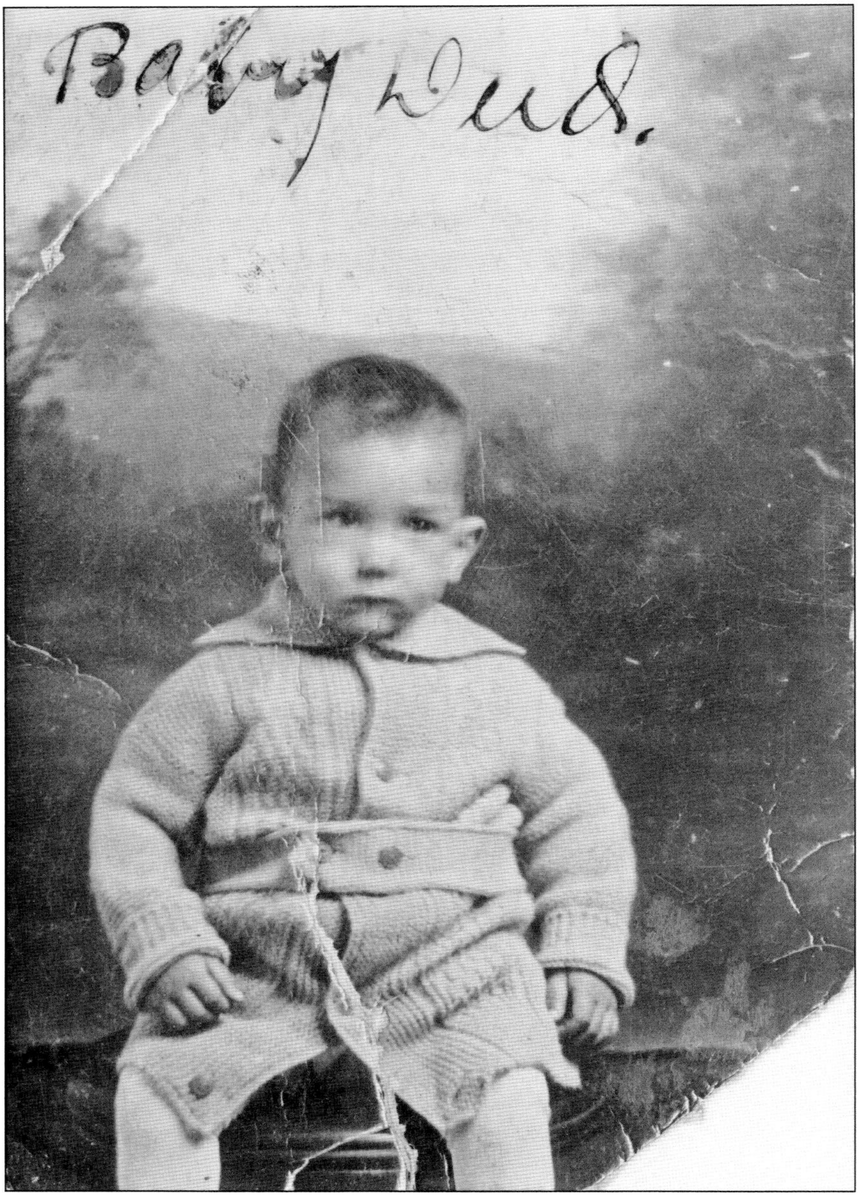

Dudley Gregory Turnbull was the son of Dudley Turnbull Jr. and Juanita Turnbull. He was born in 1925 and lived until 1980. As a child, he attended St. Francis Xavier School in South Baton Rogue. Dudley Gregory went on to serve his country in World War II. He even received a letter from Pres. Harry S. Truman thanking him for his service. The letter, which was written sometime between 1945 and 1953, reads, "To you who answered the call of your country and served in its Armed Forces to bring about the total defeat the enemy, I extend the heartfelt thanks of a grateful nation. As one of the Nation's finest, you undertook the most severe task one can be called upon to perform. Because you demonstrated the fortitude, resourcefulness and calm judgment necessary to carry out that task, we now look to you for leadership and example in further exalting our country in peace." (Courtesy of Dudley Turnbull and Family Papers, MSS 2907, Free People of Color, LSU Libraries.)

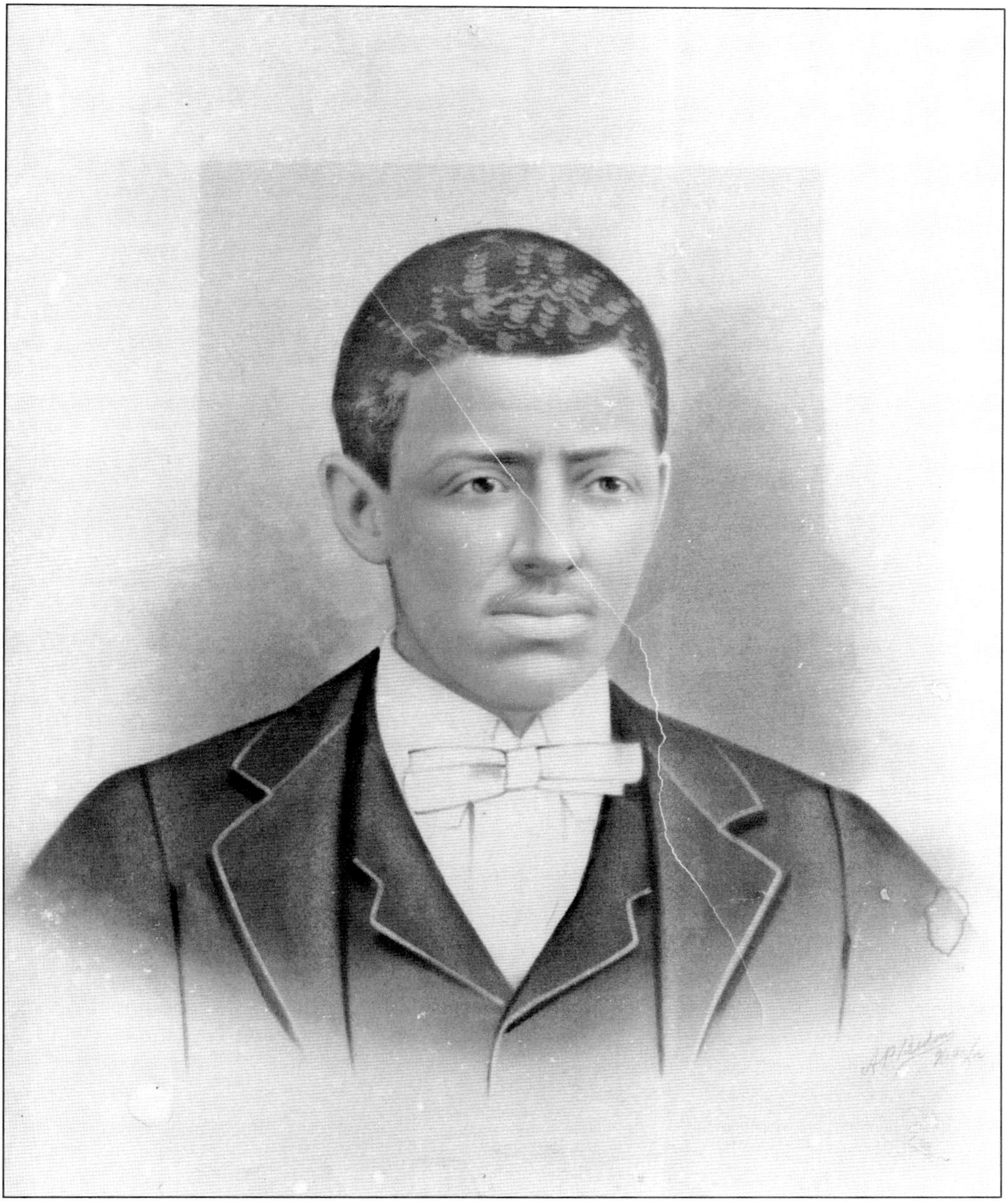

Warren Turnbull, a descendent of free people of color in South Baton Rouge, is depicted here in a collared shirt, bow tie, vest, and suit between 1887 and 1892. In September 1899, at approximately 3:00 in the morning, Warren, who was 16 years old at the time, was accidentally shot by his brother, Arthur, according to a report in the *Times-Democrat* from New Orleans. Warren died and was laid to rest in the historic St. Joseph Catholic Cemetery in South Baton Rouge. Arthur, who had graduated from New Orleans University about six years prior to Warren's death, passed away in 1948. He struggled financially while some of his other siblings were more successful. He wrote a letter to his brother Dudley in 1927, while living in Chicago, seeking financial help, and in the letter he asks his brother not to share his troubles with the "BR" (Baton Rouge) folks. (Courtesy of Dudley Turnbull and Family Papers, MSS 2907, Free People of Color, LSU Libraries.)

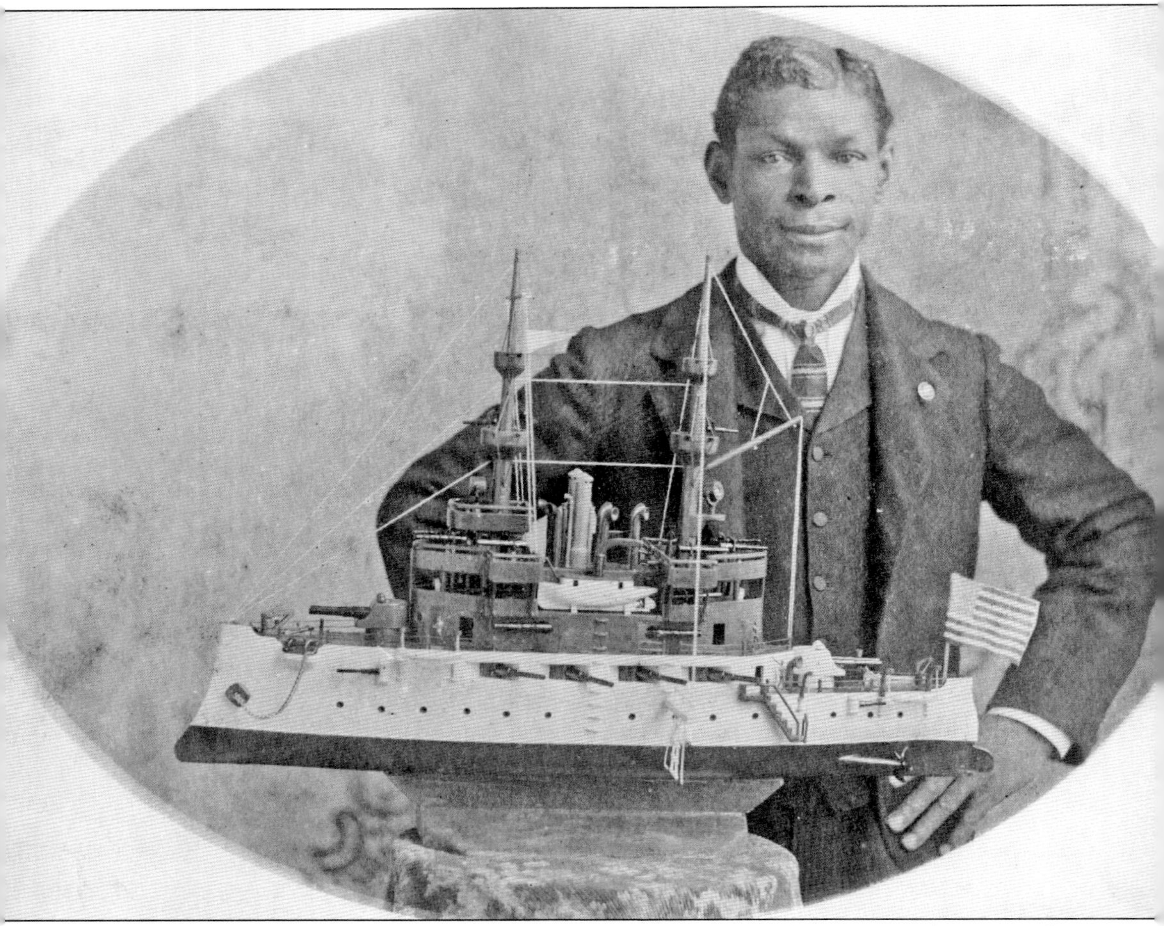

An unidentified African American man poses with a ship model in a series of portraits that are part of the collection of photographer Andrew David Lytle. Lytle was well known for capturing life and industry in Baton Rouge. His collection also includes photographs of African Americans engaged in agricultural work and captures life along the levee. Lytle's favorite subjects to photograph included Louisiana State University cadets, the Old State Capitol, and riverboats. Born in Ohio in 1834, Lytle came to Baton Rouge in 1857. Despite his affinity for photographing African Americans, Lytle had experience with a paramilitary group in Ohio and worked in 1860 to recruit and train militia for the Confederacy. Oliver Bryce Steele, a Baton Rouge banker, state auditor, and Confederate veteran, collected this image and others created by Lytle Studio and Andrew David Lytle between 1858 and 1917. (Courtesy of Andrew Lytle's Photograph Collection, MSS 2600, LSU Libraries.)

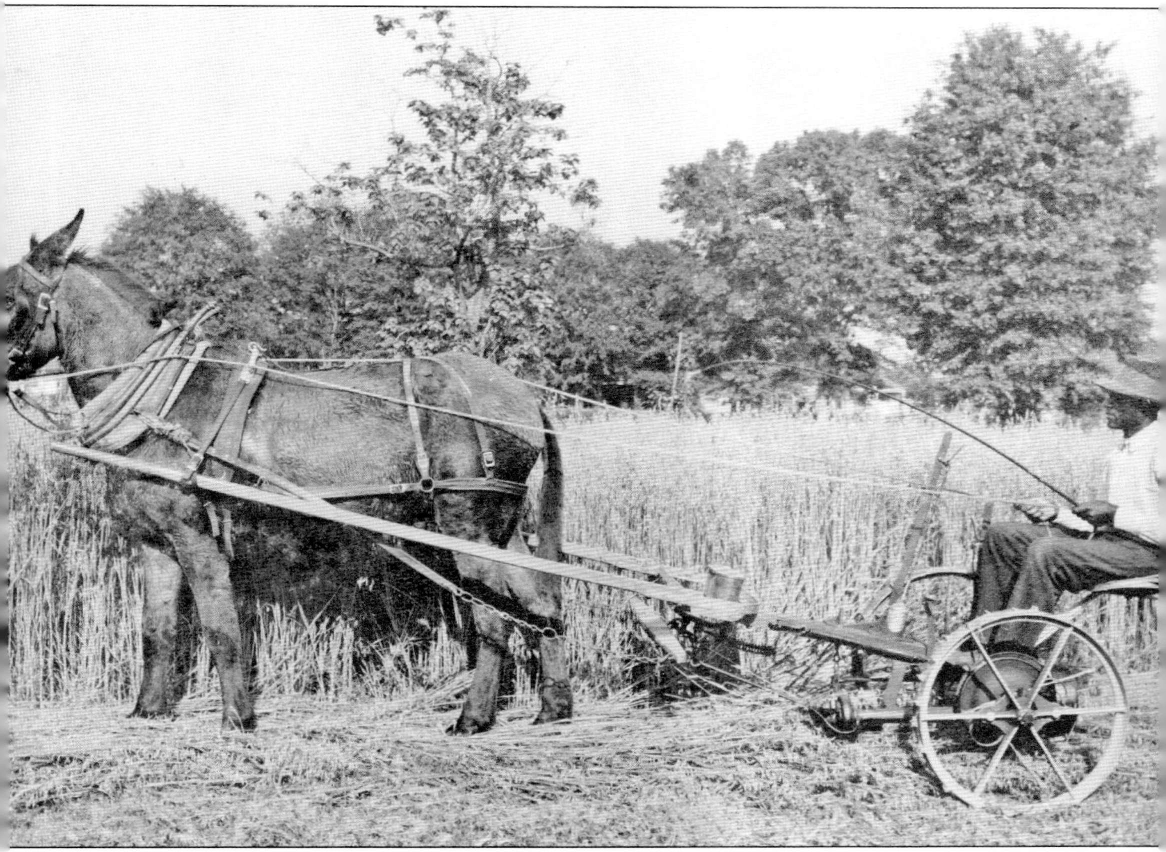

This c. 1899 photograph of an unidentified African American male was taken by Andrew David Lytle. During the 19th century, blacks in South Baton Rouge, like many other residents of Louisiana, made the things they needed for daily life, including soap and various tools. Many residents hunted and harvested food with non-mechanized tools, using animals such as mules. According to "The African American Experience in Louisiana," a report by Laura Ewen Blokker (*Southeast Preservation*, May 15, 2012) about the experiences of African Americans in Louisiana: "Where cotton was king, tenancy and sharecropping prevailed. Sharecroppers were provided with the land, tools, and seed by the landowner with an expectation that they produce a certain amount of crop. The whole family—husband, wife, and children—worked the crop together. They would not actually get paid until that crop was harvested and sold. With no source of regular income, they had to purchase their own food and clothing, etc. on credit extended by the landowner at the plantation store. These stores featured exorbitant prices and high interest that made it nearly inevitable the crop would not cover the expenses the farmer accrued during the year and kept the sharecropper in a cycle of constant debt." (Courtesy of Andrew Lytle's Photograph Collection, MSS 2600, LSU Libraries.)

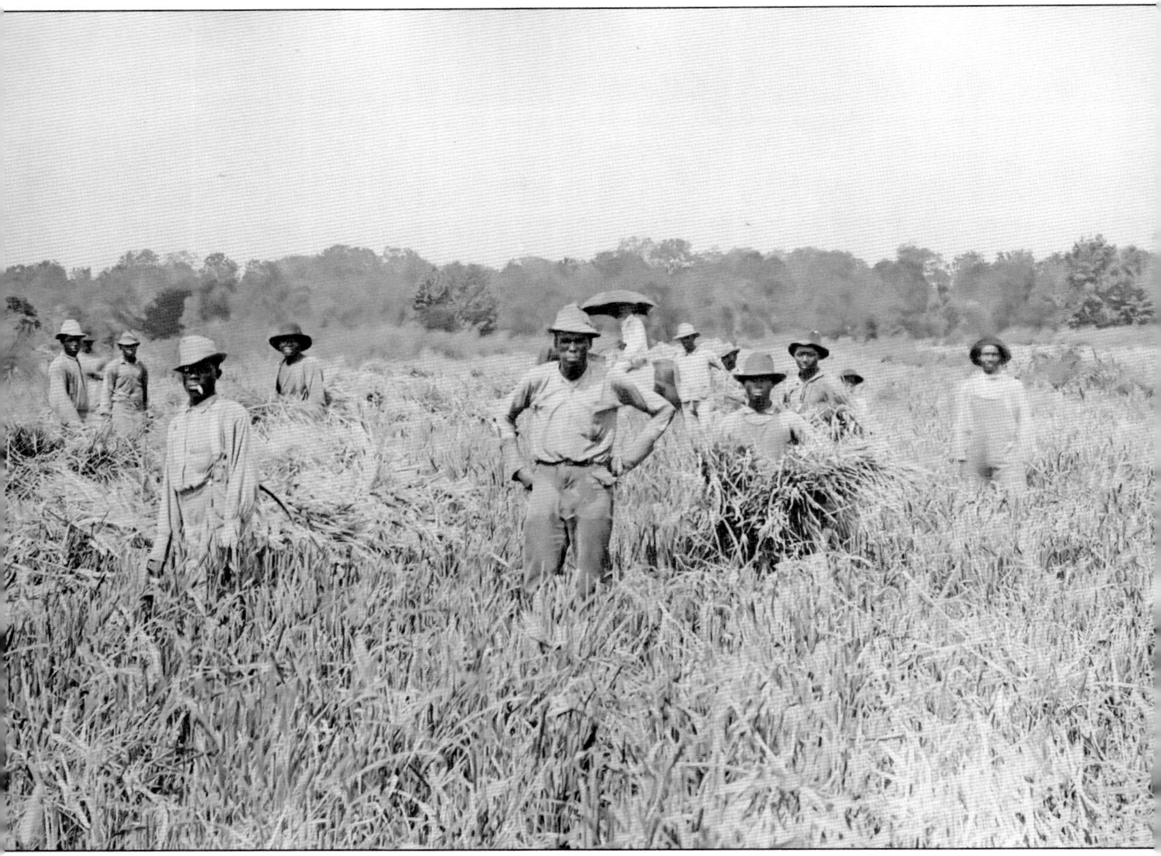

African Americans are pictured in a rice field after the harvest, with laborers gathering straw. Andrew David Lytle, noted Baton Rouge photographer and Confederate sympathizer, took the photograph at the end of the 19th century. African Americans in South Baton Rouge are part of a long heritage of individuals with expert knowledge in the cultivation of rice. Laura Ewen Blokker writes that "the enslaved Africans who came to Louisiana were not mere laborers, but people possessing valuable skills and technological knowledge. Captains of the first two slave ships to bring Africans to Louisiana were specifically instructed to purchase people who knew how to cultivate rice—something French colonists were not familiar with." (Courtesy of Andrew Lytle's Photograph Collection, MSS 2600, LSU Libraries.)

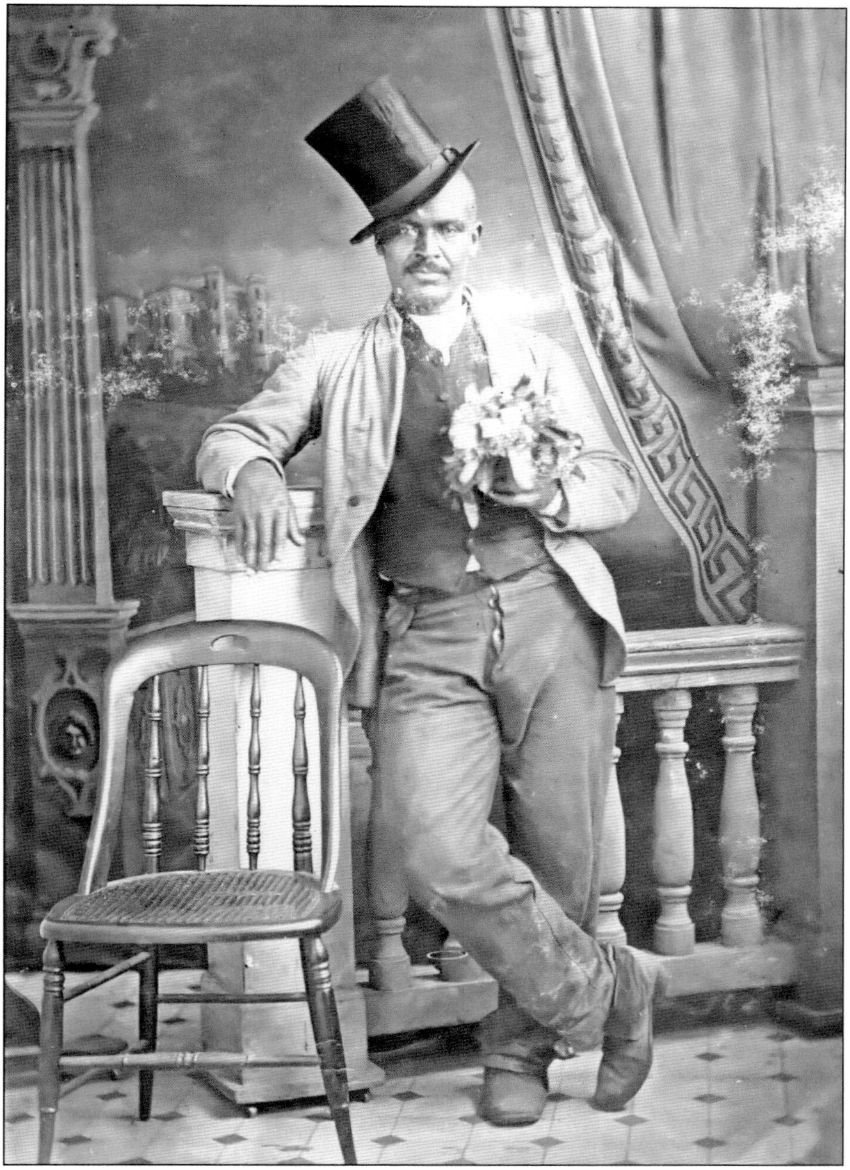

Scott Gordon, a resident of Baton Rouge, is pictured here on his wedding day in 1876. His image was captured by Andrew David Lytle in his studio. Gordon worked for Baton Rouge Water Works. According to the history of the Baton Rouge Water Company at brwater.com, the earliest known record of the local water supply dates back to 1887. On November 8, 1887, the common council adopted an ordinance contracting for the construction, building, maintenance, and operation of the city's own water system and to supply water to the city and city residents. Ownership of the company changed in 1910, and it became the Baton Rouge Water Works Company. Text on the company website states, "Meters in those days were read by men who travelled from house to house in horse-drawn buggies. Bills were prepared each night and hand-delivered the next day." Lytle's studio was located in South Baton Rouge near what was then the governor's mansion. Some scholars find it surprising Lytle allowed blacks in his studio given his strong ties to the Confederacy. (Courtesy of Andrew Lytle's Photograph Collection, MSS 2600, LSU Libraries.)

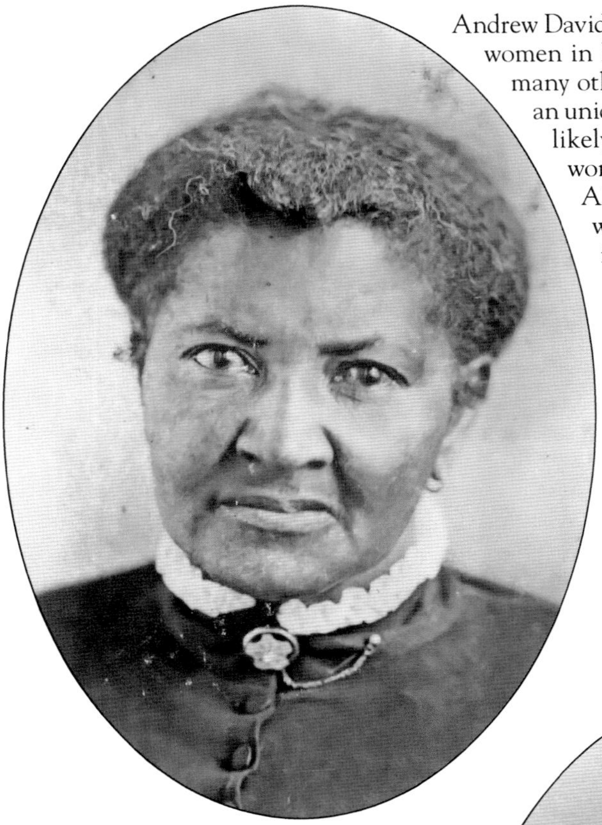

Andrew David Lytle photographed African American women in his studio in Baton Rouge, along with many other residents of the city. The picture of an unidentified African American woman was likely taken between 1880 and 1910. The woman was a contemporary of Rosemarie Aldometer Mather Turnbull. A free woman of color, Rosemarie was born in 1851 and sat for a portrait the same year this photograph was taken. She later married Dudley Turnbull Sr. and lived in Baton Rouge. Rosemarie died in 1917. (Courtesy of Andrew Lytle's Photograph Collection, MSS 2600, LSU Libraries.)

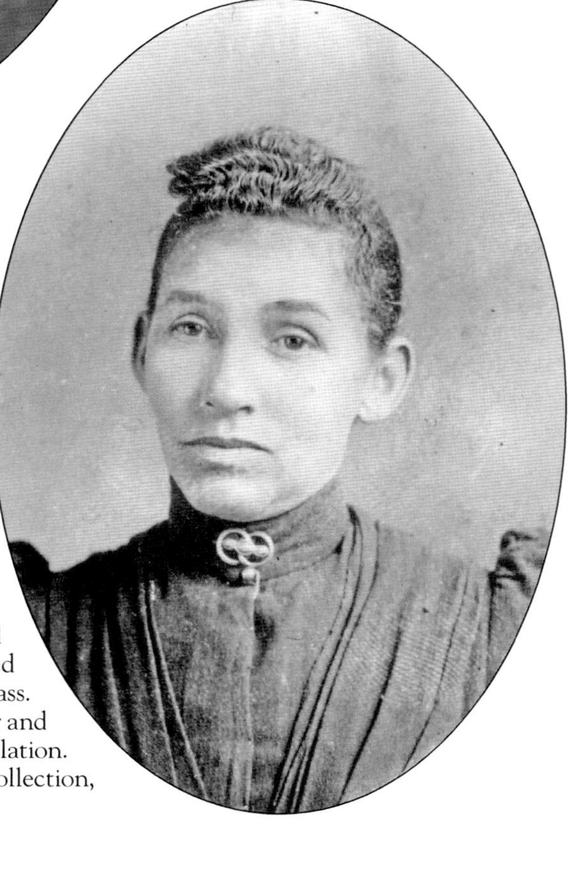

African American women played important roles in the 19th century and beyond. The woman photographed here in 1899, although unidentified, is representative of a legacy of black womanhood that endured the horrors of enslavement and endured discrimination based on race, gender, and class. Black women were exploited for their labor and were forced to reproduce the enslaved population. (Courtesy of Andrew Lytle's Photograph Collection, MSS 2600, LSU Libraries.)

Two

Churches, Schools, and Businesses

Social institutions exist to meet basic human needs and can best be understood as "systems and structures within society that shape the activities of groups and individuals," according to Kerry Ferris and Jill Stein, in the 2016 publication *The Real World* (p. G-14). Social institutions may also act as agents of socialization, as which they play important roles in communicating societal expectations of the many groups to which everyone belongs, including racial groups. Schools, faith-based institutions, and businesses were important to the history of African Americans in South Baton Rouge throughout the time period covered in this book.

According to W.E.B. Du Bois, a pioneer in sociology in North America, founder of the National Association for the Advancement of Colored People (NAACP), and author of *The Souls of Black Folks*, churches historically played a far more important role than the family or even schools in the African American experience. The disruption of the biological family resulted in the creation of kinship networks, for example. Laws prohibiting black people from learning to read or write throughout many places in the United States, including in Louisiana for a time, limited the impact of education on the lives of far too many people of African ancestry, especially during the 1800s and the first half of the 20th century.

Faith-based institutions, schools, and businesses played important roles in the lives of people living in South Baton Rouge as well as in the character of the community. This chapter includes images of free people of color during the 1800s with ties to important historically black institutions, such as McKinley High School, as well as institutions that for a time excluded blacks in South Baton Rouge altogether.

In the book *Big Box Schools: Race, Education, and the Danger of the Wal-Martization of Public Schools in America*, author Lori Latrice Martin examines the ways race was used to facilitate the unequal treatment of blacks for many years, including in Louisiana and other parts of the Deep South. In 1819, a Virginia code prohibited blacks from "assembling in schools for the purpose of teaching reading and writing" and "granted the right of officers to inflict corporal punishment on the offender or offenders at the discretion of any justice of the peace, not exceeding twenty lashes." During the 1800s, Louisiana had a law on the books that resulted in a one-year prison sentence for anyone found violating the ban on the education of free or enslaved blacks. Blacks continued to face obstacles in their quest for a quality education even as American schools were used to assimilate white immigrants from Southern, Central, and Eastern Europe who arrived en masse between the 1880s and early 1920s. These immigrants were considered less desirable than whites already in the country but were still preferable to blacks and other people of the color in the nation at the time. Schools functioned not to prepare blacks for inclusion into the larger society but to prepare them for life at the bottom of the economic and social structure. Compulsory school attendance was connected to the different approaches to education for blacks and whites.

Churches, the black church in particular, played a particularly significant role in the lives of African Americans from the days of slavery to Reconstruction to the early part of the 20th century and beyond. The black church, according to Du Bois and others, was the center of social interaction in the black experience. For much of the early history of blacks in the United States, the church was the hospital where blacks who were wounded and hurting went to get well. The black church was where people of African ancestry got information and amusement. The black church was the place where African Americans pooled their resources and mobilized their collective efforts to identify and address the challenges facing their race. It is therefore not surprising that many of the early figures and places associated with civil rights movements in America have had their origins in faith traditions.

Although the system of slavery included many prohibitions against blacks having money and placed restrictions even on blacks of free status, blacks were able to accumulate wealth and not only purchase the freedom of some of their relatives but also operate lucrative businesses. The forced separation of the races created opportunities over time for dollars to circulate within segregated black communities. The historic example of "Black Wall Street" in Tulsa, Oklahoma, is just one example of a community filled with thriving businesses. Many black businesses also thrived in Baton Rouge from the 1800s through the 1970s. Webb's Barber Shop and the Chicken Shack are among the long-standing black businesses still in existence today in South Baton Rouge. South Baton Rouge was also home to the capital city's first black millionaire, Horatio Thompson. Thompson was the first black person to own an Esso (now Exxon) station anywhere in the South. He played an important role in the history of blacks in Baton Rouge, including during the historic bus boycott.

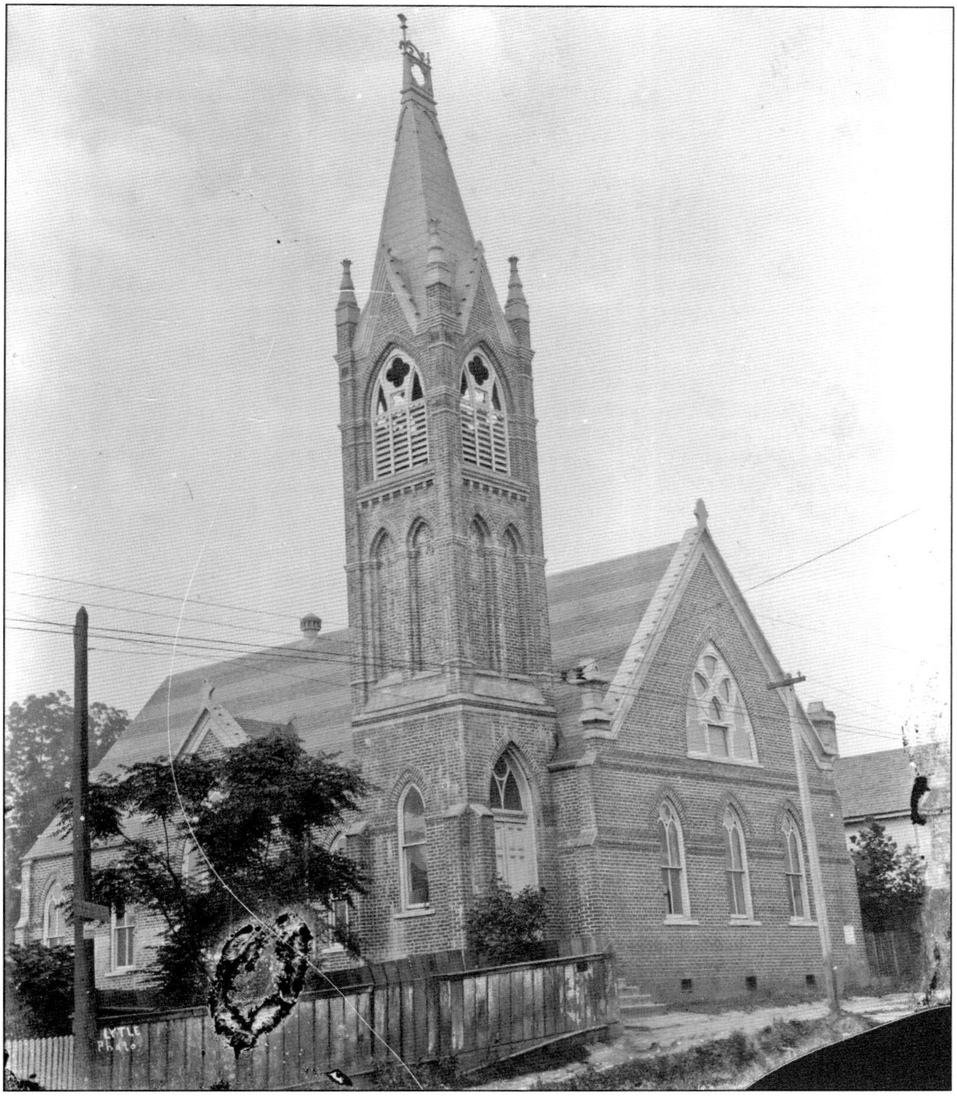

Wesley Chapel Methodist Episcopal Negro Church (now Wesley United Methodist Church) was and remains an important social institution in South Baton Rouge. It is an important place for social interaction, like many other black churches throughout South Baton Rouge and in the nation as a whole. An online history of the church states, "The beginning of Wesley was in the First Methodist Church (White) then located on the corner of Lauren and Fourth Street. When an attempt of segregation was made, a seed was planted in the minds of those who wanted something for themselves and for those who followed after them." According to archived records at the East Baton Rouge Public Library, "The Blundon School and Orphanage also had its beginning here." Mattie Carney, a well-known seamstress in South Baton Rouge, was among the black residents eulogized at the historic church in 1937. African Methodist Episcopal churches still exist in Baton Rouge. Bethel African Methodist Episcopal Church is located in South Baton Rouge and recently hosted the national unveiling of a postage stamp dedicated to one of the founders of the denomination, Richard Allen. (Courtesy of Andrew Lytle's Photograph Collection, MSS 2600, LSU Libraries.)

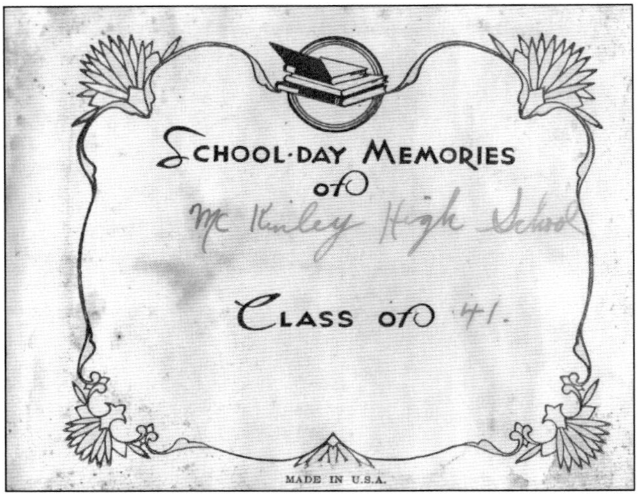

McKinley High School was the first place local blacks could earn a high school diploma. Here is a page from an autograph book belonging to Kenneth and Dudley Gregory, the sons of Dudley Turnbull Jr. and Juanita Hebert Turnbull. Kenneth served in World War II and also worked as a painter. The autograph book provides insight into the types of clubs and activities offered as well as the close community ties. (Courtesy of Dudley Turnbull and Family Papers, MSS 2907, Free People of Color, LSU Libraries.)

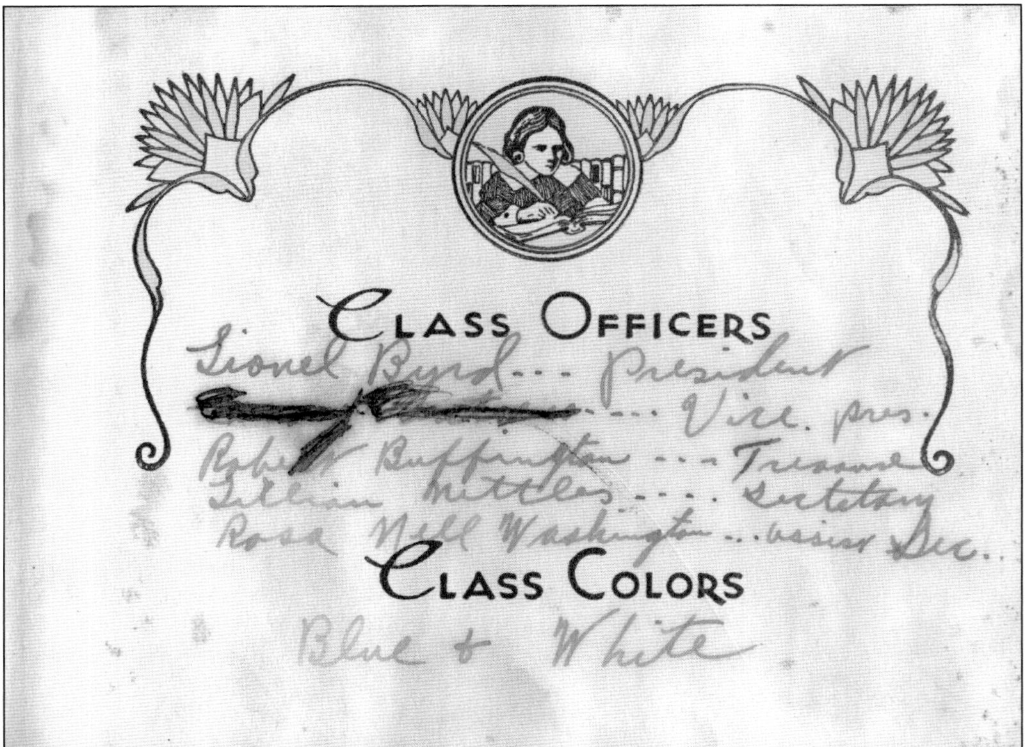

In 1907, H.K. Strickland founded the East Baton Rouge Negro School, which eventually became McKinley High School. Strickland was an 1898 graduate of Louisiana State University, where he was on the staff of the *Reveille*. He later worked as an assistant professor in English. Kenneth Turnbull's autograph book includes the names of class leaders. Officers for the class of 1941 included Lionel Byrd (president), Robert Buffington (treasurer), Lillian Nittles (secretary), and Rosa Nell Washington (assistant secretary). The school colors were blue and white and remain so today. (Courtesy of Dudley Turnbull and Family Papers, MSS 2907, Free People of Color, LSU Libraries.)

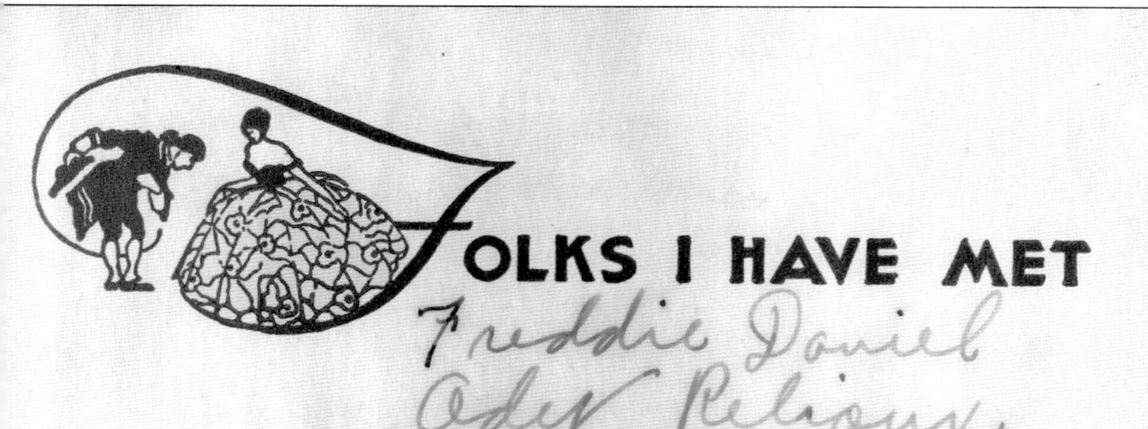

The Turnbull brothers fondly recall the names of people they encountered while students at McKinley High School. The location of the school in one of the most prominent black communities in the parish meant that the Turnbulls and others were likely to encounter people of color from all walks of life. The names include Freddie Daniel and Phillip Forbs. (Courtesy of Dudley Turnbull and Family Papers, MSS 2907, Free People of Color, LSU Libraries.)

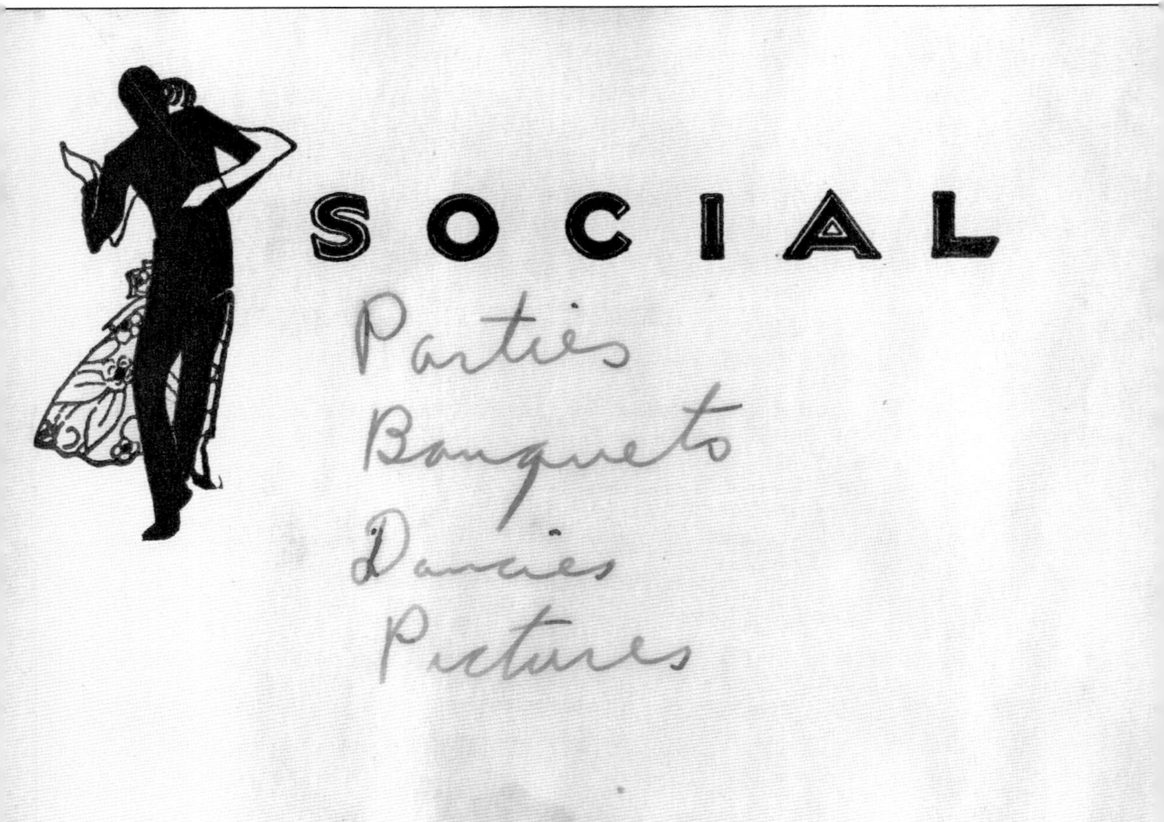

Students at McKinley High enjoyed a number of social events and athletic competition. Among the social events the Turnbulls and their classmates participated in were parties, banquets, dances, and movies. One of the most famous places to enjoy a movie was the Temple Theater. In 1924, the Grand United Order of Odd Fellows began construction of the building that would become home to the theater. The Roof Garden—housed in the same building as Temple Theater—featured local and national bands, including those led by Cab Calloway, Louis Armstrong, and Duke Ellington among others. (Courtesy of Dudley Turnbull and Family Papers, MSS 2907, Free People of Color, LSU Libraries.)

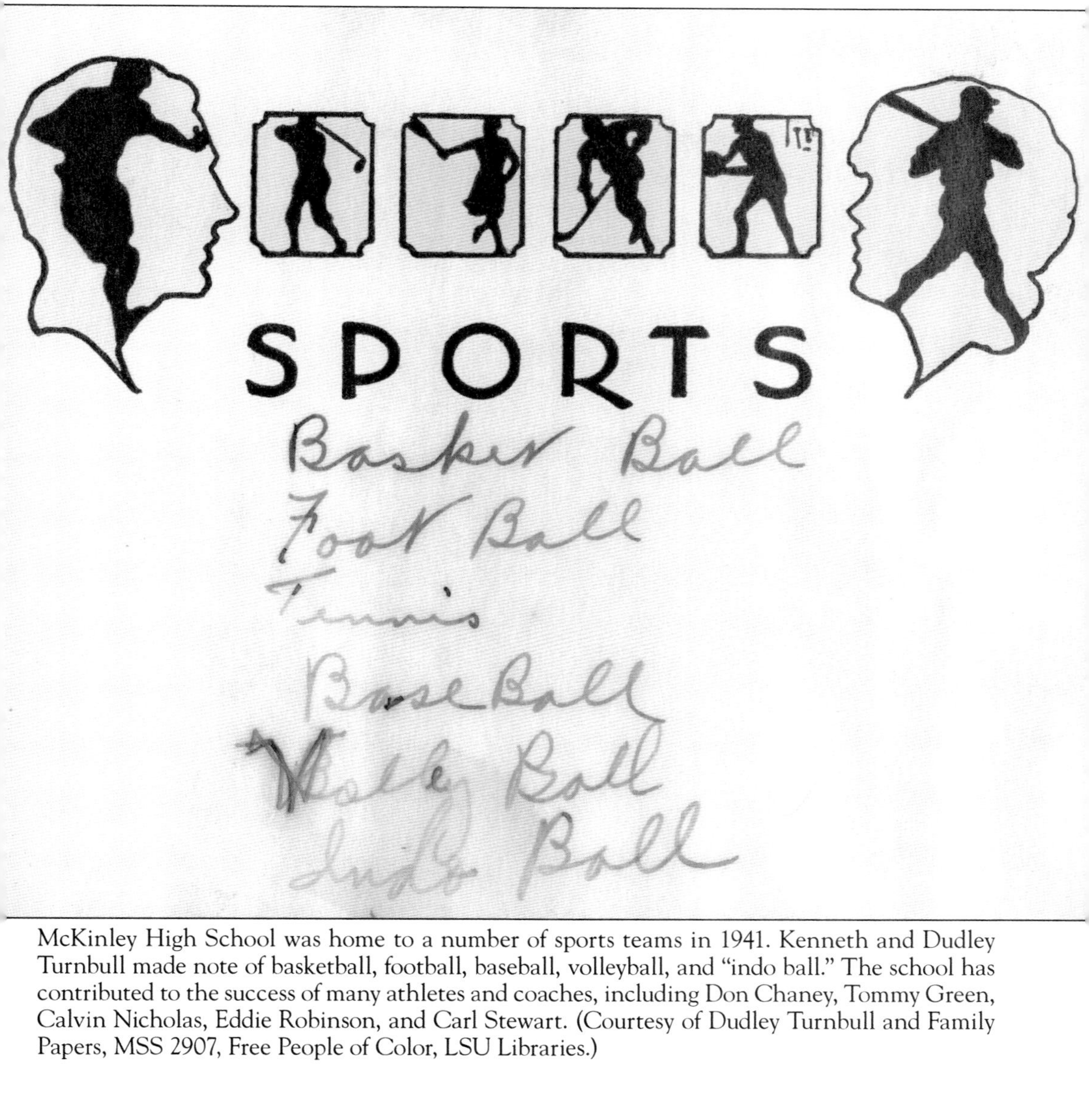

McKinley High School was home to a number of sports teams in 1941. Kenneth and Dudley Turnbull made note of basketball, football, baseball, volleyball, and "indo ball." The school has contributed to the success of many athletes and coaches, including Don Chaney, Tommy Green, Calvin Nicholas, Eddie Robinson, and Carl Stewart. (Courtesy of Dudley Turnbull and Family Papers, MSS 2907, Free People of Color, LSU Libraries.)

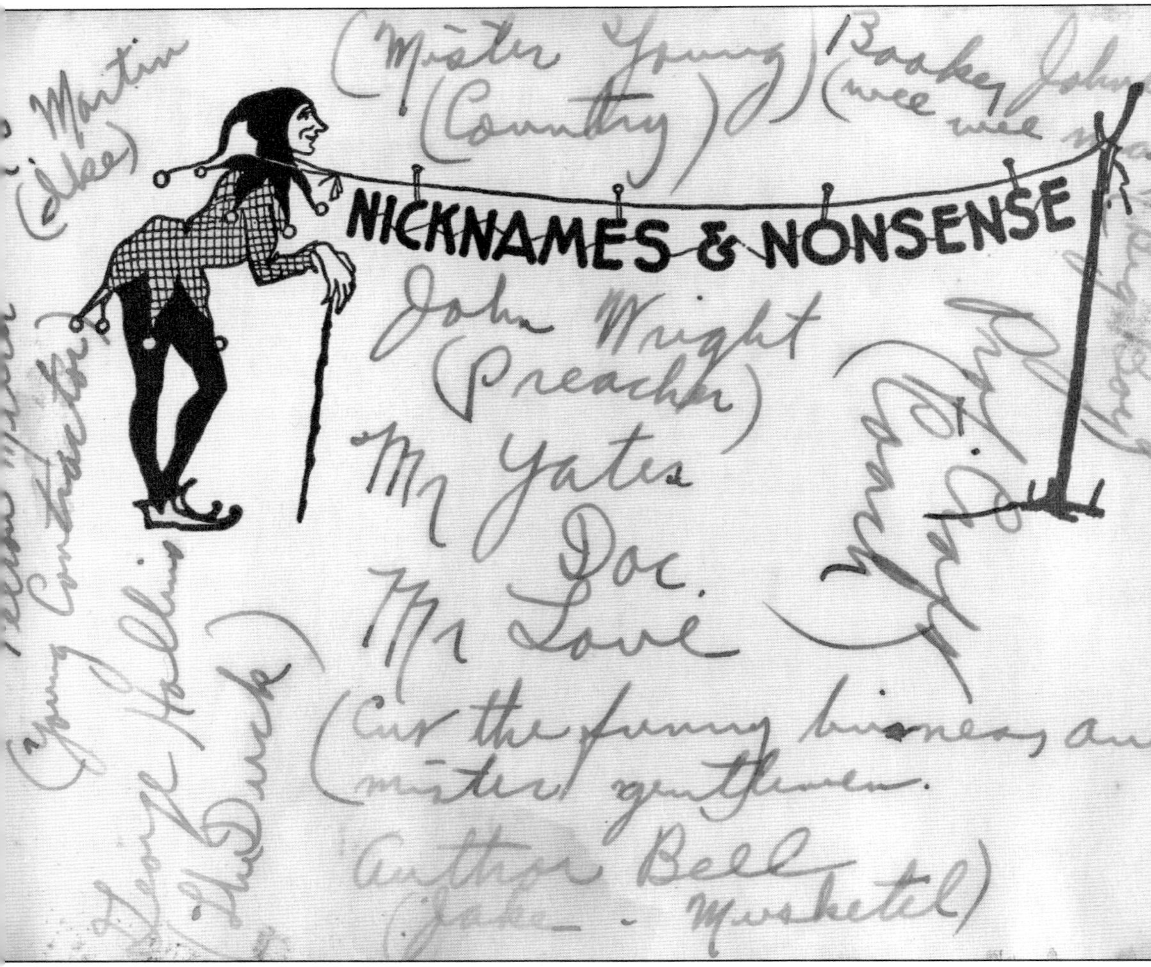

In South Baton Rouge, as in many close-knit communities, it was not uncommon for members of the community to give each other nicknames. The nicknames recorded in the autograph book belonging to Kenneth Turnbull for the McKinley High School graduating class of 1941 include "Country," "Ike," "The Duck," "Preacher," "Coach," and "Big Boy." (Courtesy of Dudley Turnbull and Family Papers, MSS 2907, Free People of Color, LSU Libraries.)

Kenneth Turnbull's parents were among the people who wrote encouraging words to their son on the event of his graduation from McKinley High School: "Remember to be honest, sincere, and truthful in dealing with your fellow man. No matter how hard the task may be, [don't ever quit]. Wishing you a full life of success & happiness." (Courtesy of Dudley Turnbull and Family Papers, MSS 2907, Free People of Color, LSU Libraries.)

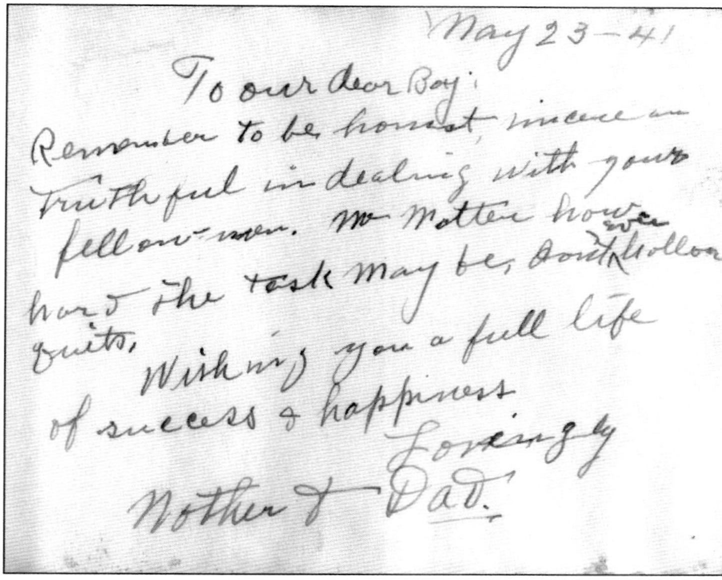

May 23-41

To our dear Boy:
Remember to be honest, sincere an Truthful in dealing with your fellow-men. no matter how ever hard the task may be, dont ever quit.
Wishing you a full life of success & happiness
Lovingly
Mother & Dad.

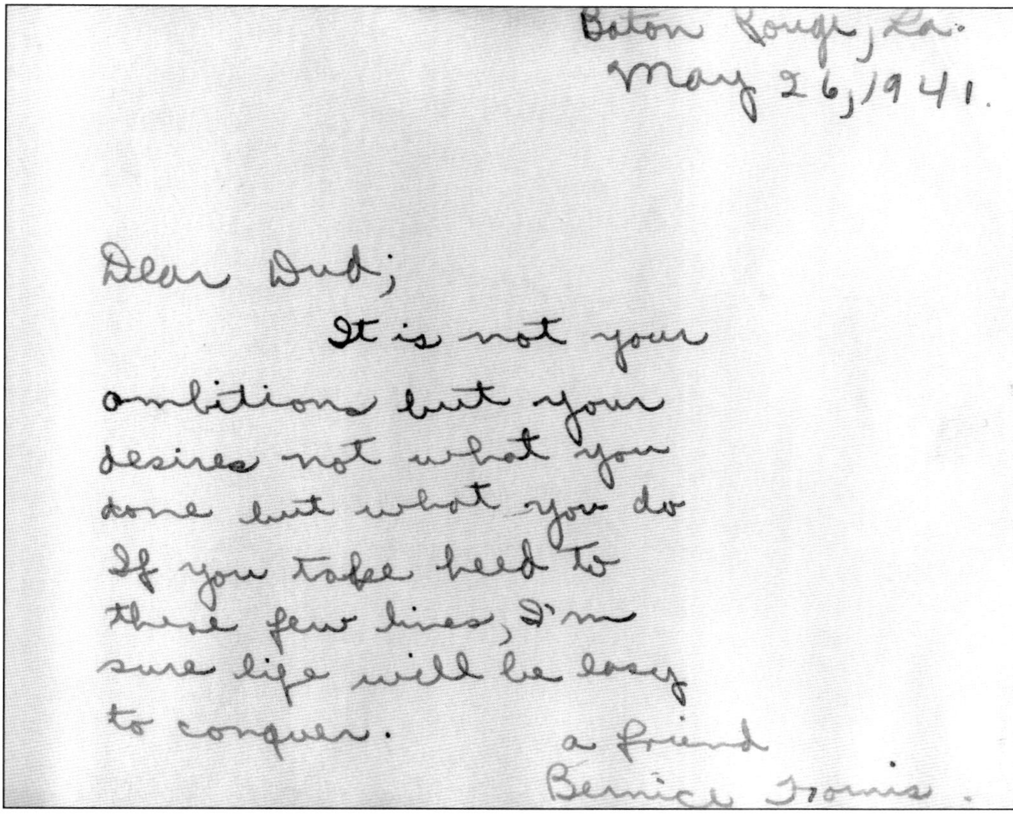

Baton Rouge, La.
May 26, 1941.

Dear Dud;
It is not your ambitions but your desires not what you done but what you do If you take heed to these few lines, I'm sure life will be easy to conquer.
a friend
Bernice Francis.

Bernice Francis wrote an inspiring note to Dudley "Dud" Turnbull: "It is not your ambition but your desires not what you done but what you do. It you take heed to these few lines, I'm sure life will be easy to conquer." (Courtesy of Dudley Turnbull and Family Papers, MSS 2907, Free People of Color, LSU Libraries.)

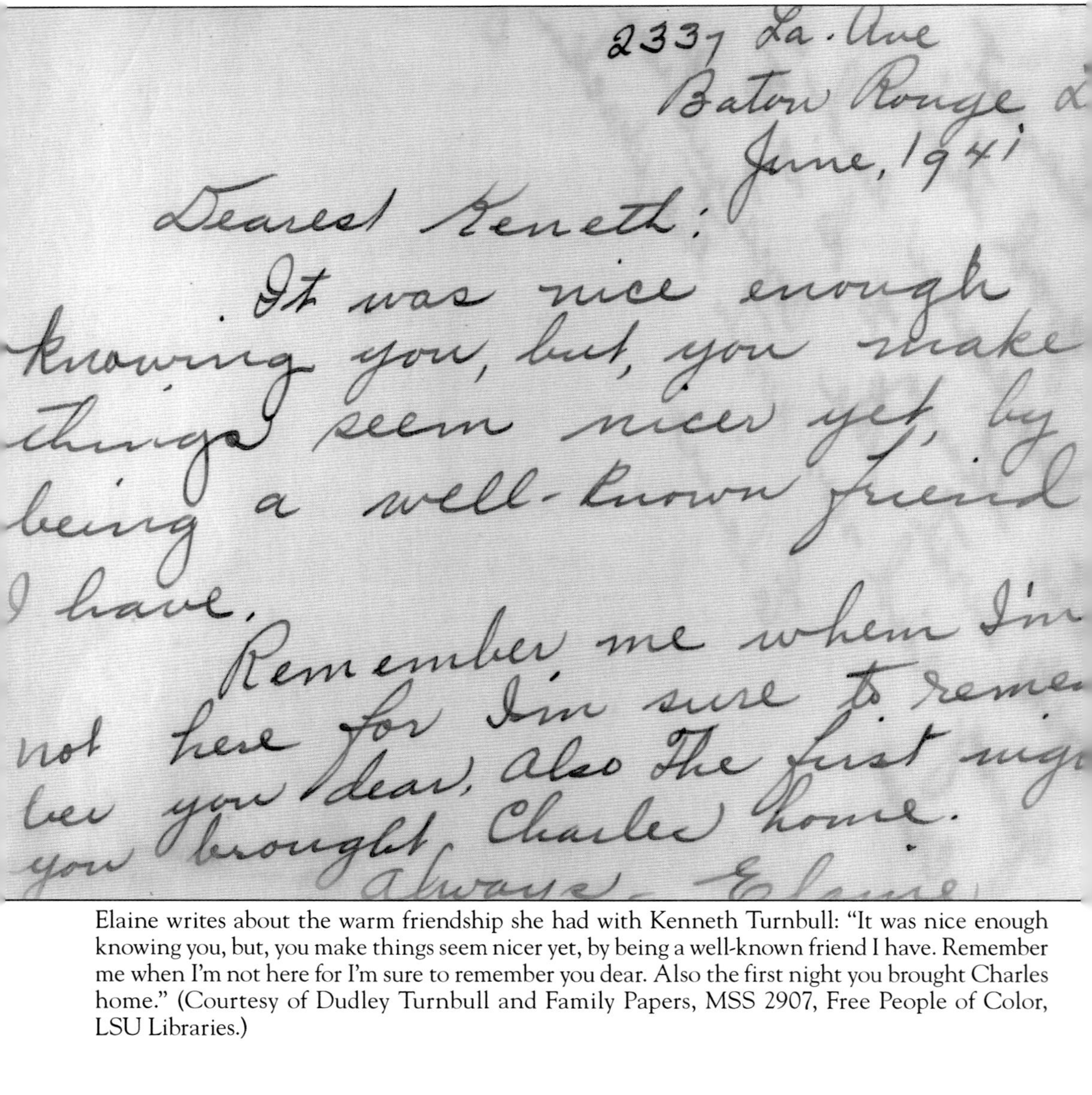

2337 La. Ave
Baton Rouge L
June, 1941

Dearest Keneth:
It was nice enough
knowing you, but, you make
things seem nicer yet, by
being a well-known friend
I have.
Remember me when I'm
not here for I'm sure to remem
ber you dear, also The first nig
you brought Charles home.
Always— Elaine

Elaine writes about the warm friendship she had with Kenneth Turnbull: "It was nice enough knowing you, but, you make things seem nicer yet, by being a well-known friend I have. Remember me when I'm not here for I'm sure to remember you dear. Also the first night you brought Charles home." (Courtesy of Dudley Turnbull and Family Papers, MSS 2907, Free People of Color, LSU Libraries.)

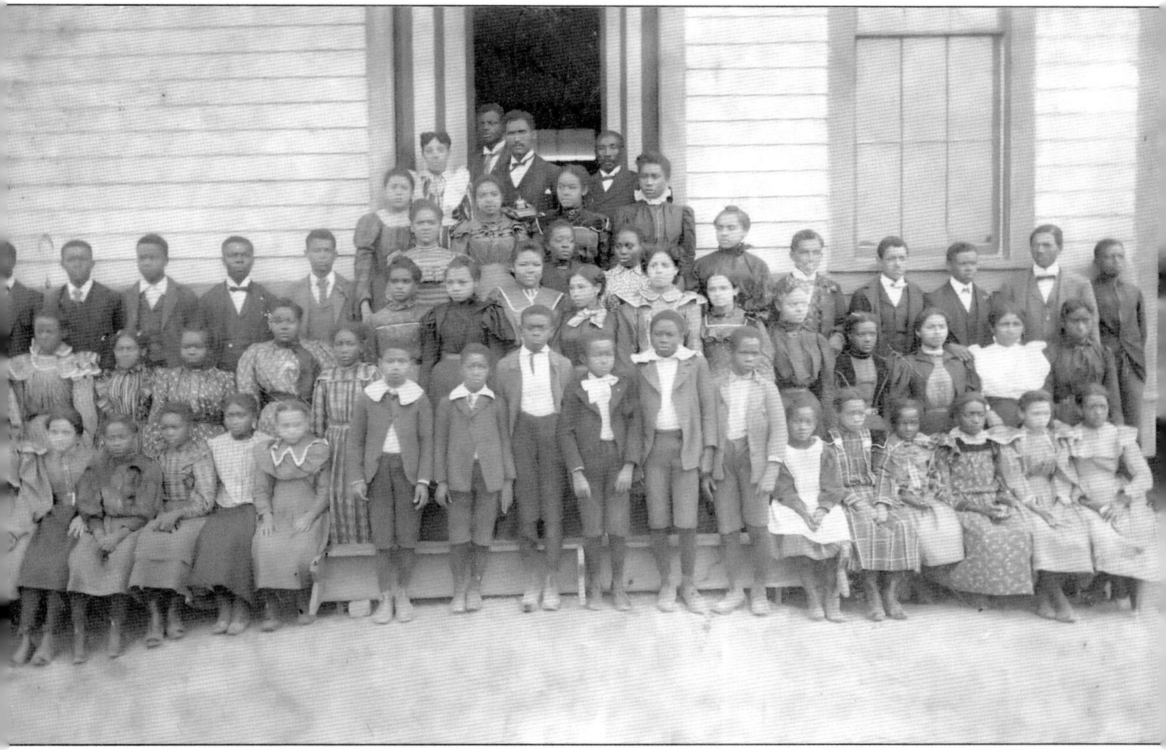

Despite informal and formal efforts to restrict black access to education, schools for black children were organized in the 1800s and grew in number after the Civil War. This photograph was taken around 1910 and includes children in front of a school. This image appears to show African American students as well as adults who likely served as teachers or in some other supportive role. Blacks created their own educational opportunities when laws and social norms placed formal and informal restrictions on their access to predominately white educational institutions. The creation of schools in South Baton Rouge, which led to the founding of historic McKinley High School, is just one example. (Courtesy of Dudley Turnbull and Family Papers, MSS 2907, Free People of Color, LSU Libraries.)

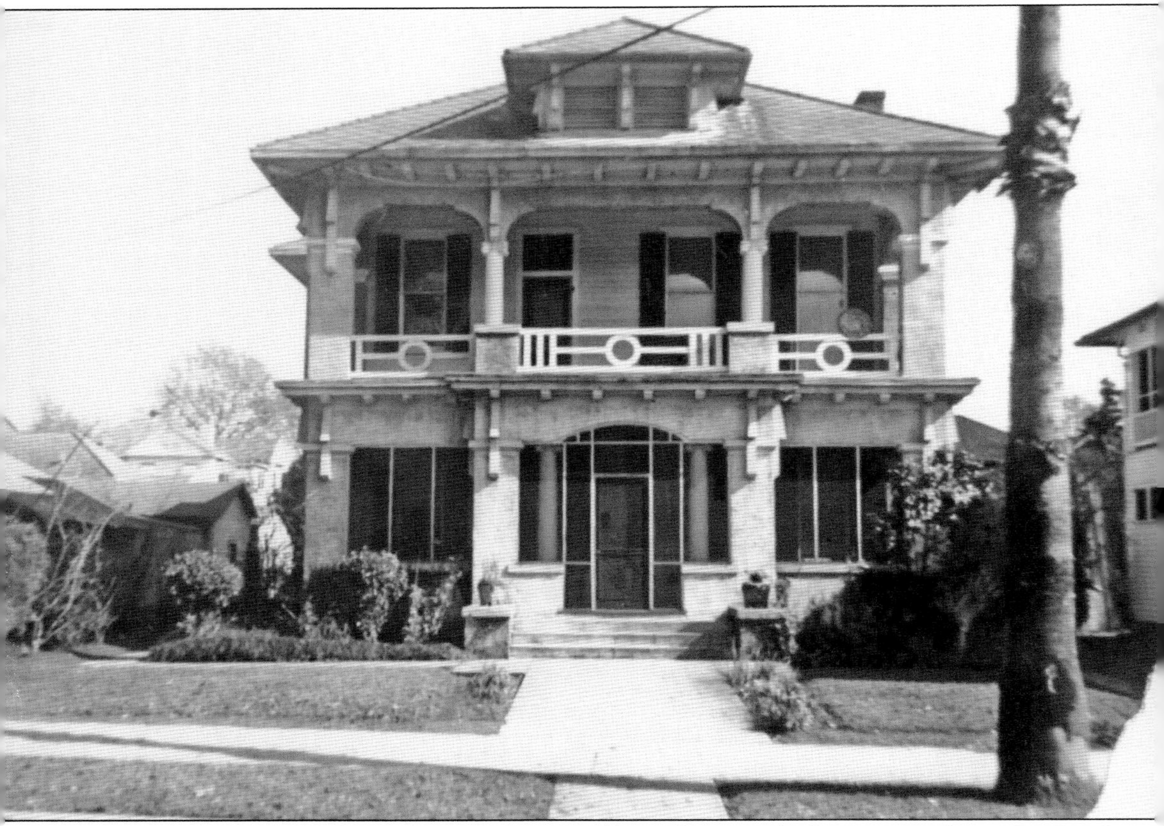

The house at 232 North Ninth Street is pictured here about 1925. The property, located in South Baton Rouge, was demolished in 1955, along with a number of other properties, to make way for Interstate 110. Highway construction, such as Interstates 110 and 10, literally changed the city's landscape. The freeway displaced homes owned by blacks and whites but had a particularly devastating impact on black households. In the mid-1960s, the Louisiana Department of Transportation and Development elected to construct I-10 through areas in South Baton Rouge with majority black populations, even in the face of staunch opposition. In "Poverty lives in LSU's culturally and historically rich neighbor," an April 2, 2014, article on the LSUNow website, Andrea Gallo notes that "around 400 houses were demolished. The long-awaited St. Francis Xavier High School, only a few years old, was bulldozed, leaving the church to stand alone. The interstate cut off Old South Baton Rouge's northeastern corner and severed the neighborhood in half." (Courtesy of East Baton Rouge Parish Public Library Digital Archive.)

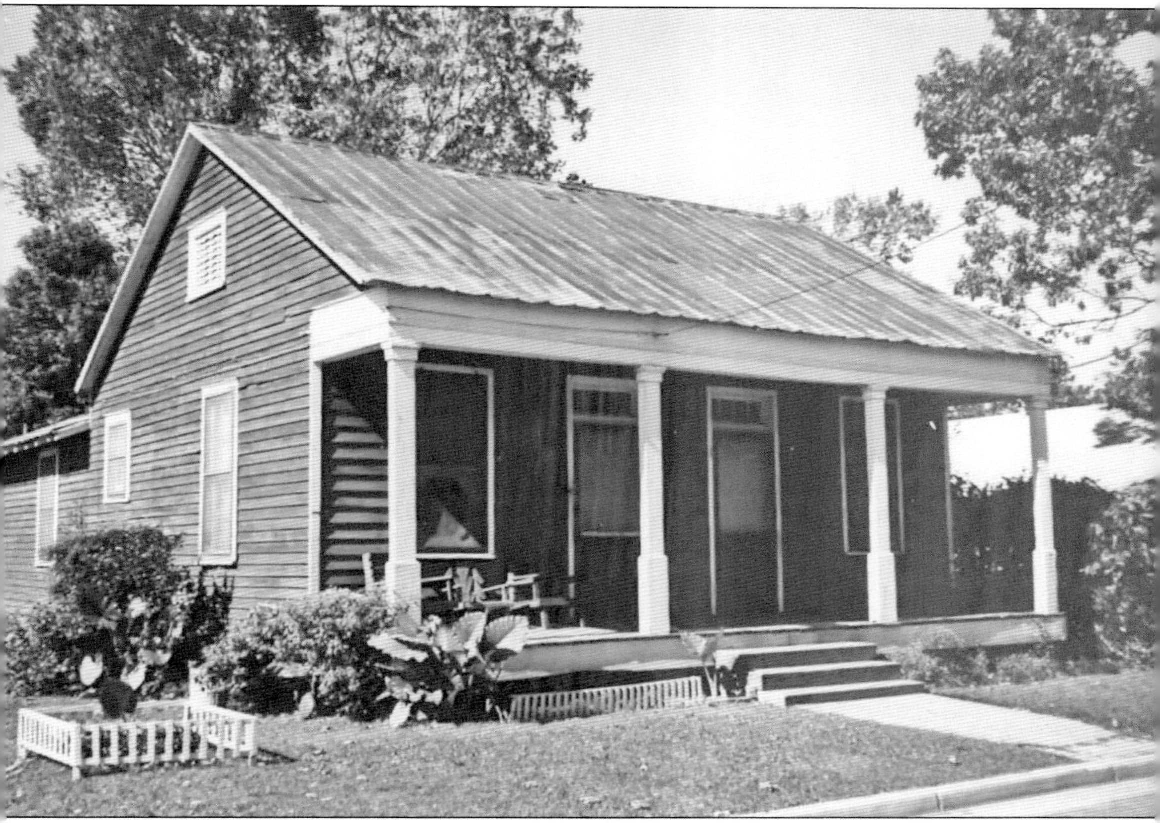

This photograph is part of the Ernest Gueymard Collection, housed at East Baton Rouge Parish Public Library. The image shows what the house looked like in the 1960s, almost a century after George Thompson built the home for his family in 1870. Thompson, an African American resident of South Baton Rouge, owned a sawmill. The house is still located at 835 North Seventh Street. According to Jim Fraiser, author of *Historic Baton Rouge Architecture,* the house was built in the Italianate style, which is recognizable by decorative boards supported by the gallery's square posts. Thompson was not alone in his role as an owner of mills. Other industrious blacks, including John Moore of Sparkill, New York, owned several mills in the late 1700s and early 1800s. (Courtesy of East Baton Rouge Parish Public Library Digital Archive.)

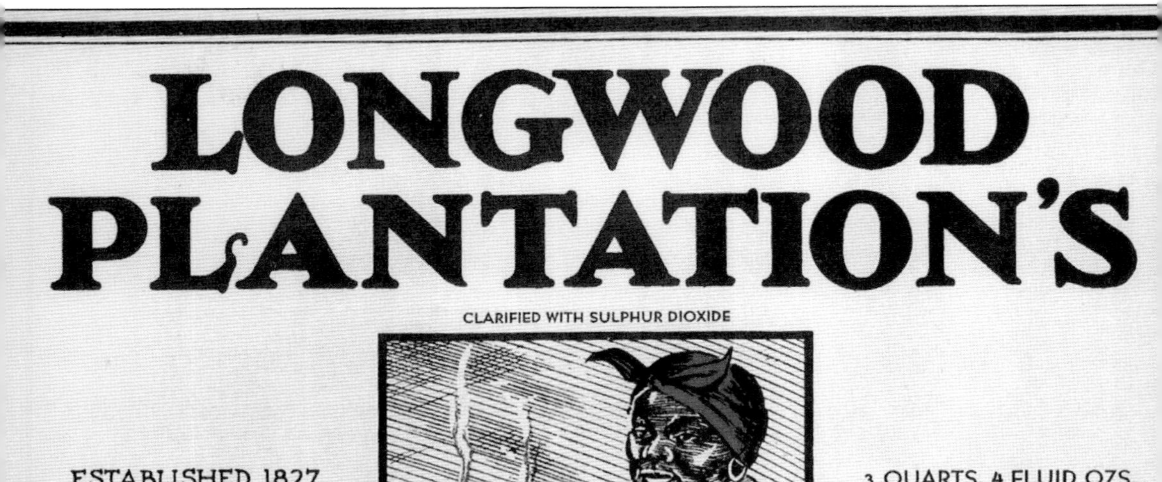

Baton Rouge was home to many active plantations prior to the Civil War. Plantations in East Baton Rouge Parish included Scotland, Magnolia, and Longwood. Longwood Plantation, a sugarcane plantation located in South Baton Rouge, was established around 1785. The first records of sugar production on the plantation are dated 1828. Over 300 hogsheads of sugar were produced that year (a hogshead was a standard unit of measurement of about 48 inches long and 30 inches in diameter). The property changed hands many times over the years. In 1845, Josiah Barker sold the plantation to his son, Thomas Hazard Barker, for the sum of $150,000. Thomas Barker sold the property, along with 93 slaves, two years later to Thomas Mille and Jacques Philippe Meffre Rouzan.

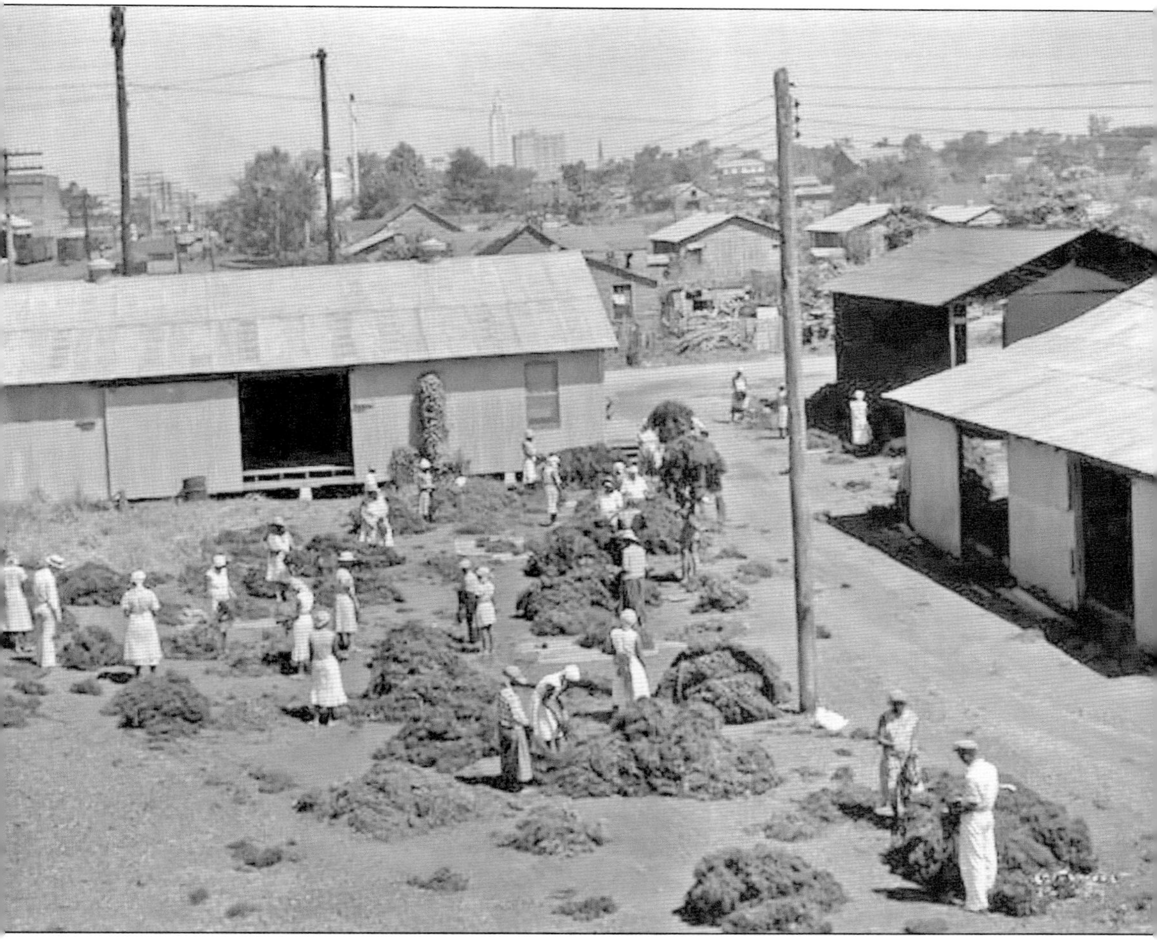

Employees are shown working at Sidney B. Webb's moss factory in the 1930s. Louisiana was a leader in the processing, distribution, and sales of Spanish moss. According to an article by Dan Gill in the January 5, 2012, *New Orleans Times-Picayune*, Spanish moss is "a flowering, epiphytic plant belonging—along with pineapples—to the Bromeliad family. It is widely distributed from southern Virginia to eastern Texas along the coastal strip of the southeastern United States. Spanish moss occurs throughout Louisiana, but is more common in some locations than others," such as South Baton Rouge. "In former times, moss had a variety of uses in upholstery. It was used to stuff everything from car cushions to horse collars, but was mainly used in furniture manufacturing. Fresh moss was gathered and cured by wetting it down and packing it in trenches or pits. It usually remained in the pits for six to eight months, in which time the outer covering rotted off, leaving the inner strand. At the factory, the moss then was sorted, cleaned and baled for shipment." The photograph is part of a collection of works by Jasper Ewing. (Courtesy of Andrew Lytle's Photograph Collection, MSS 2600, LSU Libraries.)

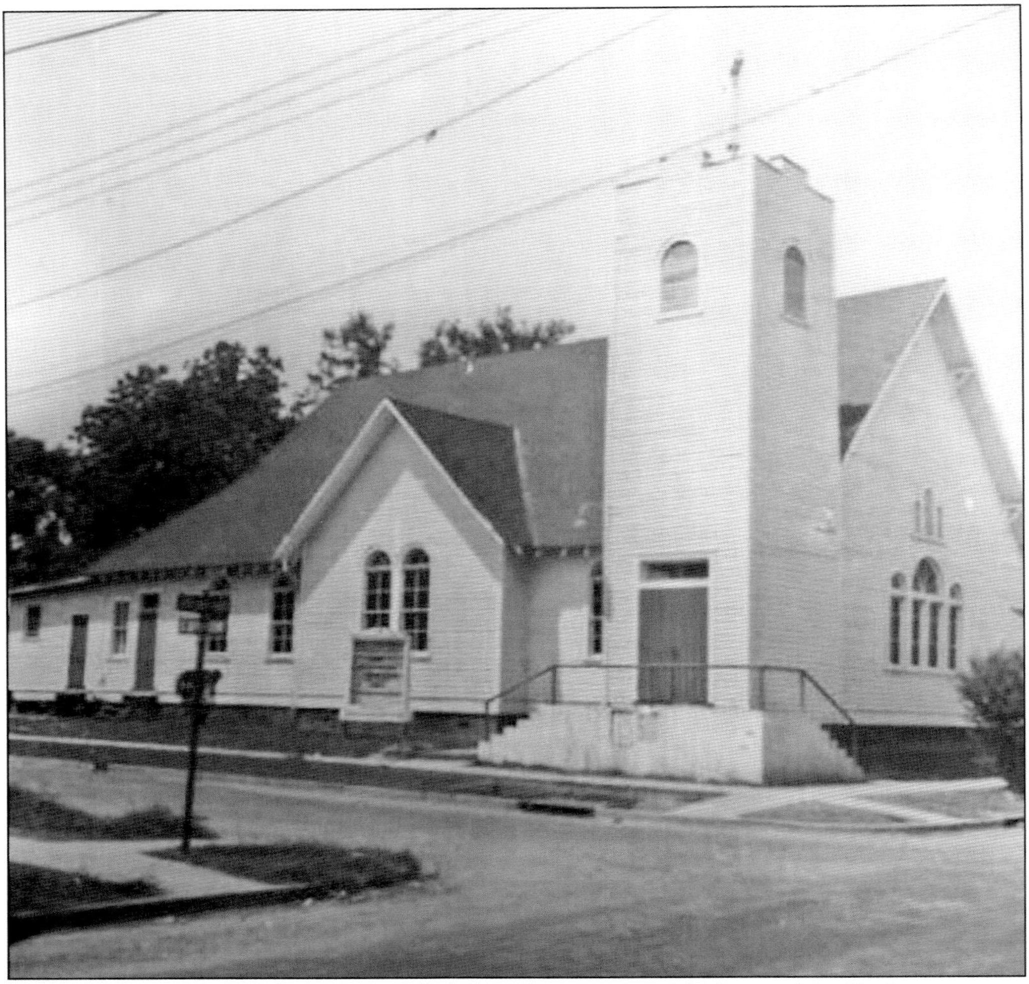

Progressive Baptist Church is a historic faith-based institution in the heart of the black community of South Baton Rouge, which is also home to a number of black churches, including Baptist and African Methodist Episcopal congregations. Organized in 1916 with over 300 members, Progressive Baptist Church is pictured here around 1948 at its current location, 998 Julia Street. The historic black church remains actively engaged in its commitment to the spiritual needs of members and to the broader needs of the surrounding community and city. The church is among a coalition of community-based organizations working to improve the quality of life for residents throughout the city, including for blacks in South Baton Rouge. The current pastor, Rev. Melvin Rushing, is a participant in an initiative called "Together Baton Rouge." (Courtesy of East Baton Rouge Parish Public Library Digital Archive.)

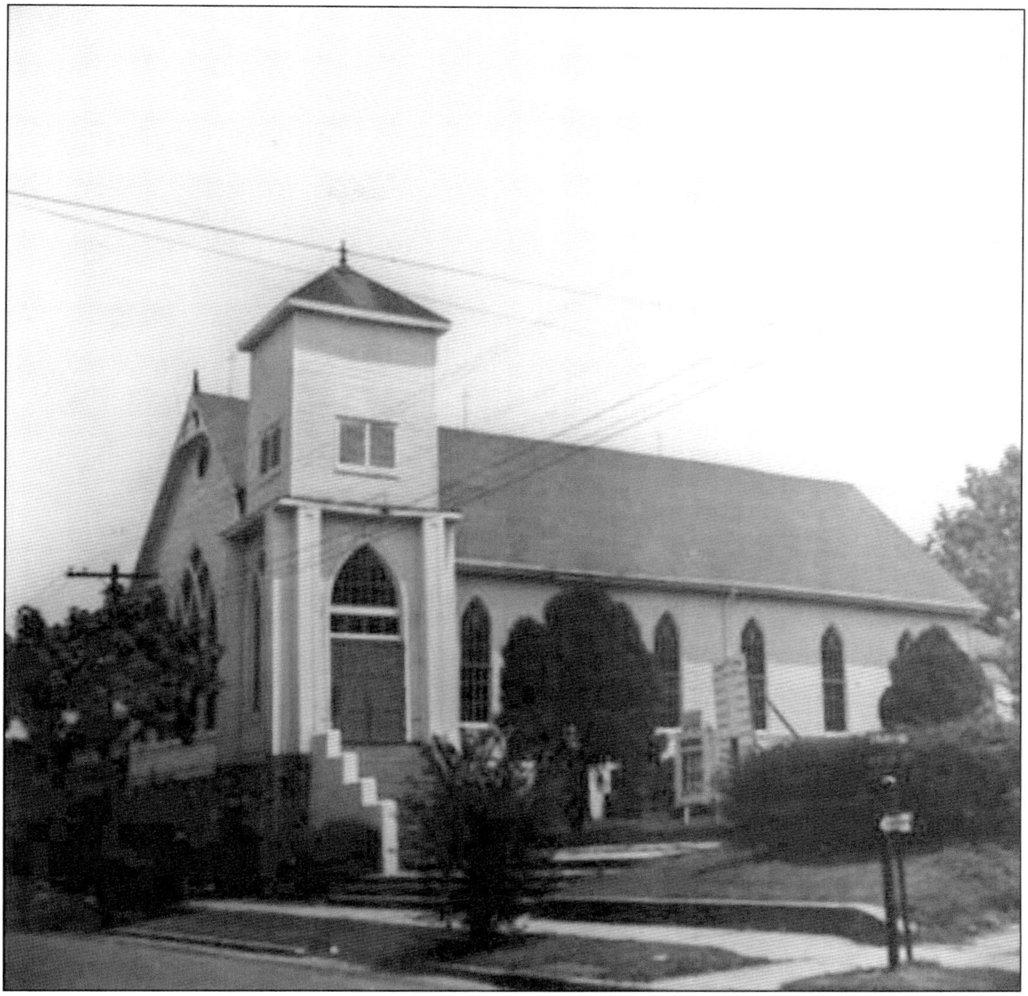

Mount Zion Baptist was organized in 1847. This photograph of the historic church was taken around 1948. A year earlier, the congregation had more than 1,000 members. The church was located at 335 Maximillian Street in South Baton Rouge. It moved to its present location at 356 East Boulevard in 1954. In December 2015, the street the church is on was renamed in honor of a former pastor of Mount Zion Baptist Church, Rev. T.J. Jemison. Jemison not only led the church for many years, he also was an important leader in national Baptist and civil rights organizations. He was one of the leaders of the historic 1953 Baton Rouge bus boycott, which served as a model for the 1955 Montgomery bus boycott. The latter boycott catapulted Rev. Dr. Martin Luther King Jr. onto the national stage in the fight for equal treatment for all Americans. (Courtesy of East Baton Rouge Parish Public Library Archive Collection.)

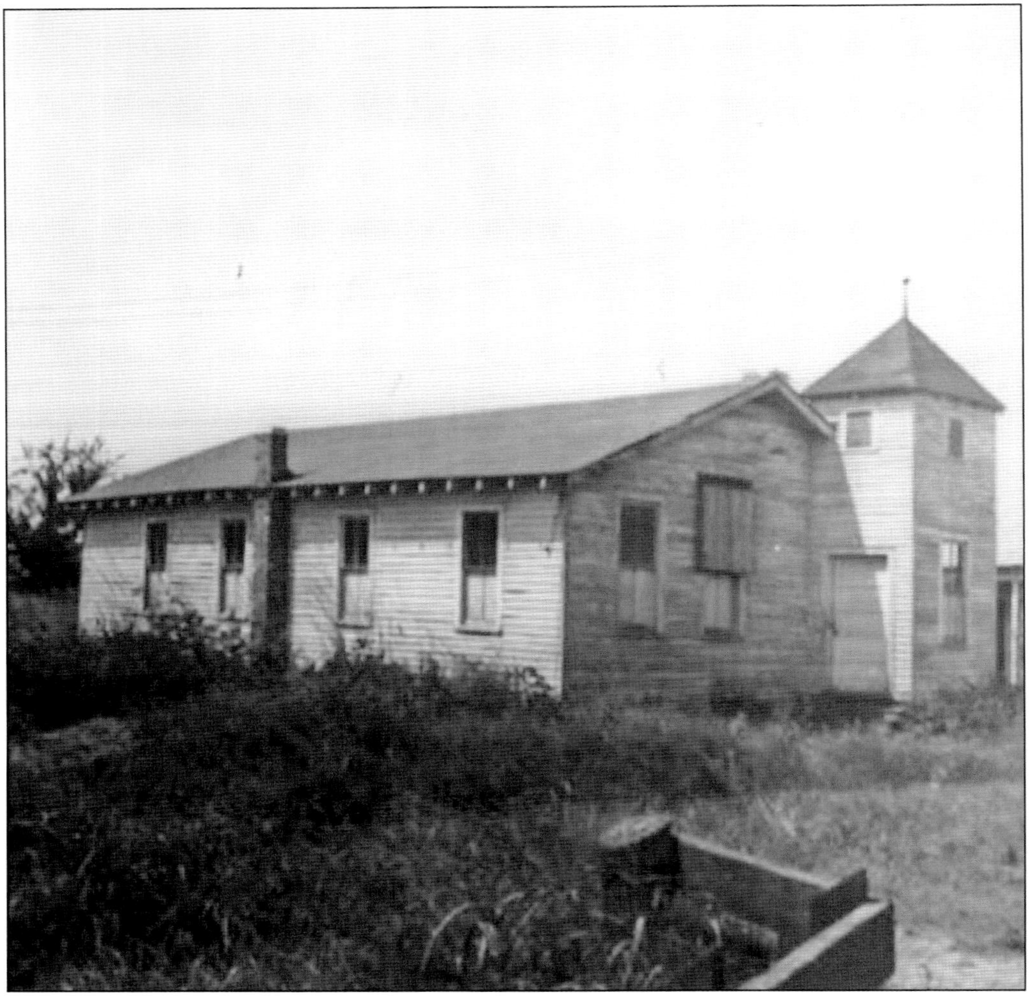

The black church has long been considered an important social institution in the lives of African Americans. It has played an important role in the experiences of African Americans throughout the nation and in Louisiana. Black residents of South Baton Rouge have worshipped at Mount Pleasant Baptist Church since the church organized in 1870. There is no shortage of predominately black churches in South Louisiana, including in South Baton Rouge. Area black churches include Bethel AME, Mount Zion Baptist, Shiloh Baptist, and Mount Pleasant Baptist Church. Church leaders were often also important community leaders. Mount Pleasant Baptist Church is pictured here in the late 1940s. Two dozen residents of South Baton Rouge were members of the congregation in 1947. Located at 1743 Convention Street, the predominately black church remains an important fixture in the community. Rev. Charlie Green Jr. is the current pastor. (Courtesy of East Baton Rouge Parish Public Library Archive Collection.)

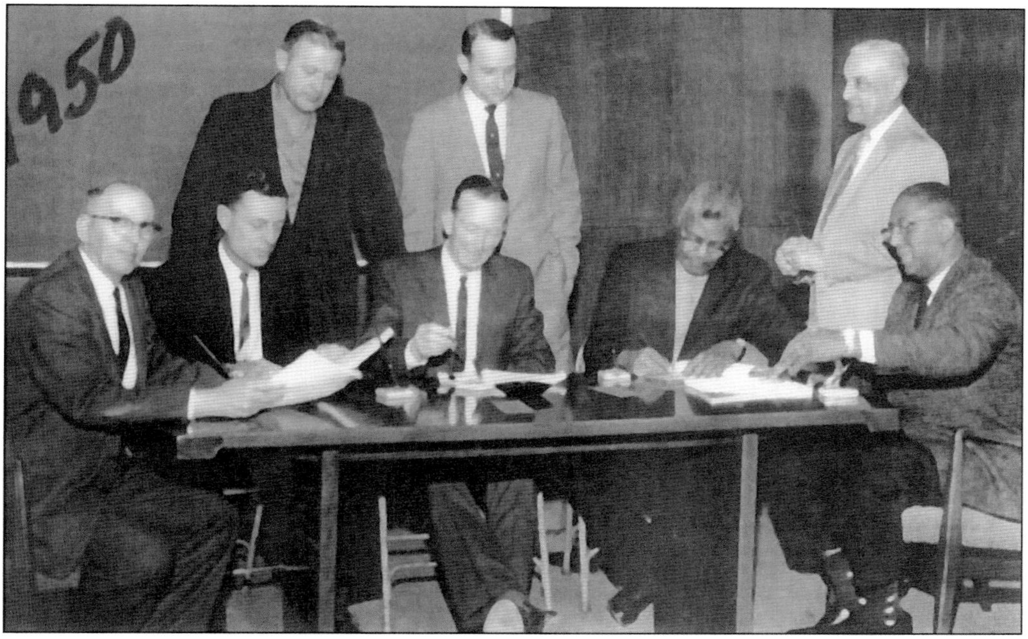

Theodore R. Smith, one of the leaders of the Baton Rouge bus boycott in 1953, was active throughout Baton Rouge over the course of his lifetime. He also played an important role in desegregating the local Esso (now Exxon) plant. Smith is pictured here signing a labor contract in 1950. Seated at left is Henry Voories, president/manager of the refinery. Unidentified officers of the white section are to the left; to the right are officers of the black section—Smith, James Cook, and Thomas Davis. Smith and his family were also active members of black churches in South Baton Rouge, which were commonly used as meeting places to mobilize for strategies around issues of social justice. (Courtesy of Russell Kelly.)

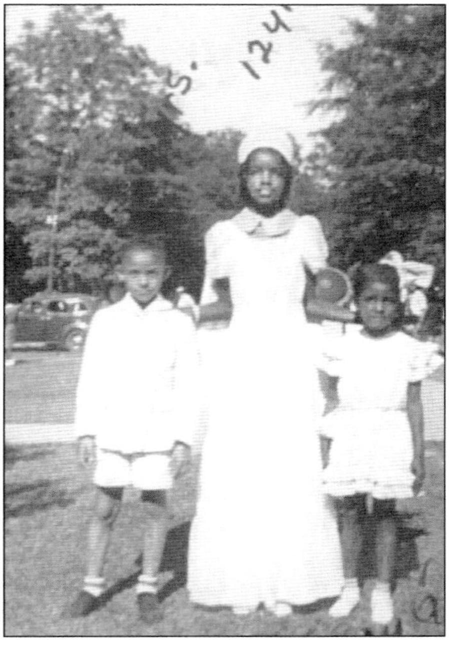

A young Theodore R. Smith, champion of civil rights and social justice in South Baton Rouge and beyond, is pictured here at the age of 9 in May 1939 with his sisters, Constance Smith (Lamotte) and Yvonne Smith (Brunner). The Smith family attended church in South Baton Rouge. Theodore was a longtime member of Bethel African Methodist Episcopal (AME) Church, which is still located in South Baton Rouge. (Courtesy of Russell Kelly.)

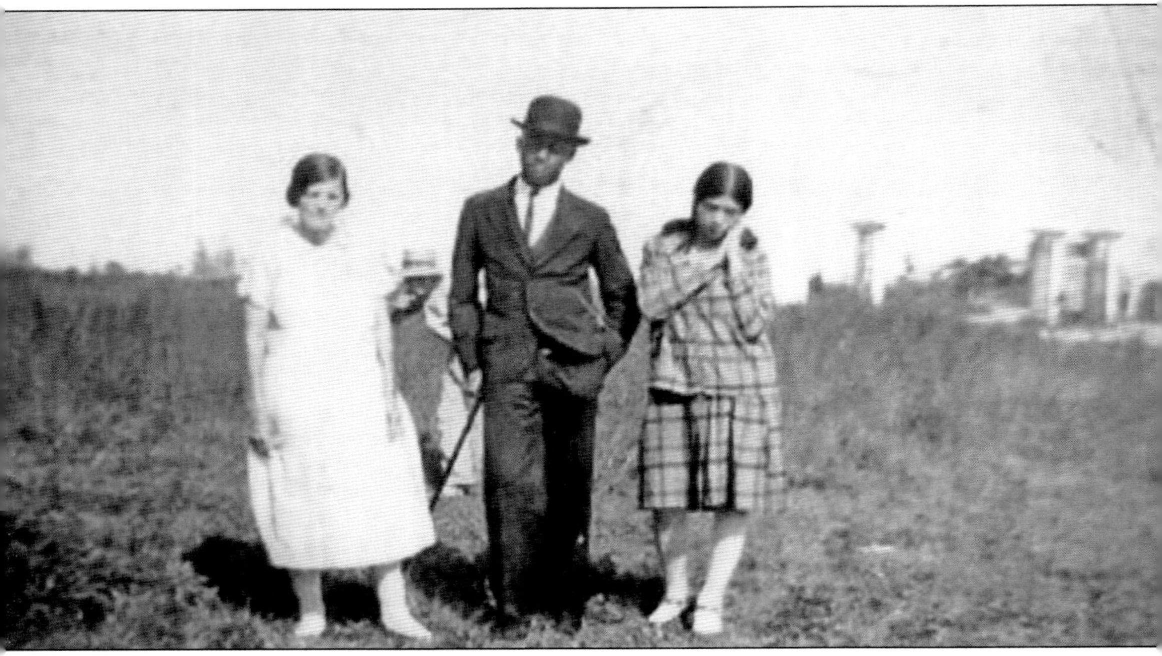

Pictured are relatives of Smith's. Many members of the Smith family lived in South Baton Rouge or attended important institutions there and in other parts of the city, such as Southern University, which was the only university in Baton Rouge blacks could attend for a time due to segregation. (Courtesy of Russell Kelly.)

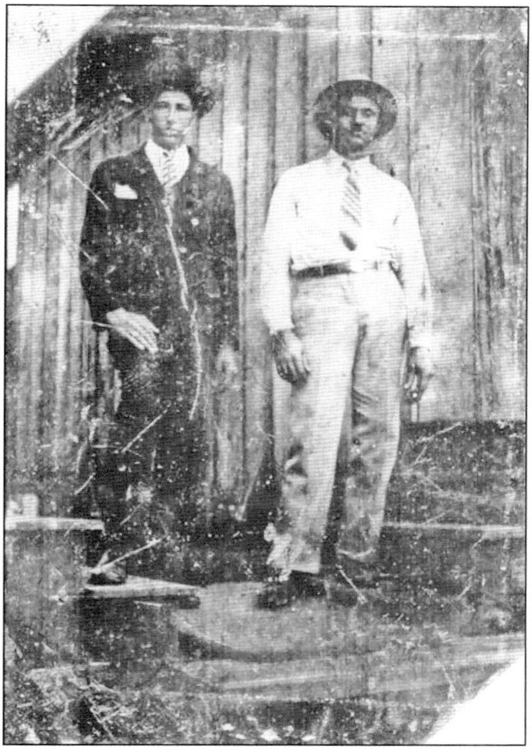

The two men pictured together and the woman pictured alone are also relatives of T. Roosevelt Smith, who played an important role in the 1953 Baton Rouge bus boycott, among his many other important contributions. Smith was the executive chairman of the board of the United Defense League, the organization responsible for mobilizing much of the community's resources during the boycott. The group collected over $1,000 in black churches to pay for a free-ride system, which was critical to the local boycott and which was replicated two years later in Montgomery, Alabama. Arther Donaldson, a member of the Smith family, is pictured at right with his brother-in-law Lloyd; below is Marie Gradney in the late 1940s. (Both, courtesy of Russell Kelly.)

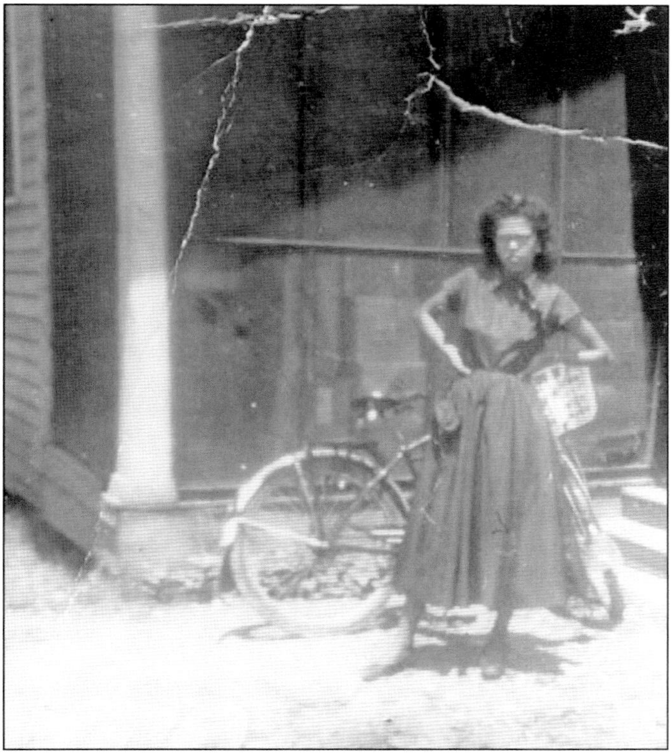

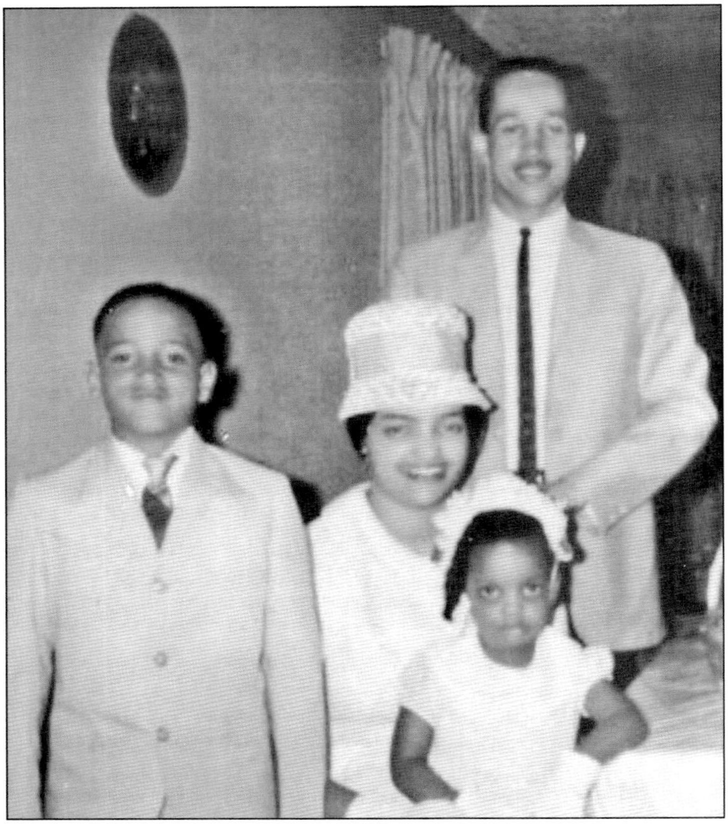

Members of T. Roosevelt Smith's family are pictured here. At left is Russell Kelly with his parents and sister. Below is Russell Kelly as a youngster with four generations of his family. A driving force behind the 1953 Baton Rouge bus boycott. Smith was born and raised in Baton Rouge. His standing in the community was not only evidenced in the media coverage he received outside of Louisiana but was also evident when the community gathered to remember his life when he passed away. Honorary pallbearers included judges and other prominent local people. (Both, courtesy of Russell Kelly.)

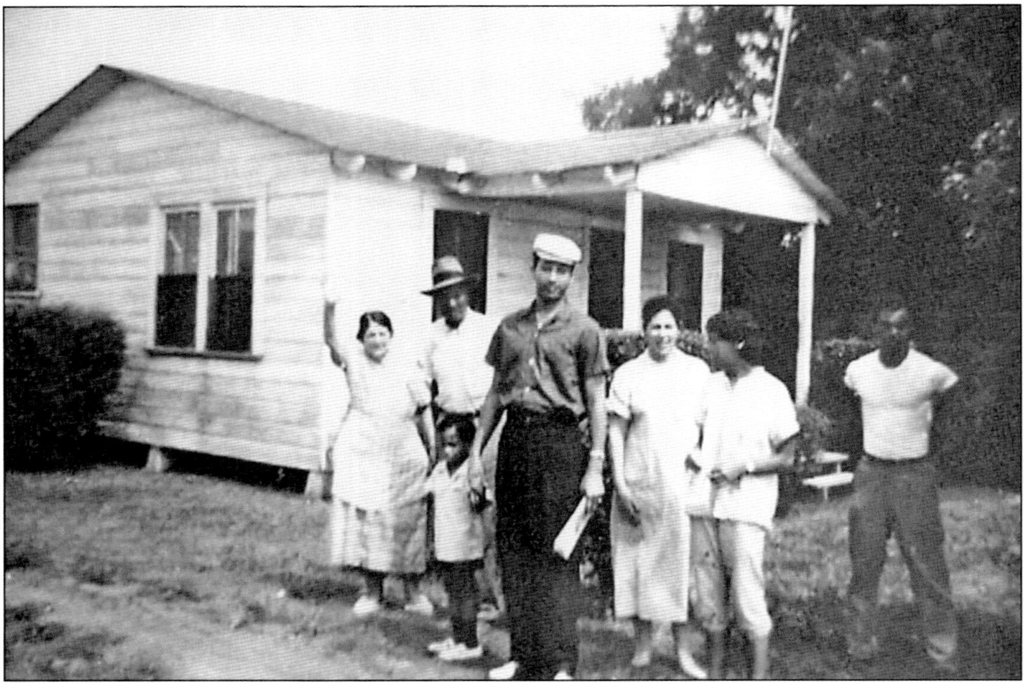

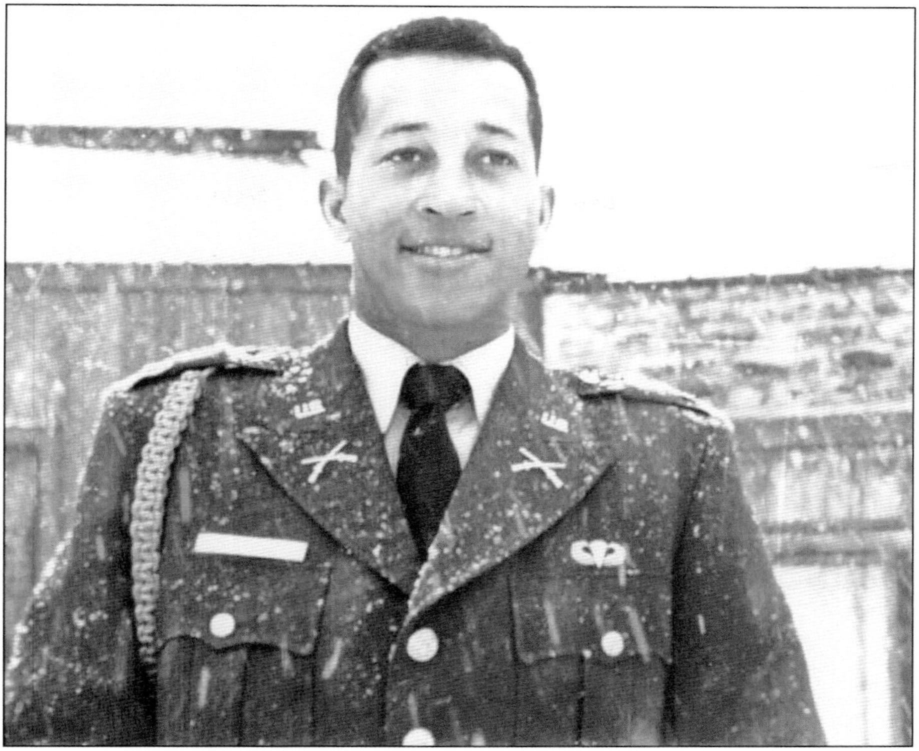

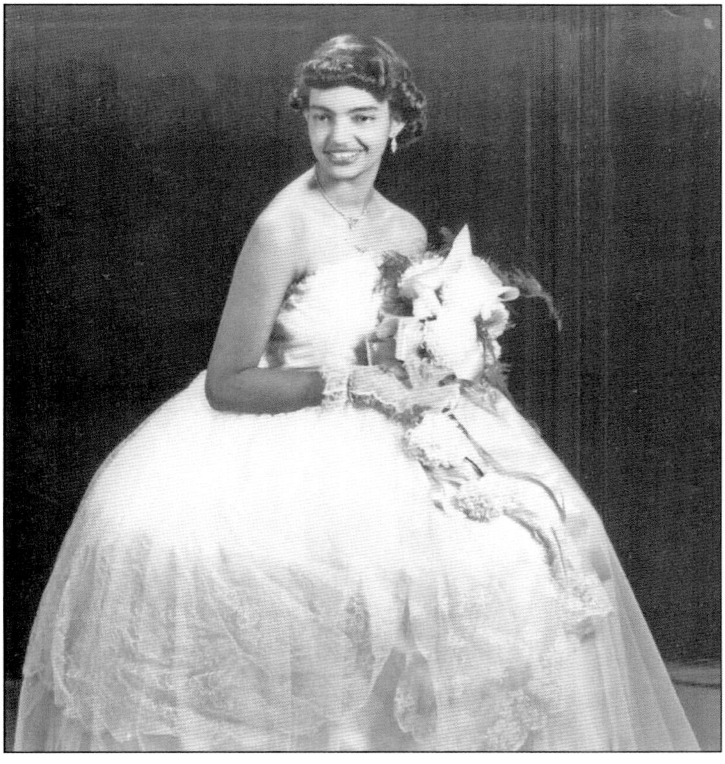

Many black residents in South Baton Rouge served valiantly in the military, including in the Civil War and every war thereafter. Russell Kelly is a descendant of T.R. Smith. Kelly's father, Nolan Kelly, is pictured above while stationed in Korea. The photograph is representative of the men of the era who were willing to sacrifice their lives for others. Smith's youngest granddaughter and Russell's mother, Jewell Amelia Smith Kelly, is pictured at left. T.R. Smith was involved in many organizations, often serving as president, which earned him the nickname "Prezy." (Both, courtesy of Russell Kelly.)

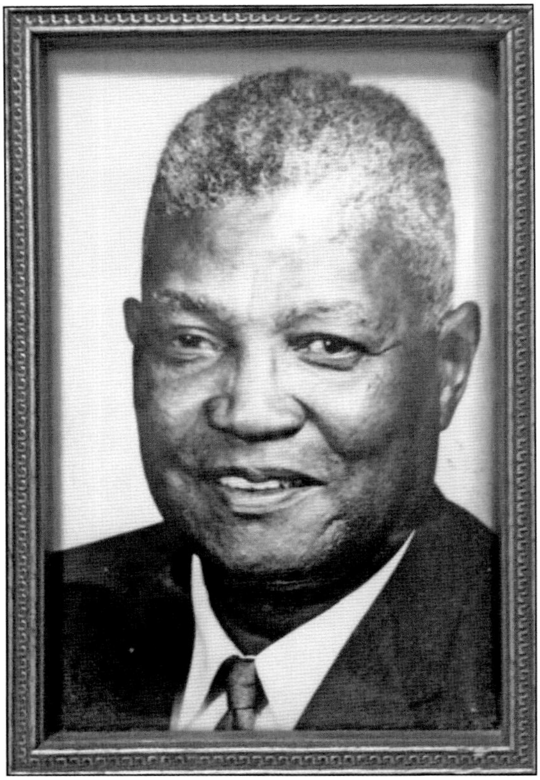

Theodore R. Smith is pictured at left. Smith was a founding member of the organization that helped organize black churches and residents to participate and fund the Baton Rouge bus boycott. Smith was also one of the founders of the Purple Circle Club and was an active member of Bethel AME Church. Other members of the Smith family attended Shiloh Baptist Church, which was organized in 1872. The church was originally located on Boyd Street and moved to South Fourteenth Street in 1932. Below is a picture of the intersection bearing the name of another one of the leaders of the Baton Rouge bus boycott, Rev. T.J. Jemison. (Both, courtesy of Russell Kelly.)

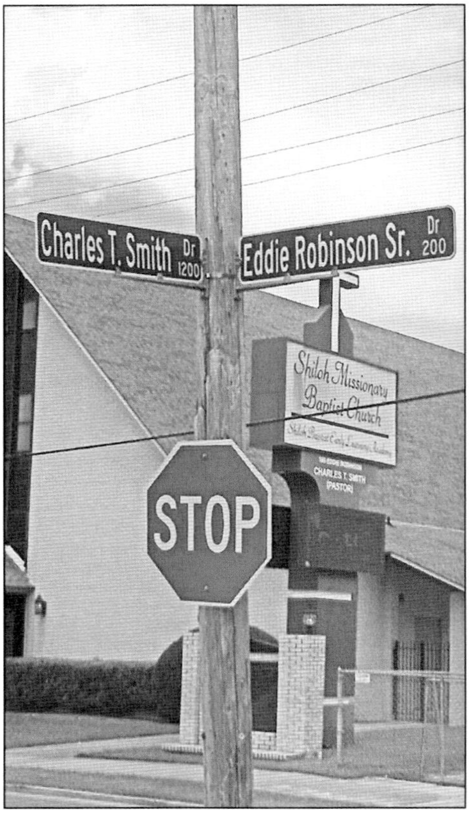

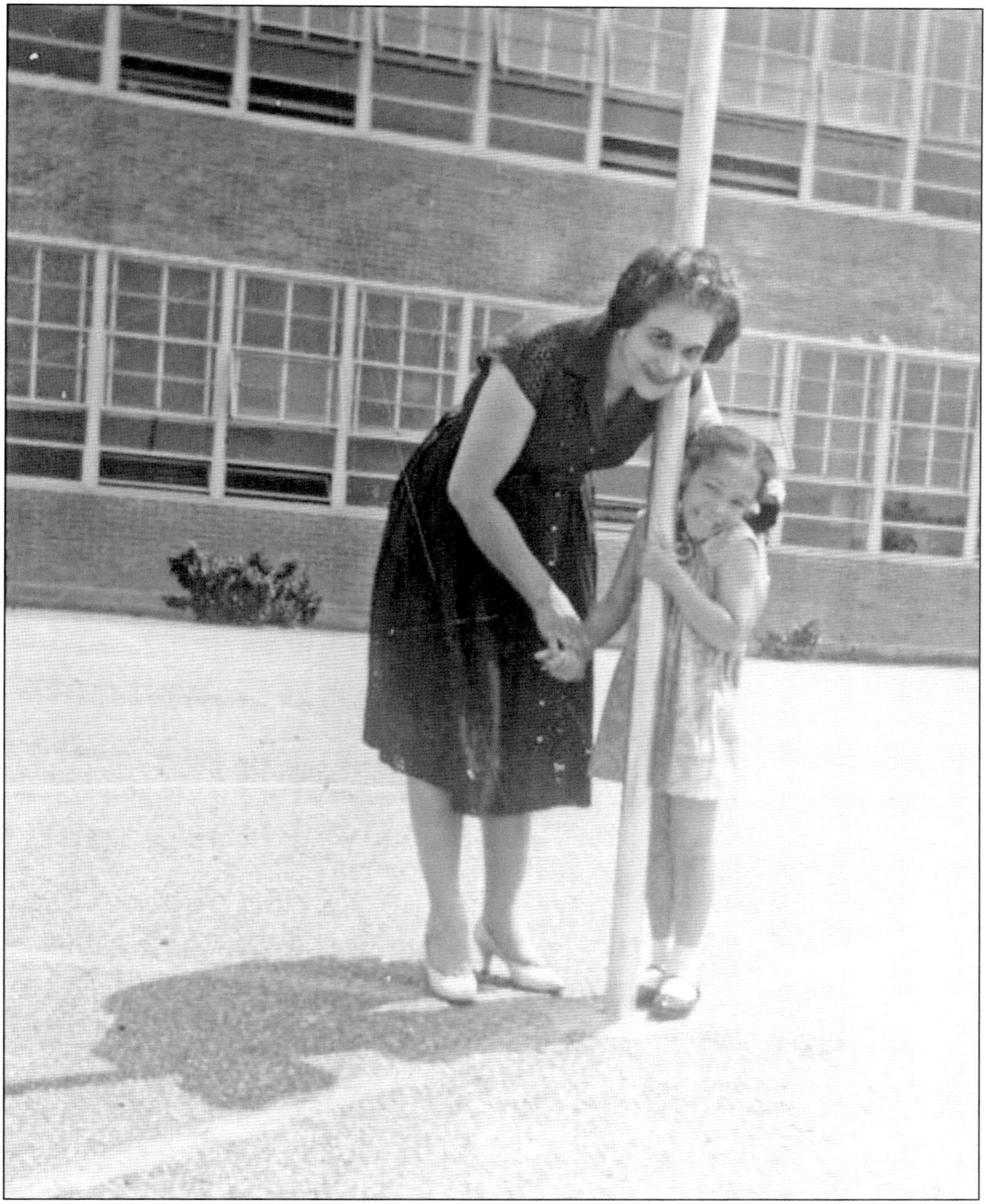

South Baton Rouge is well known not only for its families and its historically black churches and schools but also for its dedicated, highly intelligent, and committed black educators. These educators not only communicated knowledge, they also set high expectations and provided students with the love, guidance, and discipline required to meet and exceed those expectations. Sadie Connor Keel (1914–2010) is pictured in the mid-1960s with a student. Keel was an educator in Baton Rouge for many years. A teacher and principal at Reddy Street Elementary School for nearly three decades, she graduated from McKinley High School in 1930 and earned degrees from Michigan State and Southern Universities. (Courtesy of East Baton Rouge Parish Public Library Digital Archive.)

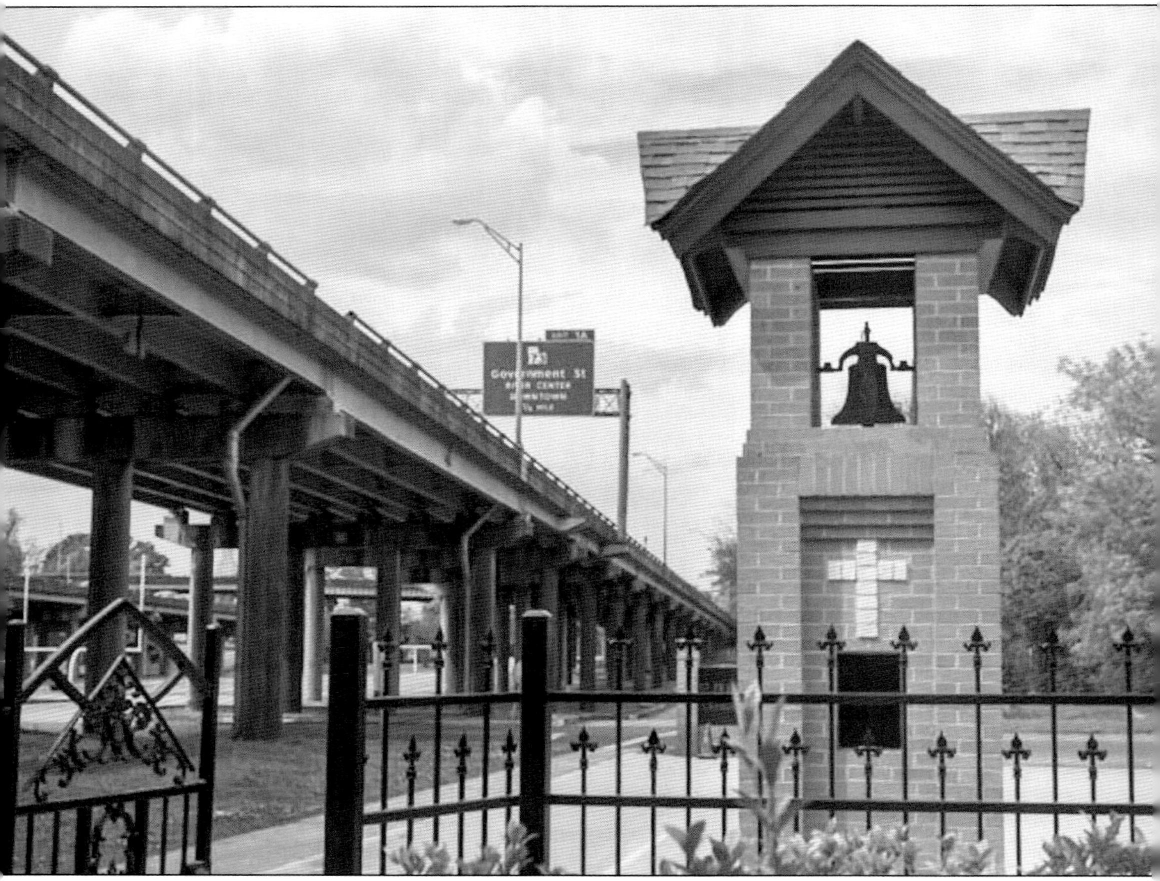

St. Francis Xavier Catholic School is a fixture in South Baton Rouge. It is the only African American Catholic school in the Diocese of Baton Rouge. The school, which opened its doors in 1920, educates students from prekindergarten to the eighth grade. According to the school's website, Holy Family Academy, the first Catholic school for blacks in Baton Rouge, was sold and the money received was loaned to the parish to build St. Francis Xavier Catholic School, the first parochial school in the diocese. The school draws students from the immediate neighborhood and from areas such as Zachary and Gonzales, Louisiana. St. Francis High School opened in 1955 but was torn down in 1961 to make way for the interstate system. Text on the school's website states, "That same year the old elementary school, which had also served as the convent, was moved to the site of the present Saint Francis Xavier Church. A new school was constructed on the property, and opened its doors in 1963." (Courtesy of East Baton Rouge Parish Public Library Digital Archive.)

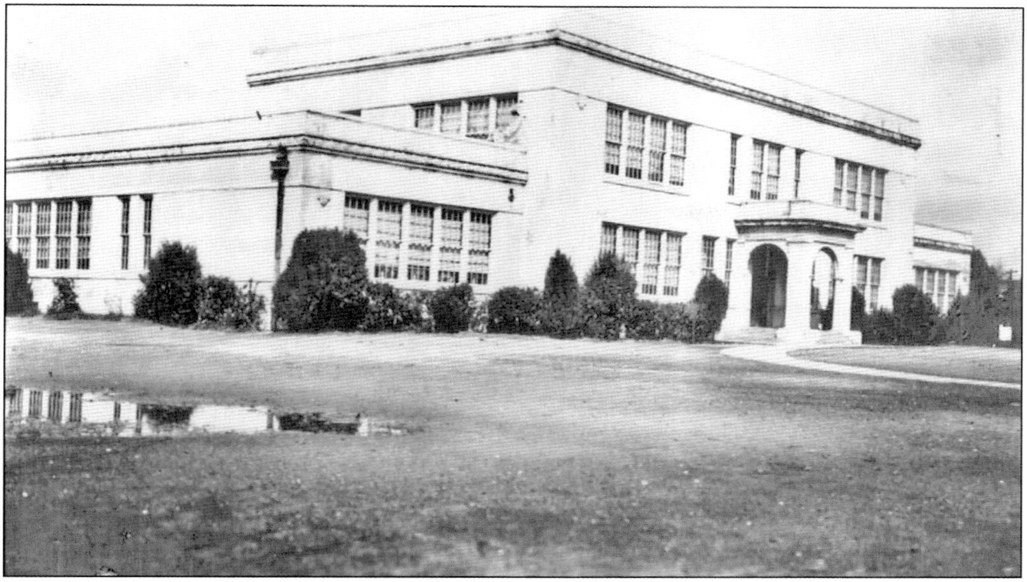

Perkins Road African American School appears in the 1930s photograph above. The school replaced the original Baton Rouge Colored High School, which was damaged in a fire in 1928. After the fire, the city tore the building down and built the structure pictured here. James Monroe Frazier served as the head of the black portion of the city's segregated school system for two decades. Frazier's master's thesis is on the history of African American education in East Baton Rouge Parish. Another school that drew black students from South Baton Rouge was the Rosenwald school, pictured below in the 1920s. It was one of more than 5,000 Rosenwald schools throughout the South funded in part by the Julius Rosenwald Foundation. The foundation's aim was to improve the quality of public education for blacks in the early part of the 20th century in the South. (Both, courtesy of State Library of Louisiana.)

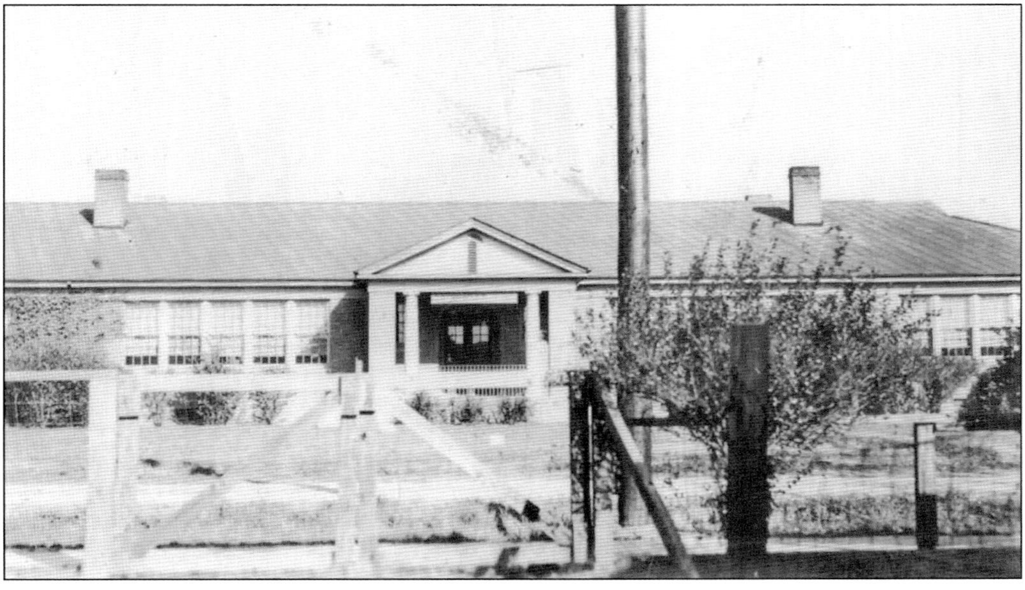

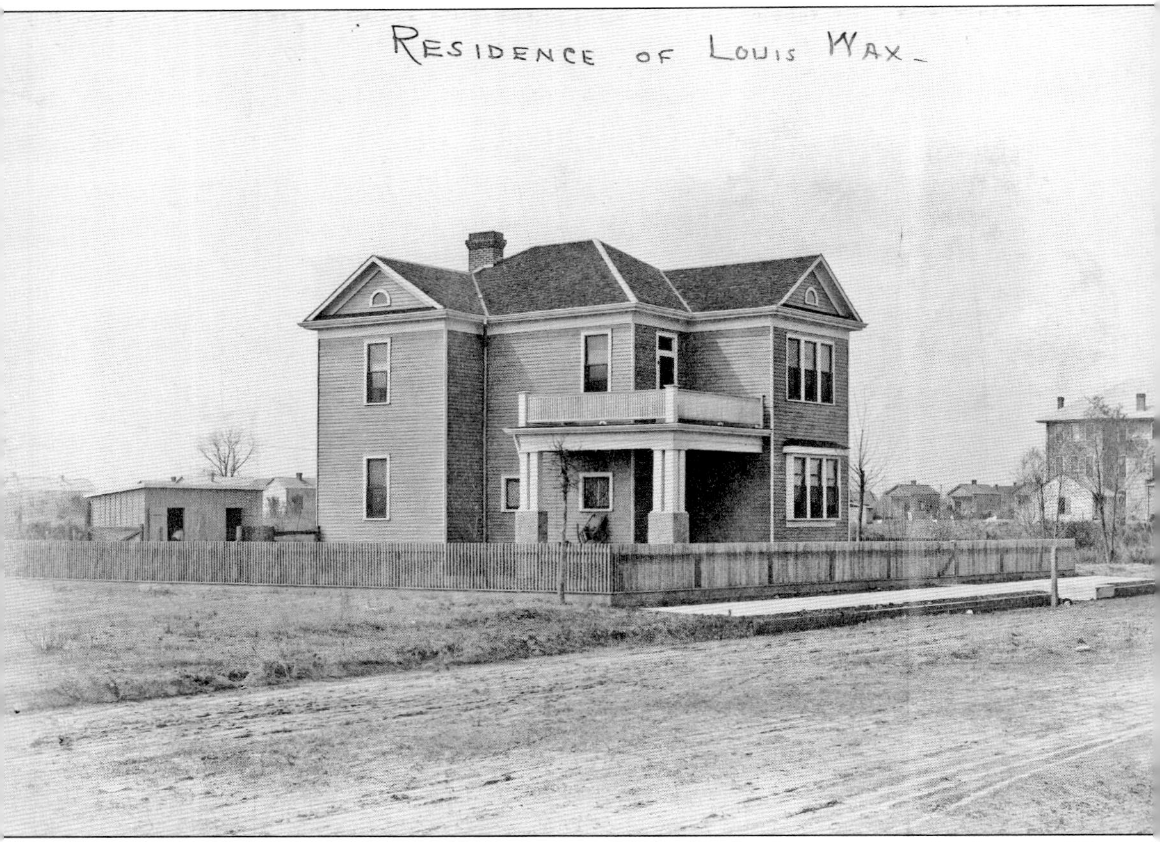

Baton Rouge Academy, an African American school, is the brick structure in the distance. This photograph was taken in 1915. The Fourth District Baptist Association ran Baton Rouge Academy beginning in 1906. A suggestion was made in the early 1890s for the association to buy a tract of land for a denominational school. The Fourth District Baptist Association purchased land referred to as the O'Connor Tract on Perkins Road. The doors opened on September 23, 1893, to educate black boys and girls. Prof. J.L. Croosiey was the school's first principal. (Courtesy of East Baton Rouge Parish Public Library Digital Archive.)

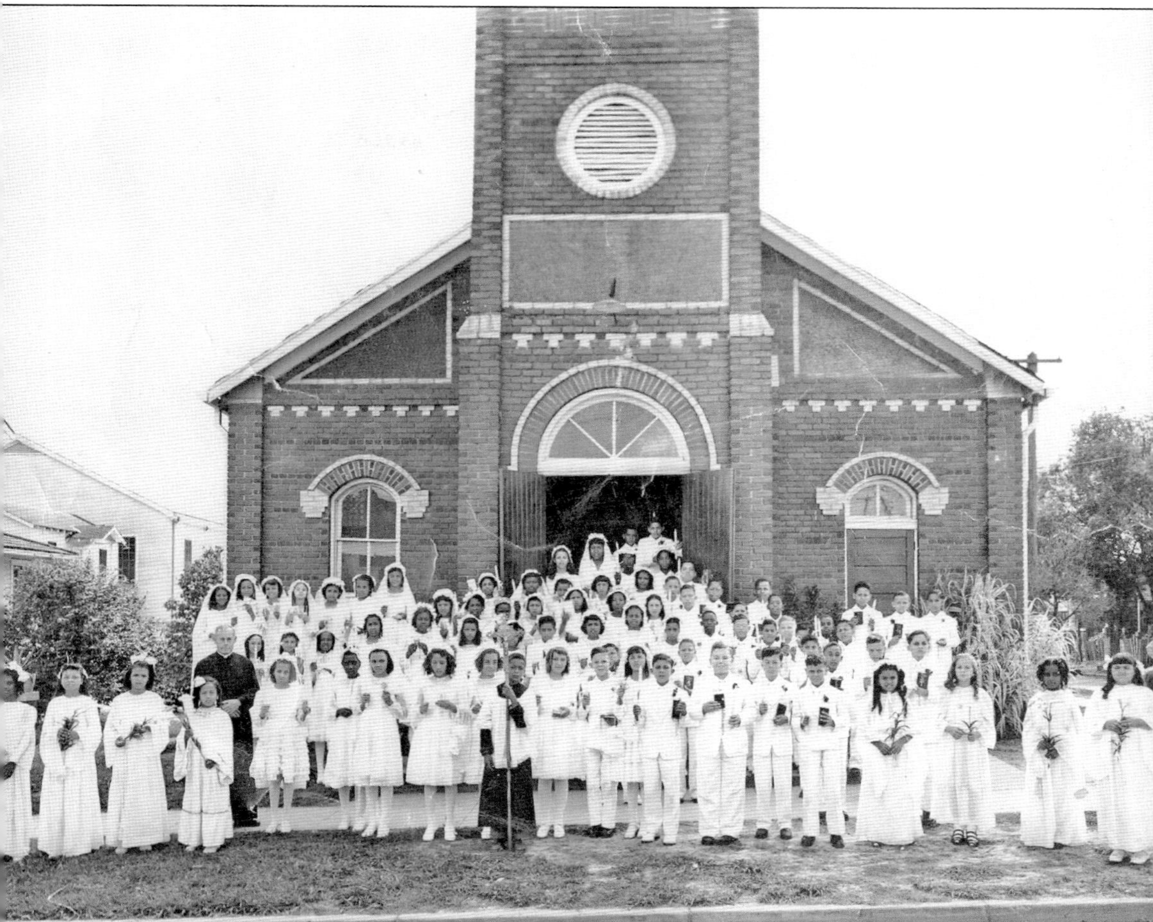

Parishioners of St. Francis Catholic Church in South Baton Rouge celebrate First Communion in this 1949 photograph. The predominately black parish not only provided for the spiritual needs of black Catholics in the diocese, it provided schools for them as well. The church's history is indicative of the history of race relations in Baton Rouge. The church provided educational opportunities for blacks when they were excluded from predominately white institutions and suffered when the predominately black community was literally divided by the construction of the interstate system, with little regard for the immediate and long-term effects of the decision on the historic black neighborhoods and their residents and institutions. (Courtesy of East Baton Rouge Parish Public Library Digital Archive.)

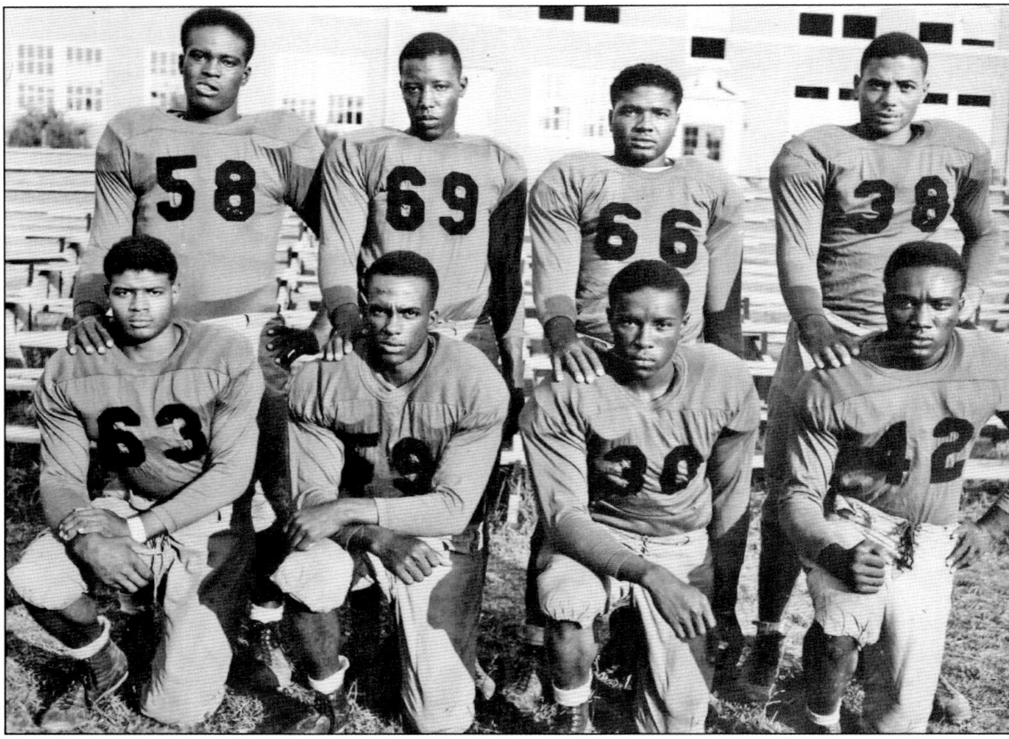

Educational facilities in South Baton Rouge produced legendary people in a wide array of fields, including one of the most successful college coaches. Eddie Robinson Sr. graduated from McKinley High School in South Baton Rouge, and he went on to coach football at Grambling University, a historically black university in Louisiana that counts among its thousands of graduates men and women who were raised in South Baton Rouge. These pictures of players from the storied athletic program were taken in the 1940s. Robinson coached at Grambling University for nearly six decades from 1941 to 1997. The athletes seen in these images are unidentified. (Both, courtesy of East Baton Rouge Parish Public Library Digital Archive.)

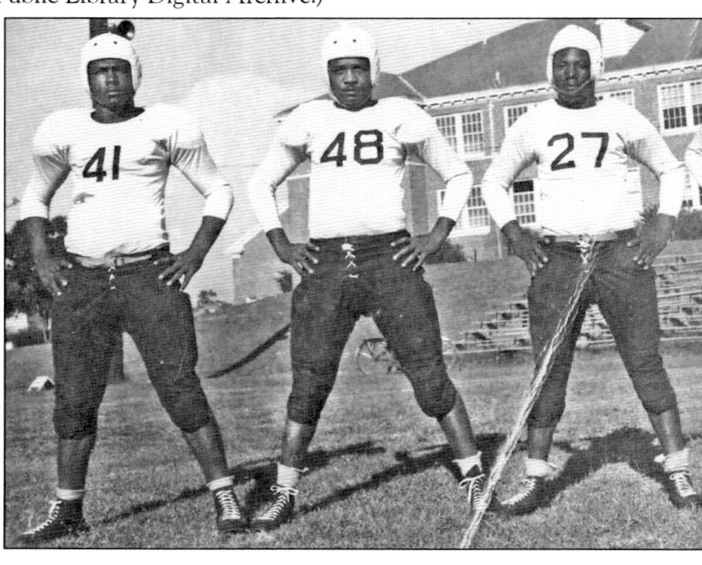

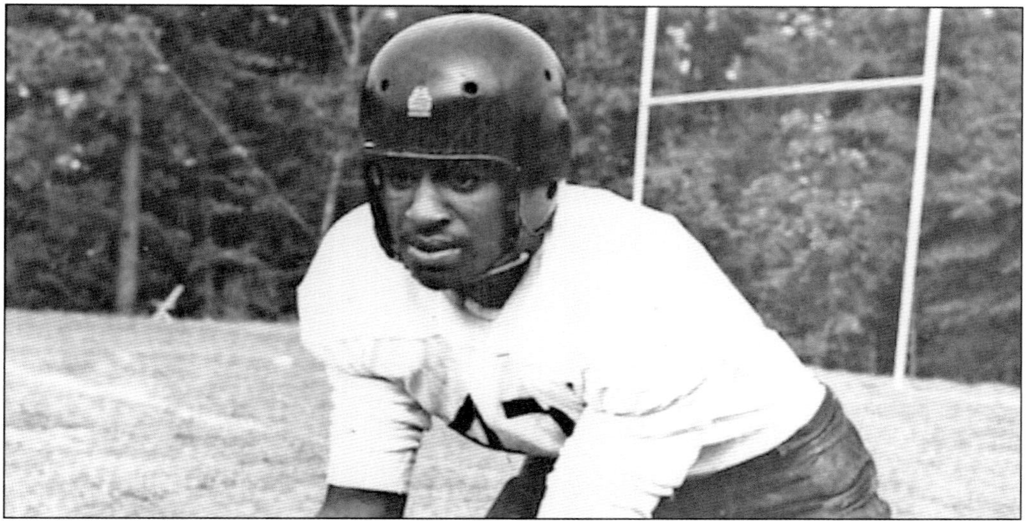

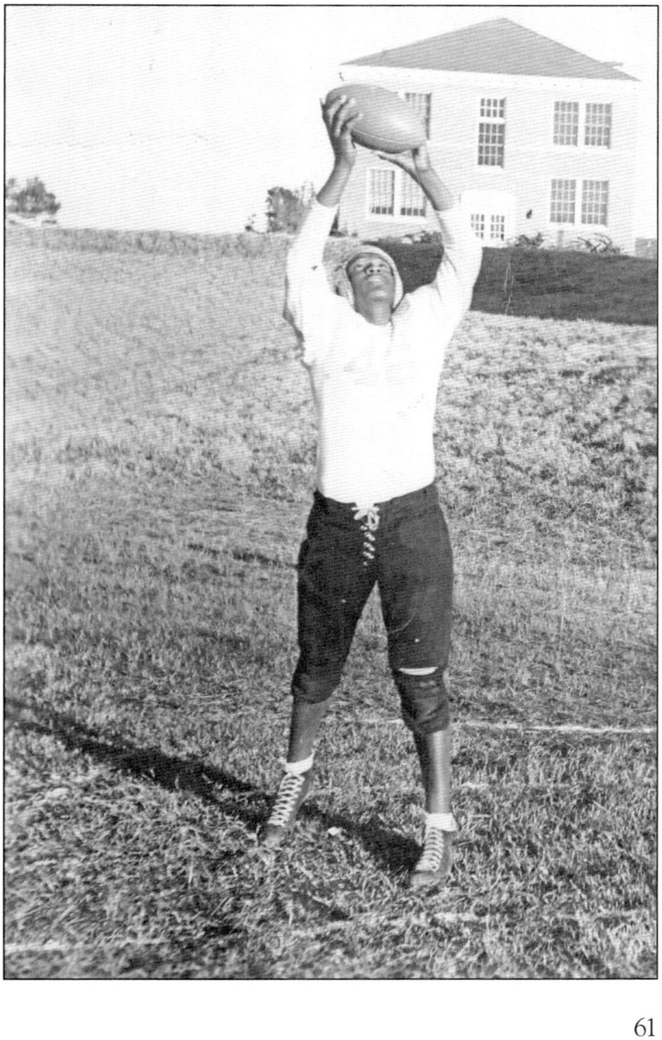

Photographs of Grambling University football players during the 1940s are presented here. In the 1940s, coach Eddie Robinson Sr. started his long reign with the program. Legolian "Boots" Moore is pictured above, and an unidentified teammate is pictured at right. Moore is considered one of the best Grambling football players of the decade. He is credited with helping Grambling University defeat Southern University for the first time in the program's history—by a score of 21-6 in 1947, which Robinson said put the program on the map. Moore also toured for a time with the world-renowned Harlem Globetrotters. (Both, courtesy of East Baton Rouge Parish Public Library Digital Archive.)

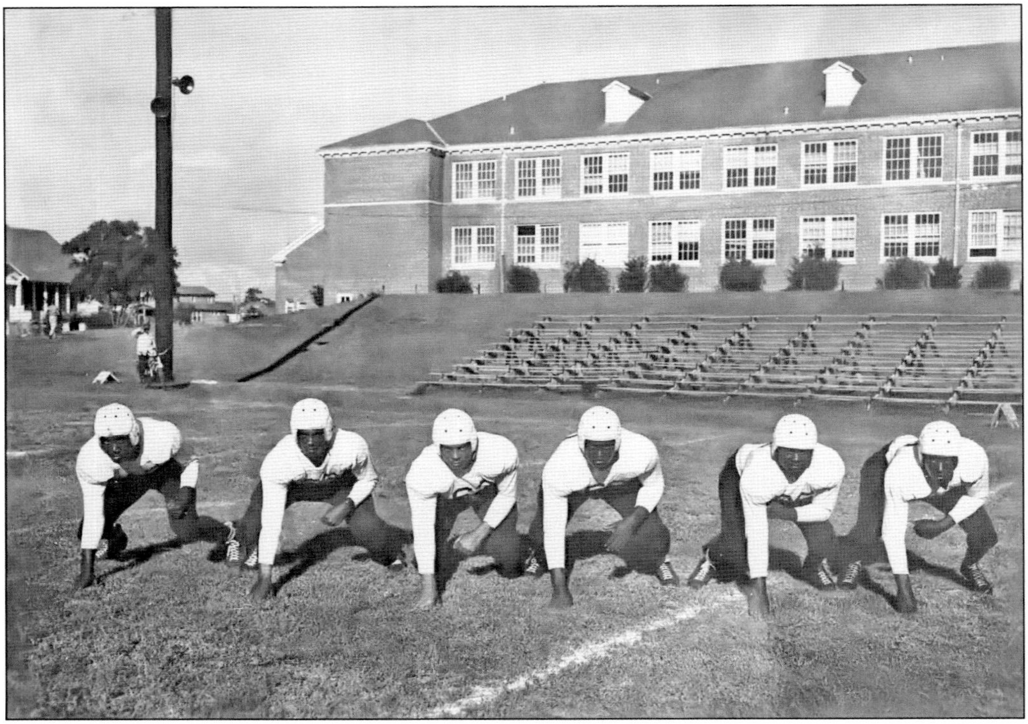

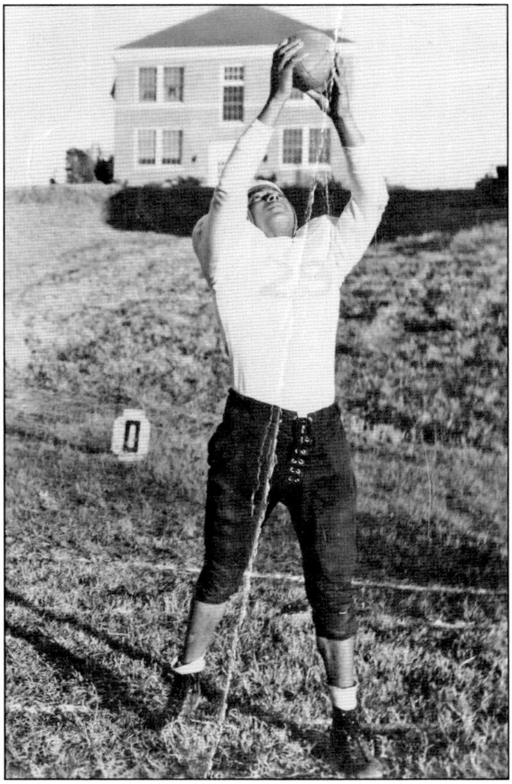

Grambling University football players from the 1940s are pictured here. The players above are tackles. A teammate is also pictured at left. Eddie Robinson Sr. is one of the most recognizable names in college sports. The McKinley High School graduate coached more than 200 players who went on to play in the NFL. Doug Williams, a Super Bowl champion, is just one of the professional players Robinson coached over the course of his career. On October 7, 1995, Robinson became the first college football coach to break the 400-win barrier. None of the individuals pictured are identified. (Both, courtesy of East Baton Rouge Parish Public Library Digital Archive.)

Additional Grambling football players are pictured at right, and a team photograph is included below. No one in either photograph is identified. Both images are from the 1940s, when Eddie Robinson Sr. began his career. Robinson was the son of parents who never earned high school diplomas. Nevertheless, they encouraged him to pursue his desire to get a college education. After graduating from McKinley High School, Robinson attended Leland College, where he excelled as quarterback. Robinson wanted to coach after his college career, but coaching opportunities were few and far between. Robinson found a job working in a feed mill in Baton Rouge. He soon became aware of an opening for a football coach at Louisiana Negro Normal and Industrial Institute, which later became Grambling University, and the rest is history. (Both, courtesy of East Baton Rouge Parish Public Library Digital Archive.)

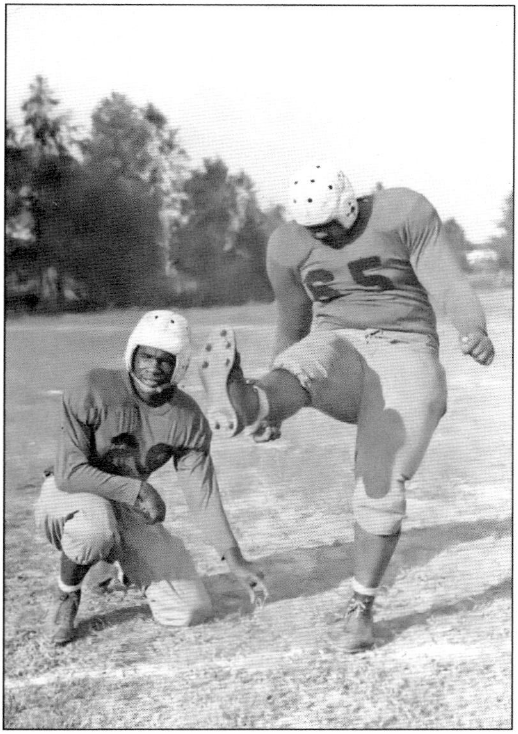

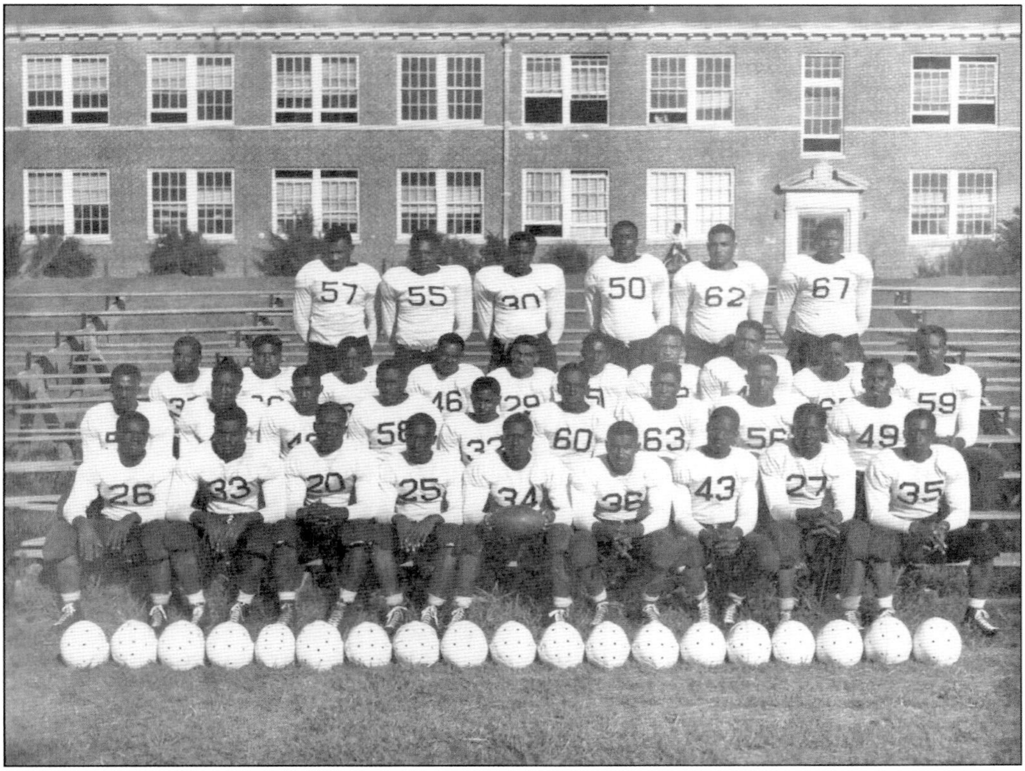

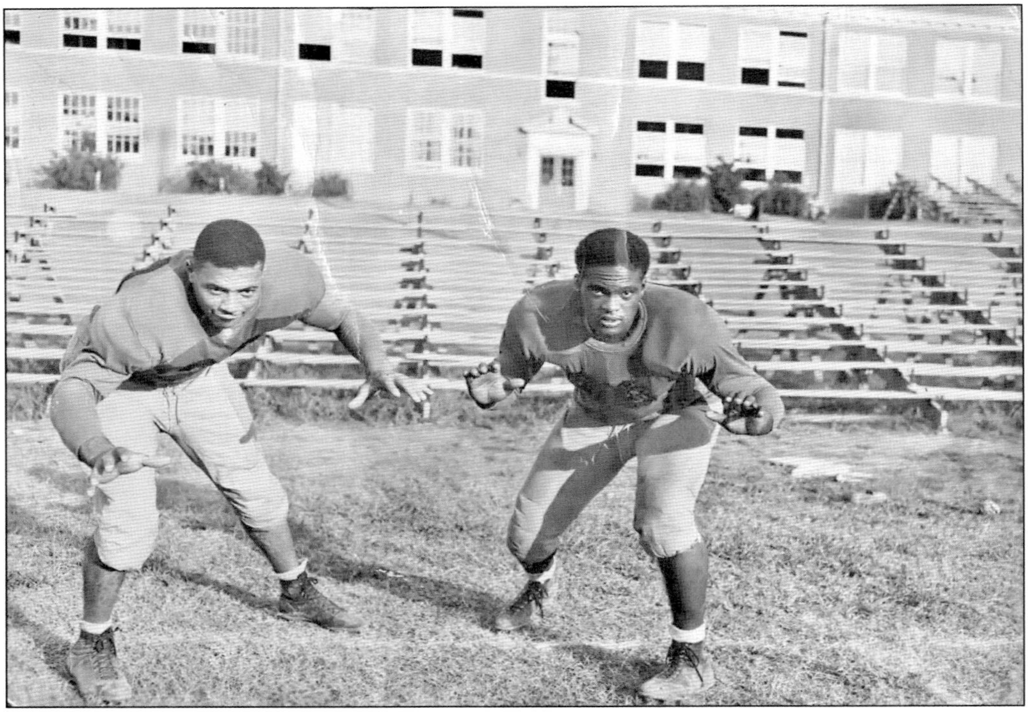

Eddie Robinson Sr. coached many of the young men in the following photographs and many more after them. According to the Eddie G. Robinson Museum website: "It didn't take Coach Rob, as he is affectionately known, long to prove his worth. Following his initial season, Coach Robinson took command and dismissed some players who he felt were not living up to expectations. The results came soon thereafter, as the next season Coach Robinson's team posted a perfect 9-0 season with the team going undefeated, untied, and unscored upon. Grambling was only the second collegiate team to have shut out every opponent, a feat which has not been repeated since." No one in these images is identified. (Both, courtesy of East Baton Rouge Parish Public Library Digital Archive.)

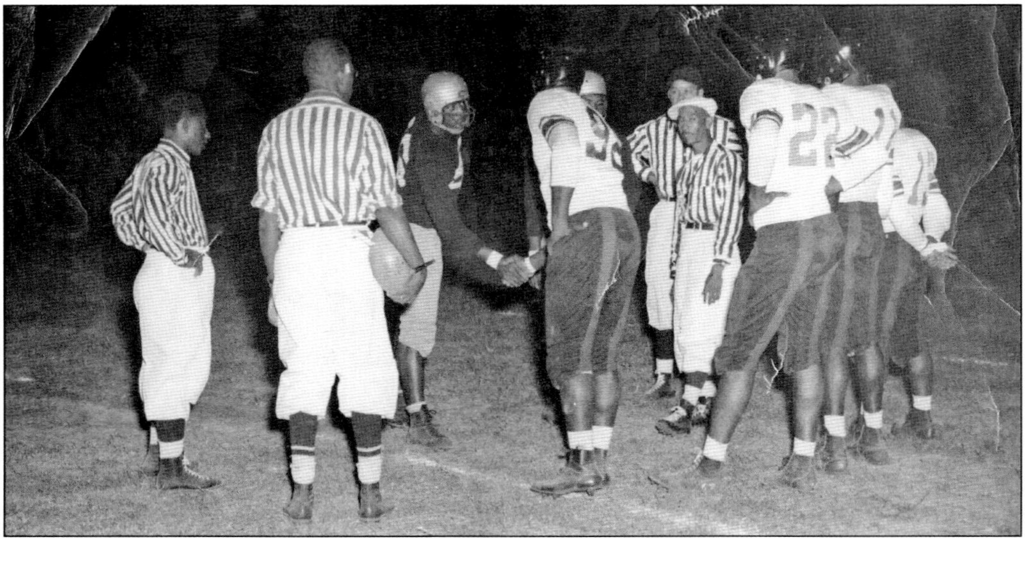

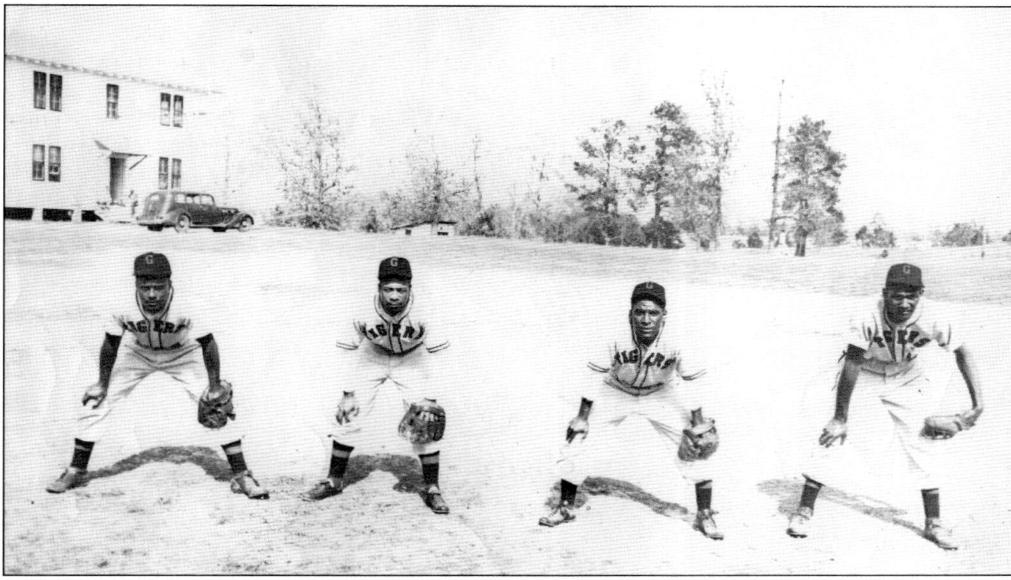

Grambling University is not only known for its fine athletic programs and for its connection to the life and legacy of Eddie Robinson Sr. Rigorous academic programs also attracted black college students from South Baton Rouge and across the nation and the globe. Grambling also fielded other athletic teams, including the baseball team shown above from the 1940s. Grambling football players are pictured below in the 1940s. By 1949, the football program at Grambling received national attention after Paul Younger signed with the Los Angeles Rams of the NFL. Younger, a running back, was affectionately known as "Tank." He had the distinction of becoming the very first player from a historically black college or university (HBCU) to sign with an NFL team. No one in these photographs is identified. (Both, courtesy of East Baton Rouge Parish Public Library Digital Archive.)

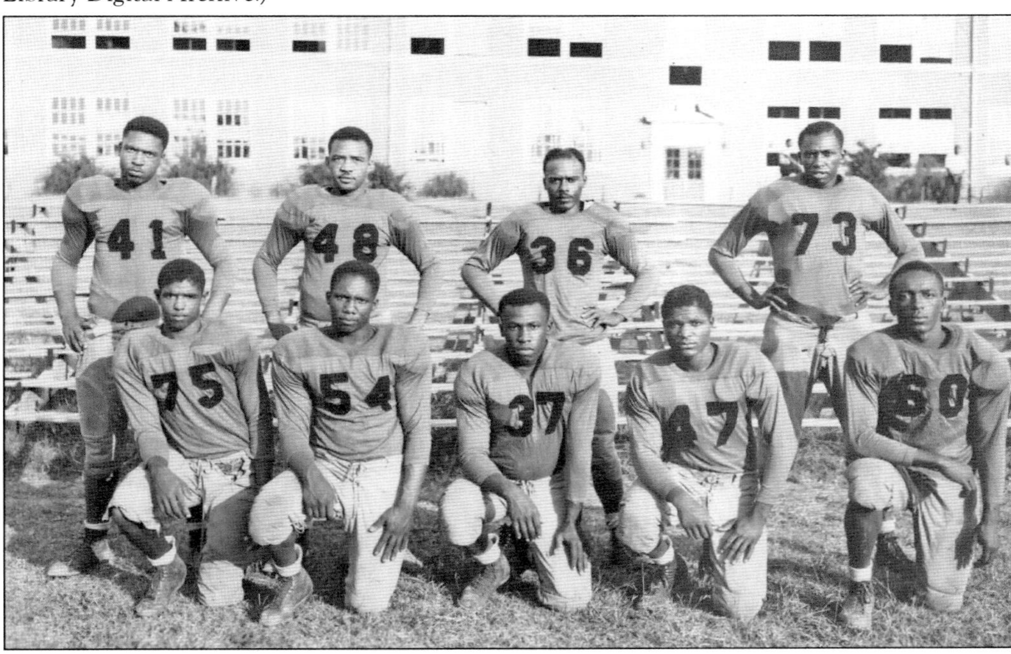

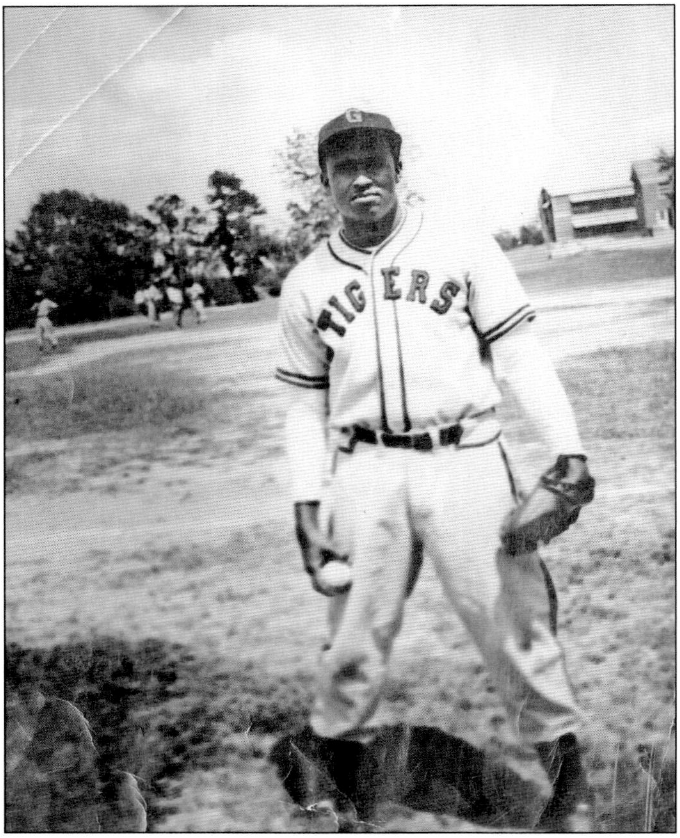

Grambling University athletes are pictured here. Grambling was synonymous with Eddie Robinson Sr. for many years and will likely be associated with him for many years to come. The South Baton Rouge neighborhood surrounding the high school Robinson graduated from now has a street named in his honor. The community also boasts a number of public artworks, which adorn columns under the interstate that divided the community decades earlier. One of the columns is dedicated to Robinson. The nearby Odell S. Williams Now and Then African American Museum also includes artifacts and exhibits about the legendary coach. (Both, courtesy of East Baton Rouge Parish Public Library Digital Archive.)

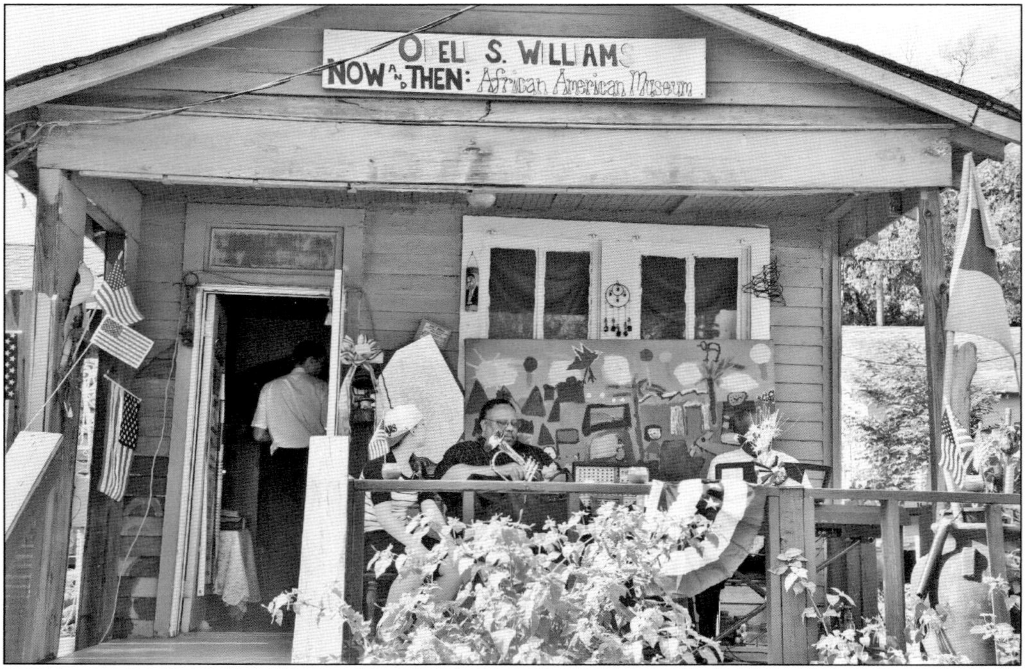

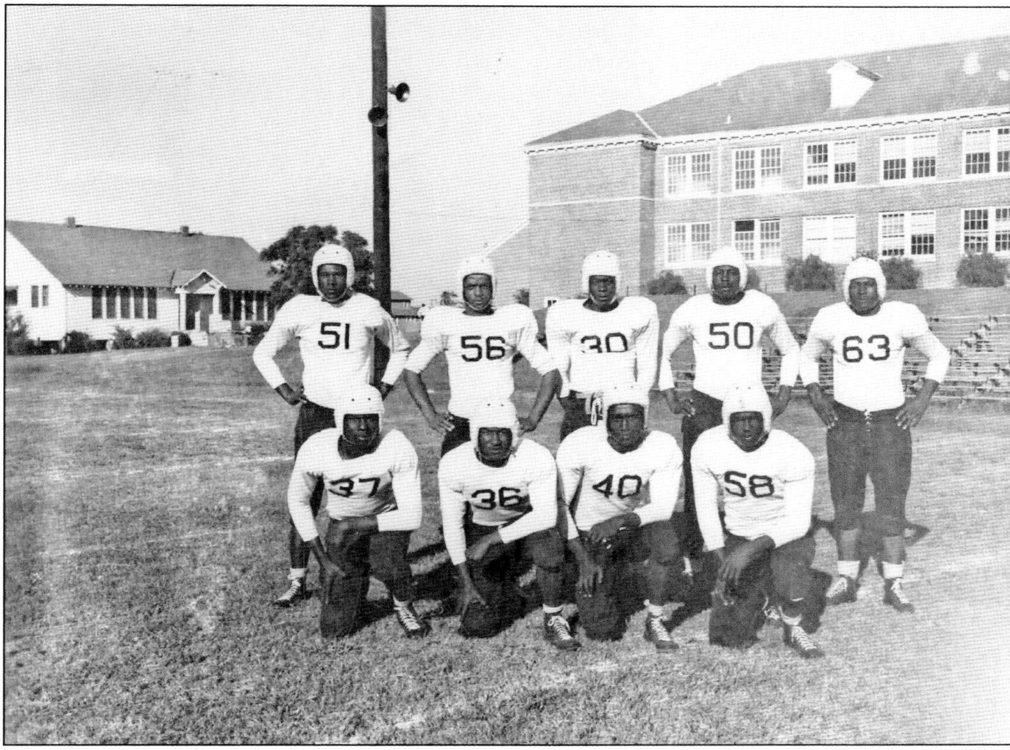

Sports are an important part of American life, and they are also an important part of student life on college campuses. Grambling is no exception. Members of the football team are pictured above in the 1940s. The photograph at right shows two Grambling student-athletes. Black students from across Baton Rouge, including South Baton Rouge, were provided with opportunities at Grambling to learn and to participate in many student organizations, groups, and clubs. Organized in 1896 by a group of African American farmers who wanted a school for African Americans in their region of the state, the university continues to live up to the vision of the founders. (Both, courtesy of East Baton Rouge Parish Public Library Digital Archive.)

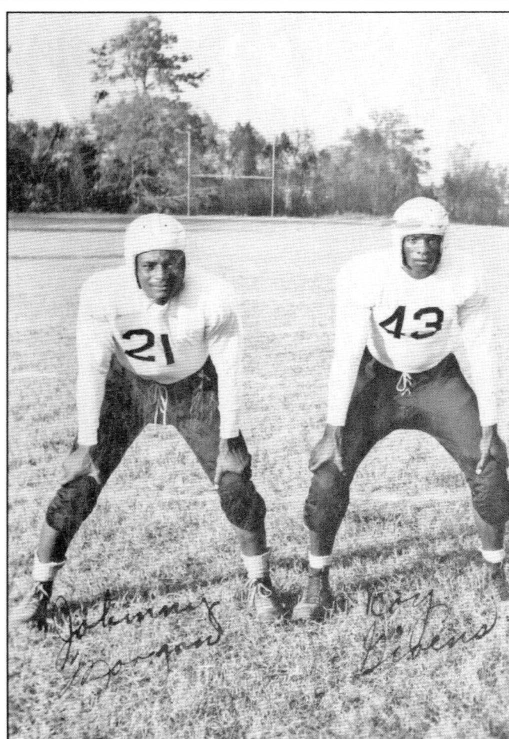

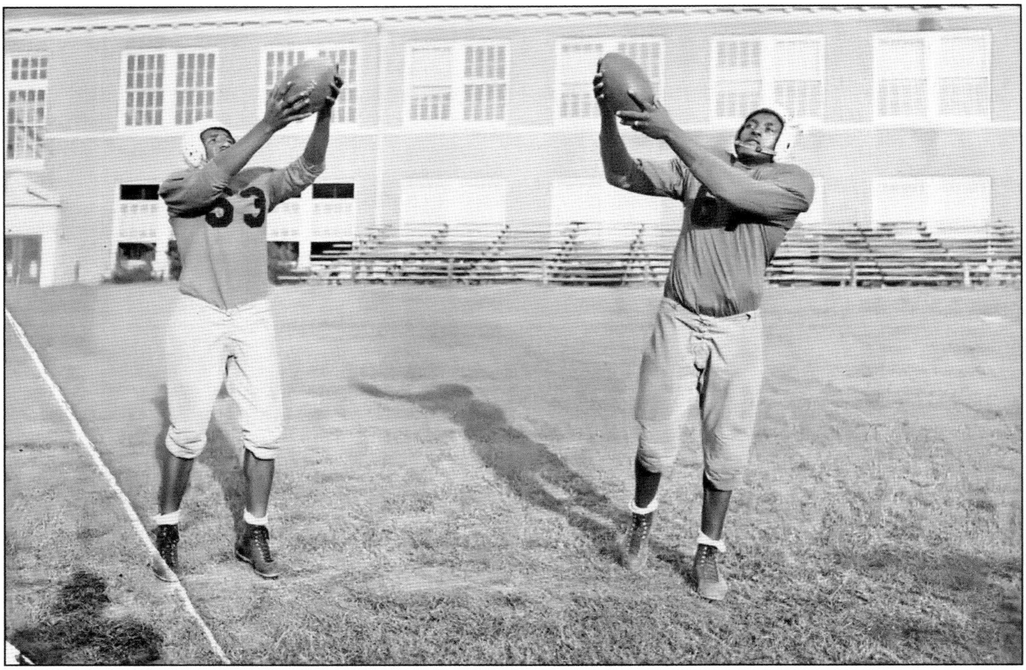

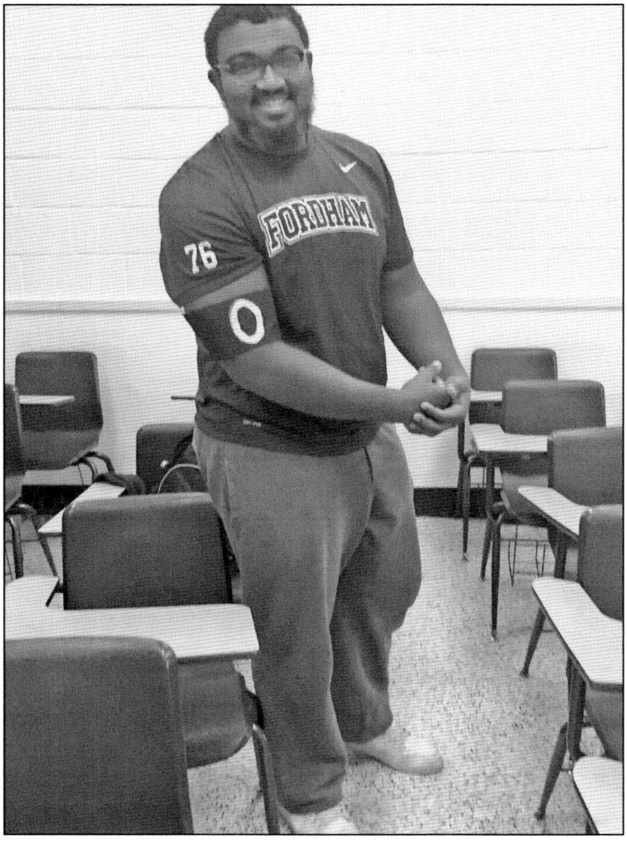

College football is serious business throughout the United States, and South Baton Rouge is no exception. Colleges and universities throughout the country look to places like southeast Louisiana for elite high school football players. Storied programs like Grambling University's have recruited from predominately black high schools in Baton Rouge for many years, including from the very high school Eddie Robinson Sr. attended, McKinley. The tradition of excellence in football carries on today. Garrick Mayweather Jr., a 2012 graduate of McKinley High School and a 2016 graduate of Fordham University in New York City, signed with the Kansas City Chiefs, and he is featured in an extensive article in the April 23, 2016, *New York Daily News* about his successes on and off the field. (Above, courtesy of East Baton Rouge Parish Library Digital Archive; left, courtesy of Mark Naison.)

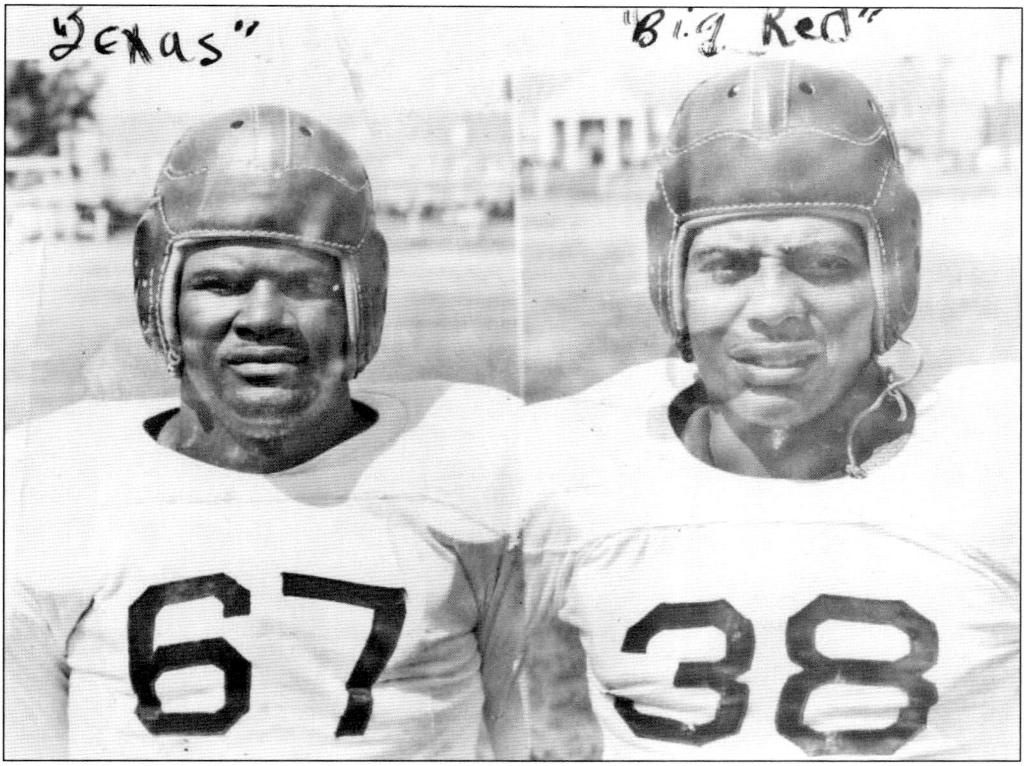

College football players are among the most recognizable students on campus. The fame and notoriety bestowed upon them was evidenced in the 1940s, when McKinley High School graduate Eddie Robinson Sr. began coaching at Grambling University. Black residents, including those in South Baton Rouge, followed the careers of players at local HBCUs, such as Southern University and Grambling University. Many of the players were known by their given names, while others were better known by the nicknames given to them by friends and family members or by fans, coaches, and teammates. Pictured above are two players from Grambling University who were affectionately known as "Texas Smith" and "Big Red." A. Walters, another student athlete at Grambling, is pictured below. Both pictures were taken in the 1940s. (Both, courtesy of East Baton Rouge Parish Public Library Digital Archive.)

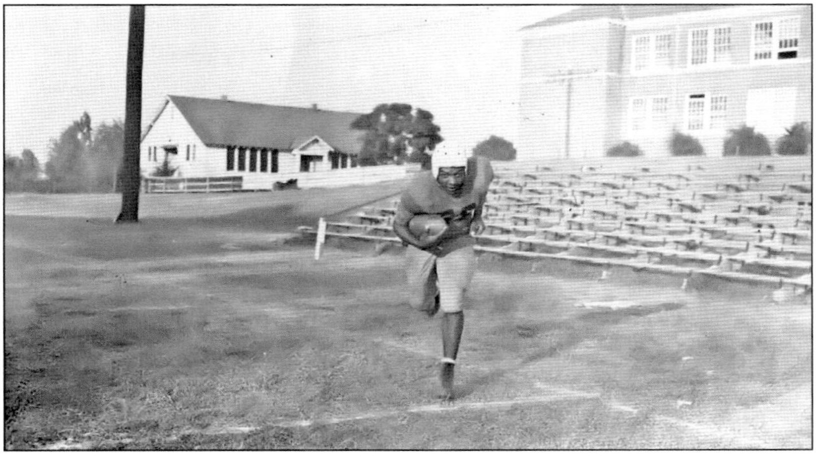

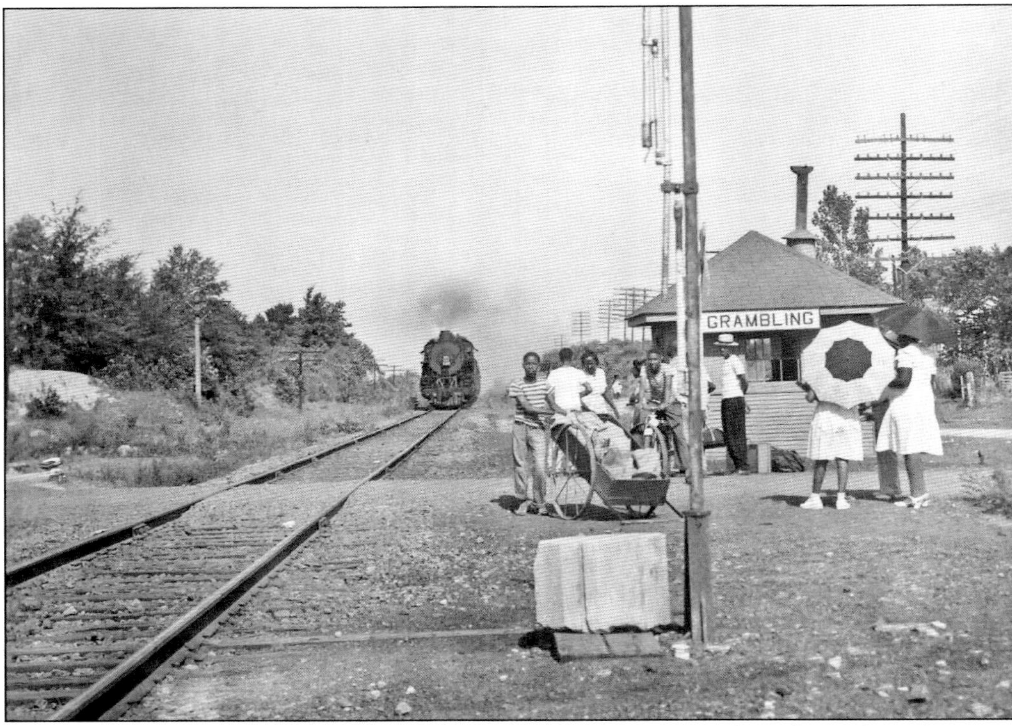

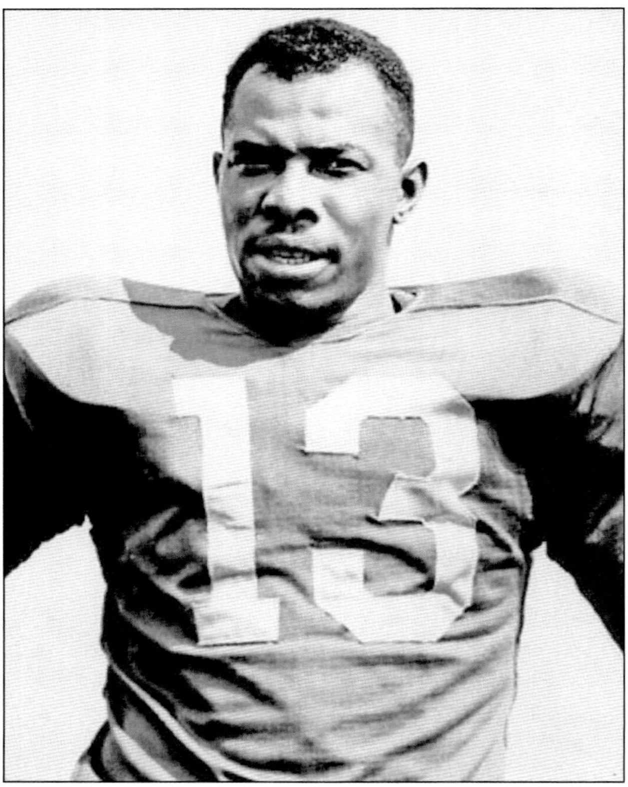

Trains brought students from across the state to Grambling University for classes and for sporting events. Above is the train station at the university. At left is Paul Younger, the first athlete from an HBCU to play in the NFL, who enjoyed a long football career. In an article about his death in 2001 at the age of 73, the *New York Times* describes him as "the first star player turned out by the renowned coach Eddie Robinson" and one of the greatest players in the history of black college football. (Both, courtesy of East Baton Rouge Parish Public Library Digital Archive.)

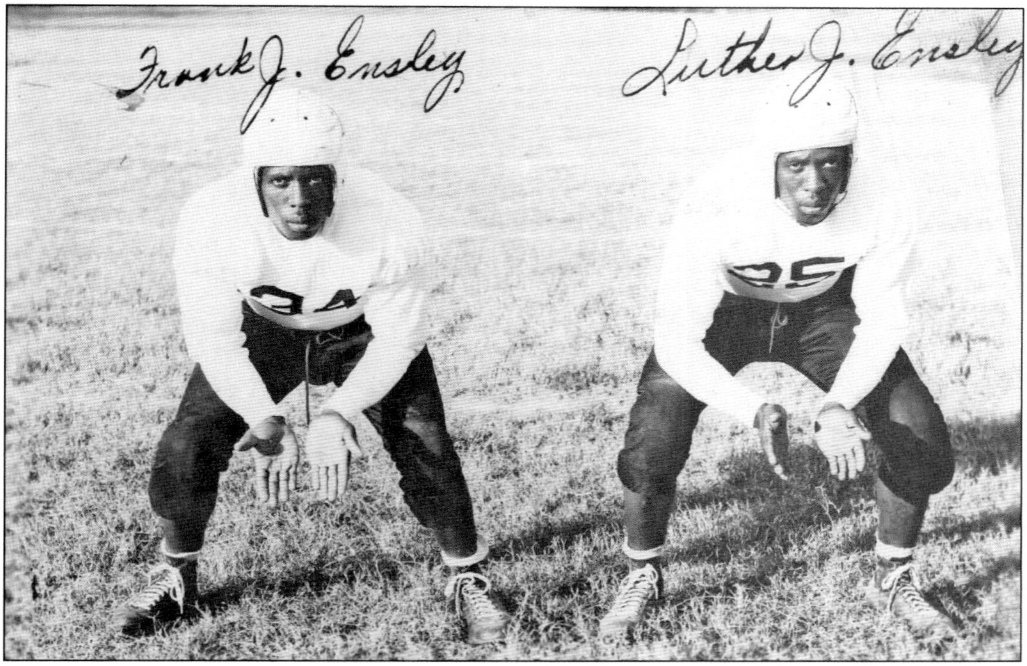

Frank and Luther Ensley were among the hundreds of black men given the opportunity to play for and learn from coach Eddie Robinson Sr. at Grambling University. The pair played in the 1940s. Robinson certainly had an eye for talent. Frank and Luther Ensley, for example, were multisport athletes at Grambling. The Friends of the Eddie Robinson Museum acknowledged Frank Ensley's passing at the age of 84 in 2011. The acknowledgement states that Ensley attended school at Grambling College from elementary school through college. (Grambling operates a laboratory school on campus, which educates students K–12.) He played professional baseball for the Indianapolis Clowns and Edmonton Braves and ended his baseball career with the Kansas City Monarchs. Like Robinson, Frank Ensley went on to coach. Ensley's teammate, Texas Smith, is pictured below. (Both, courtesy of East Baton Rouge Parish Public Library Digital Archive.)

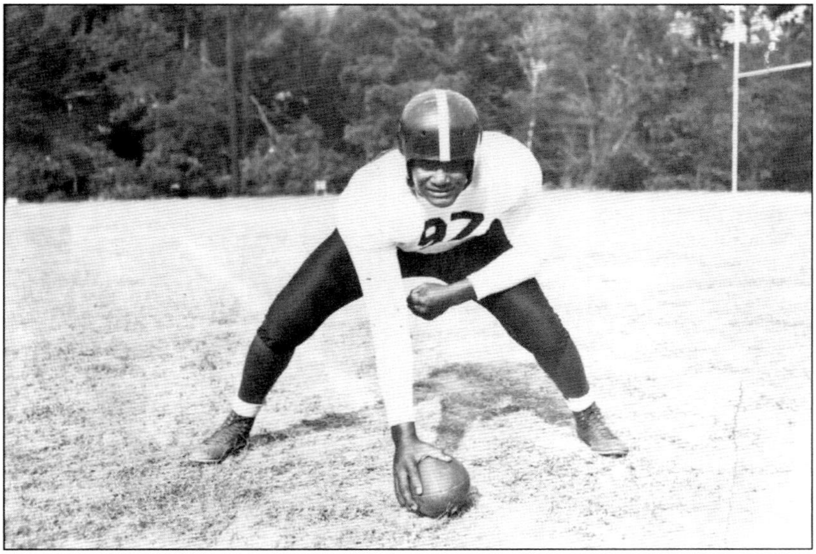

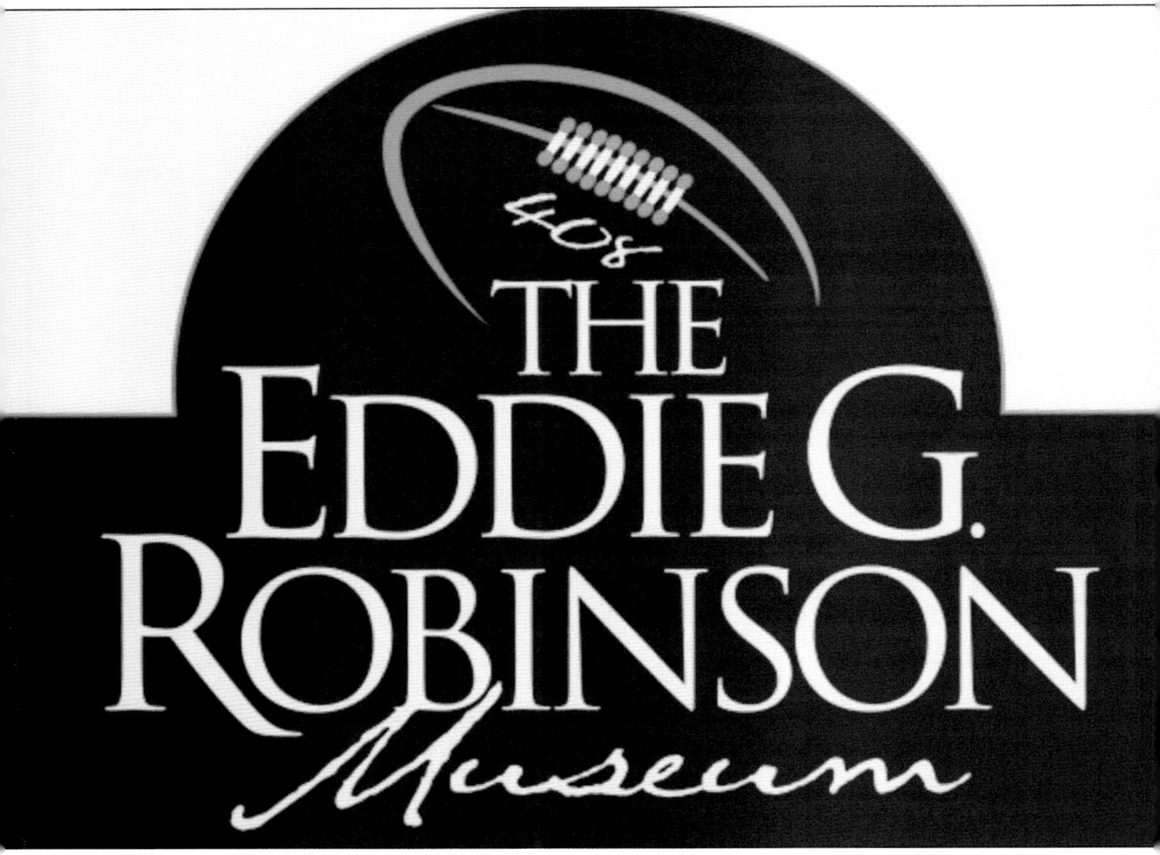

At the time of Coach Robinson's death, tributes poured in from all over the globe. In a *New York Times* article, Samuel Freedman writes about opening day for a museum in the coach's honor and reflects on Robinson's experiences growing up in South Baton Rouge. Freedman observes that the only way a black person in love with the game of football could attend a game at the state university was to show up at 5:00 a.m. on Saturdays to clean the stadium. Three years after Robinson's death at the age of 88, Louisiana appropriated $3.3 million for the museum. Over the entrance to the museum on Grambling's campus is a replica of the Temple Theater's marquee, which is a landmark in South Baton Rouge and the place were Robinson played basketball and watched Westerns as a young person. (Courtesy of East Baton Rouge Parish Public Library Digital Archive.)

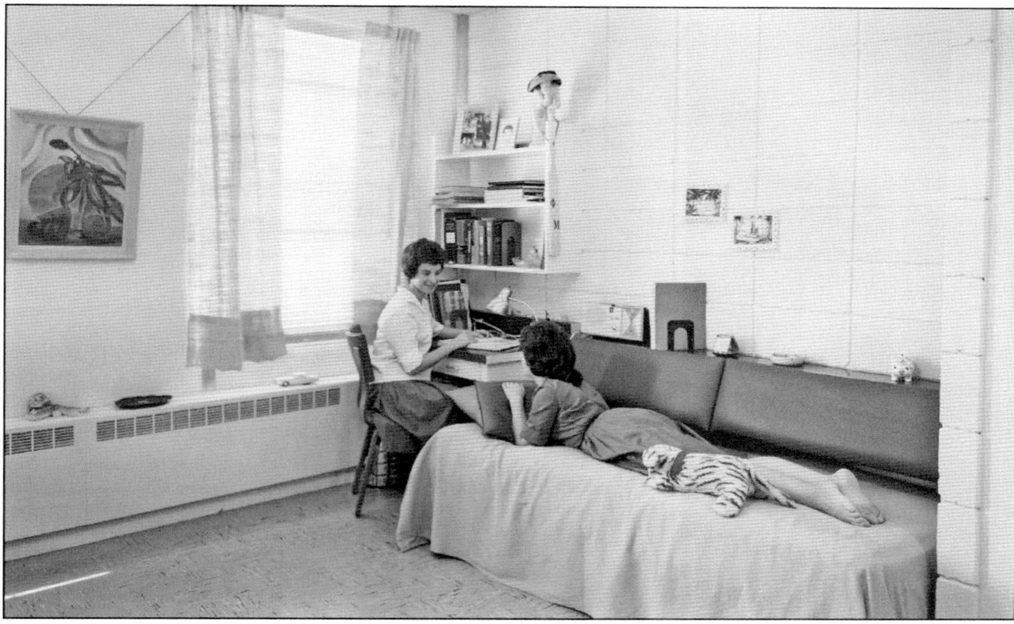

Louisiana State University's flagship campus is within a stone's throw of black residents in South Baton Rouge. Unfortunately, the campus has not always been accessible to local black residents. Above is a room in the girls' dormitory in the 1920s. The first black female student to live in a dorm on campus was Maxine Crump, founder of Dialogue on Race Louisiana, in the 1960s. Not only were black residents in South Baton Rouge excluded from attending games in Tiger Stadium, the home of the university's football team, but black undergraduates were prohibited from attending the school until the 1960s and blacks were prohibited from playing on any of its athletic teams until the 1970s. (Both, courtesy of LSU University Relations Archive.)

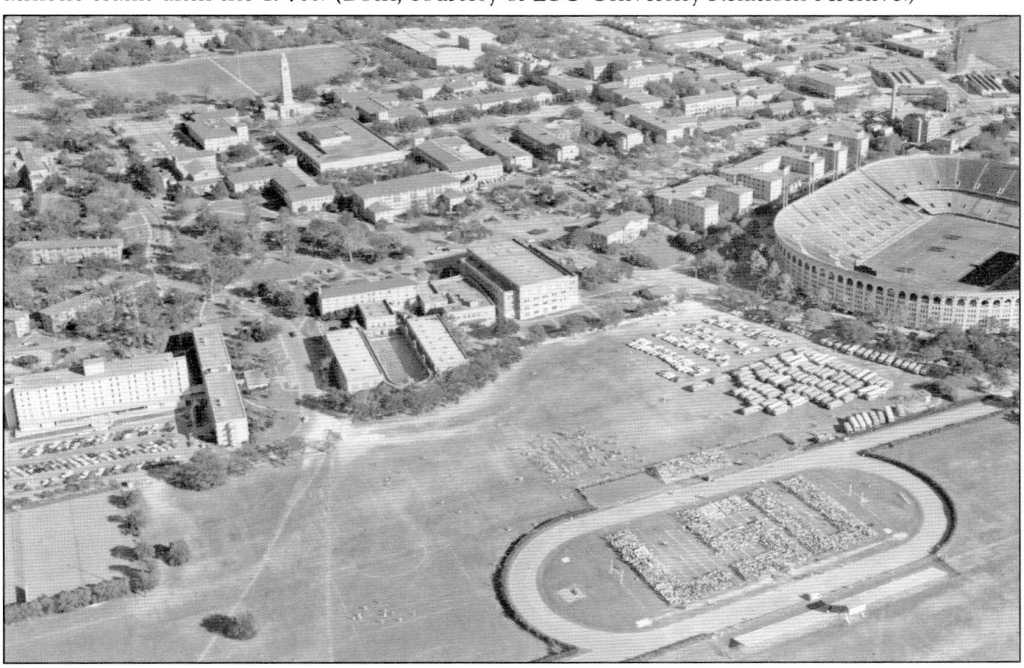

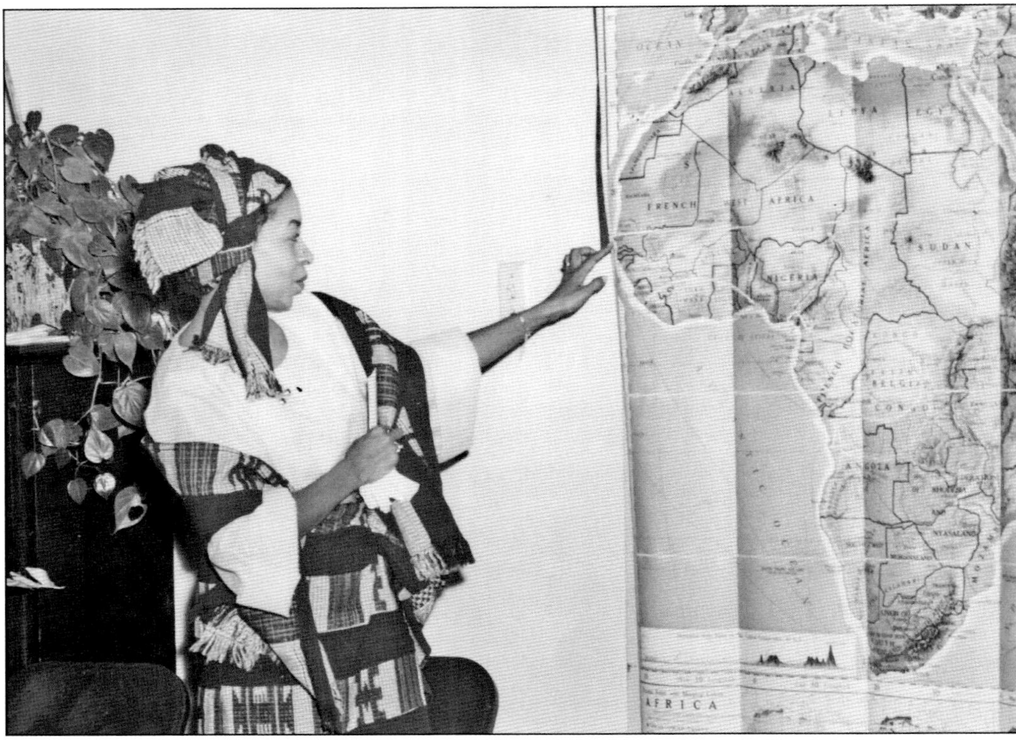

Although Louisiana State University was off-limits for black residents in South Baton Rouge, Southern University was an option for many dating back to the 1800s. Southern University has conferred degrees to students from such historic South Baton Rouge schools as McKinley High School for generations. Southern was established in New Orleans in 1880 with just 12 students, five faculty, and a total budget of $10,000. The university relocated to Baton Rouge in 1914. Allene Clark, wife of the second president of Southern University, Dr. Felton Grandison Clark, is pictured above giving a talk in the 1960s. Coach Larry Owens of Southern University is shown below speaking with students in 1965. (Both, courtesy of East Baton Rouge Parish Public Library Digital Archive.)

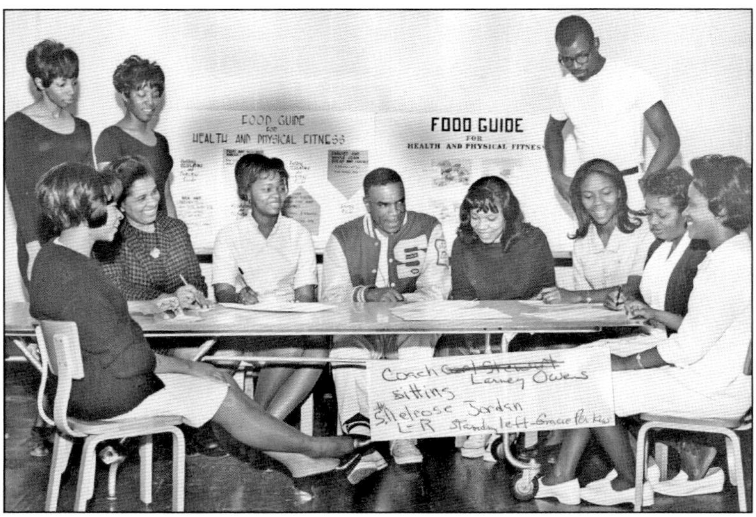

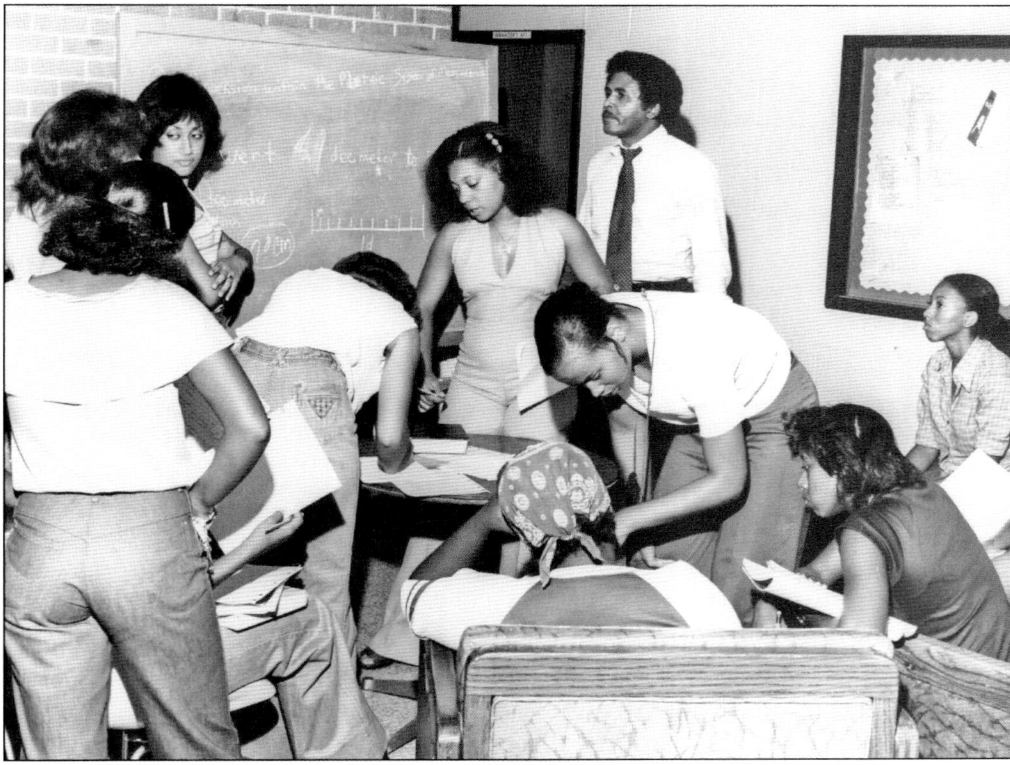

Biology instructor Dr. Clyde Johnson is pictured above with students at Southern University in the 1960s. Johnson later received tenure. In 1984, former student Felton Valdry announced he was seeking a position on the city council. Graduates of Southern University remain active in the community and in political positions in South Baton Rouge and throughout the capital city. Alumni created Southern University Alumni Federation to support their beloved university. According to the official web page, the federation's mission is to support the goals and objectives of the university through recruitment, financial support, public relations, community outreach, talent loyalty, dedication, and commitment to the highest standards. (Both, courtesy of East Baton Rouge Parish Public Library Digital Archive.)

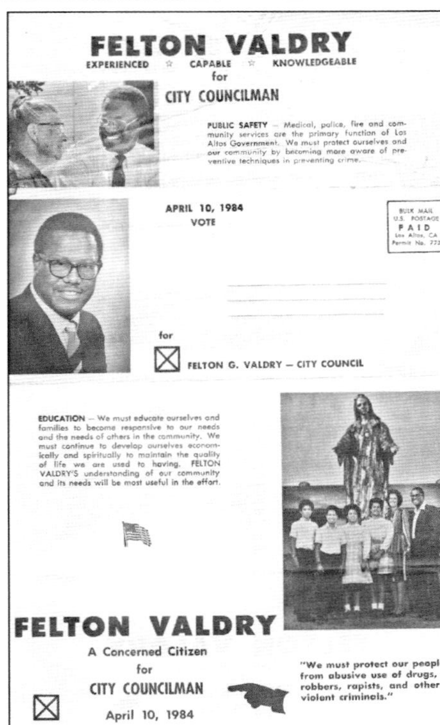

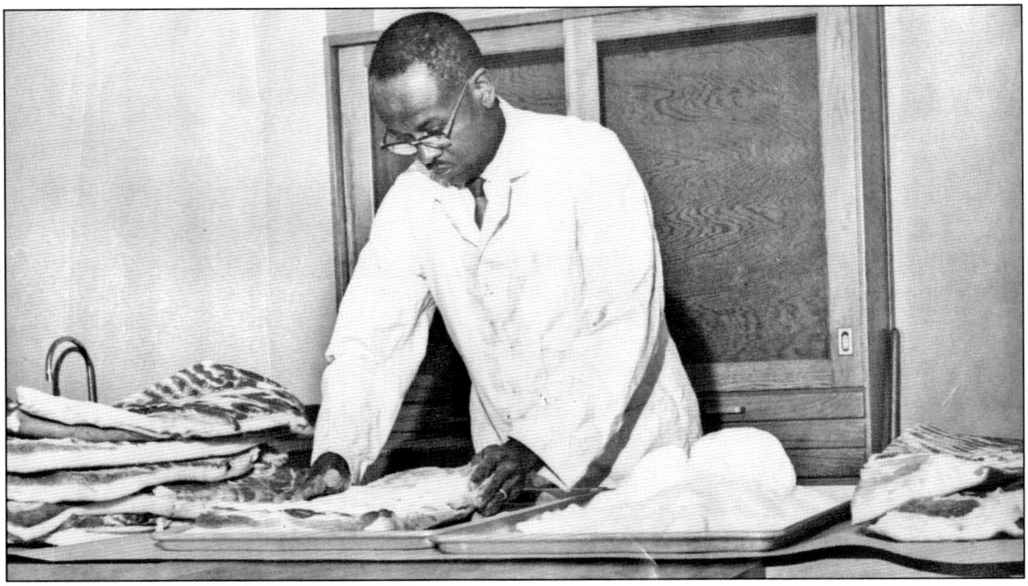

George Robinson, a professor at Southern University, is pictured above in the 1960s. Pinkie Smith is pictured below speaking with administration at Southern University in 1965. The administration came under fire from many black residents in Baton Rouge during the 1960s because the university was at the center of the civil rights struggle. Students enrolled at Southern University regularly supported and led efforts to integrate places of public accommodation, but the university was not always supportive of the student protests. Threats of expulsion were made and realized in some cases, including at sit-ins staged at local lunch counters. The sit-ins were inspired by similar acts of civil disobedience throughout the South, including in Greensboro, North Carolina. Protestors were welcomed into black churches in South Baton Rouge to share their stories and receive encouragement. (Both, courtesy of East Baton Rouge Parish Public Library Digital Archive.)

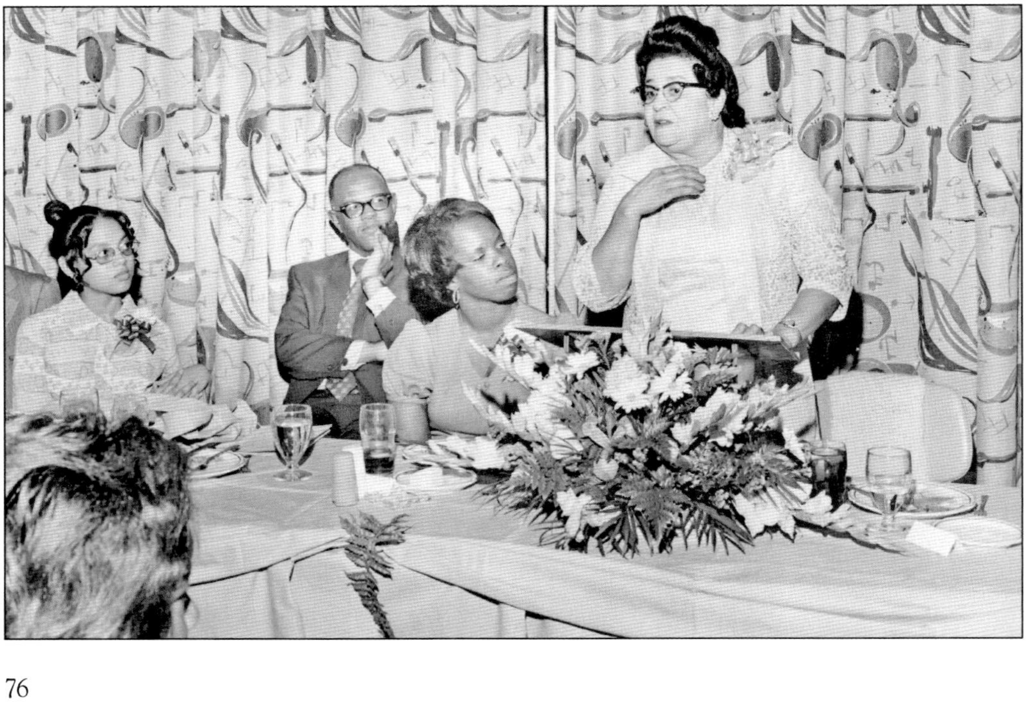

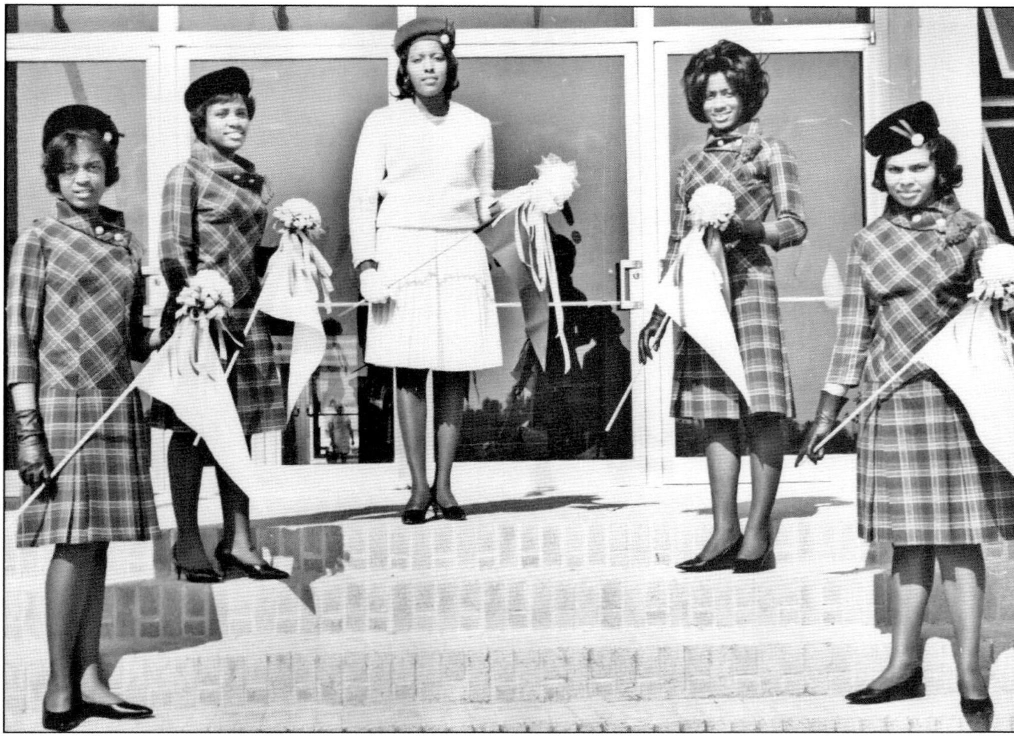

Despite the racial turmoil and tensions facing the city of Baton Rouge and the nation in the 1960s and the controversies over Southern University's official response to student protests, students at the historic university continued to find opportunities to learn and grow personally and intellectually. The students pictured in the photograph above of the court for Southern Lab, a preparatory school on the campus of Southern University, are, from left to right, Carolyn Mitchell, Sandra Hayes, Brenda Spears, Judith James, and unidentified. The photograph was taken during the 1964–1965 academic year. Southern University home economics students are pictured below during the 1960s. (Both, courtesy of East Baton Rouge Parish Public Library Digital Archive.)

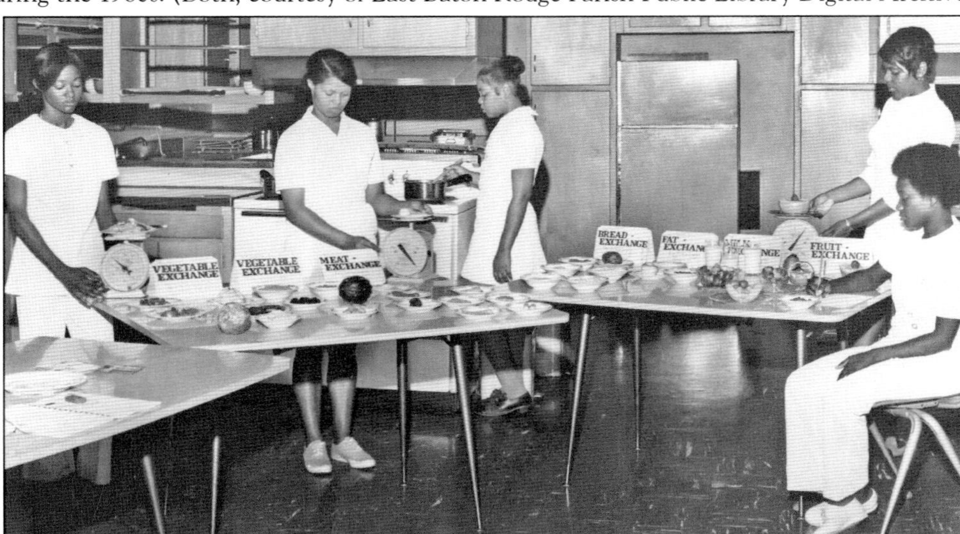

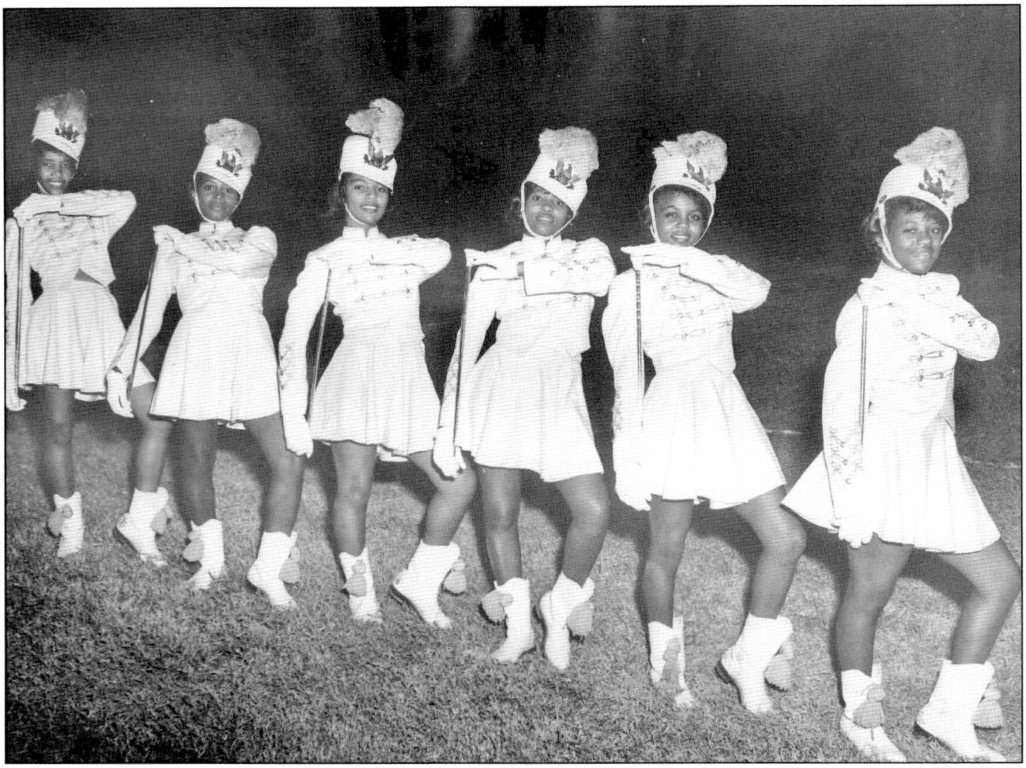

Black residents of South Baton Rouge have enjoyed taking in and participating in many of the activities that make Southern University a special place for alumni and for the surrounding community. Southern University Drum Corps and Dancing Dolls are just two examples. Both groups are pictured here in performances from 1965. The Dancing Dolls have the privilege of dancing to the music of the world-renowned Southern University band, of which the drum corps is an important part, known the world over as the "Human Jukebox." Students must audition and perform tap, jazz, modern dance, and ballet and meet academic requirements. (Both, courtesy of East Baton Rouge Parish Public Library Digital Archive.)

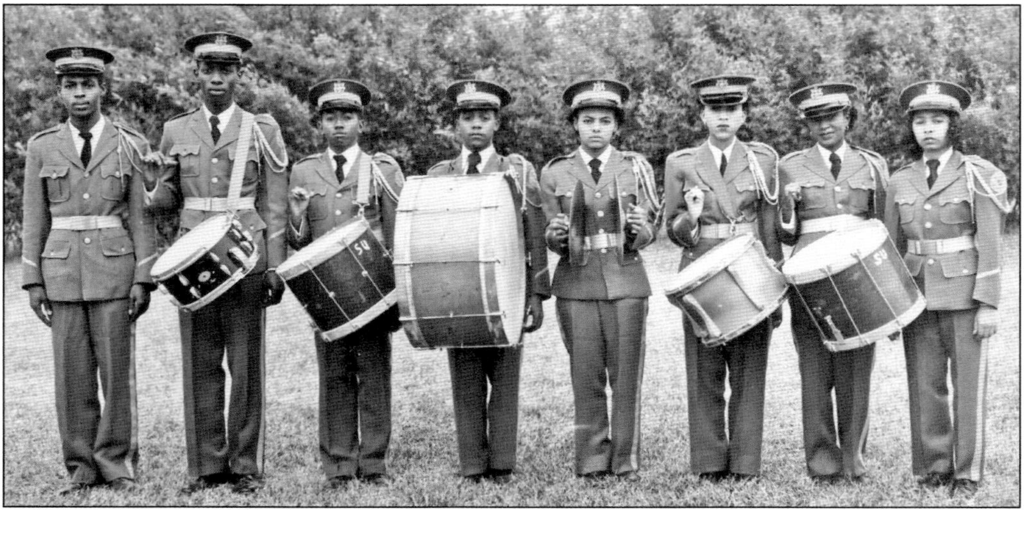

Southern University's legendary Drum Corps and Dancing Dolls are fixtures at home and away games, especially for the football program. University football players are pictured in 1960 (at right) and 1970 (below). The university's program boasts a long list of student-athletes who proudly wore the Jaguar uniform and later played professionally in the NFL. Players from the 1960s and the 1970s include Pete Barnes, Al Beauchamp, Donnie Davis, Alvin Haymond, Frank Pitts, and Clyde Williams. Mel Blount, another prestigious alumnus of the football program, was inducted into the National Football Hall of Fame in 1989. He played for many years with the Pittsburgh Steelers. (Both, courtesy of East Baton Rouge Parish Public Library Digital Archive.)

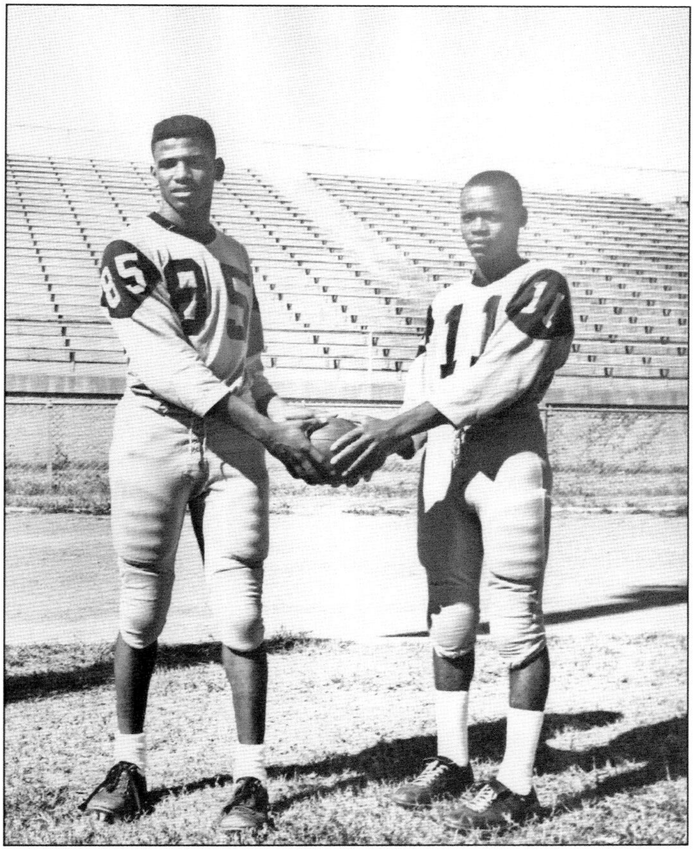

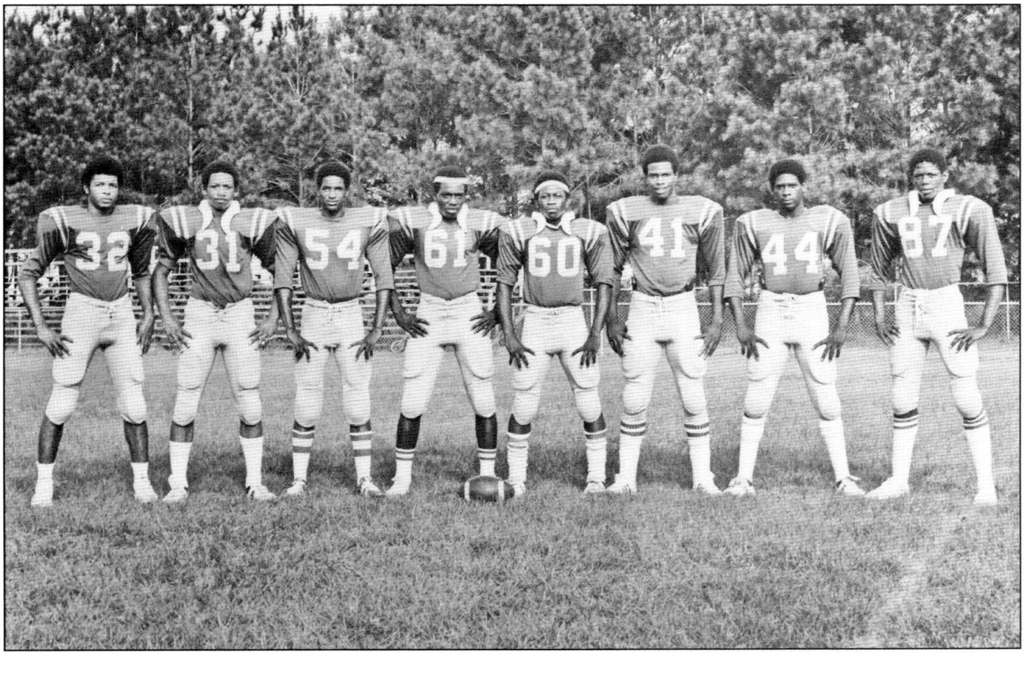

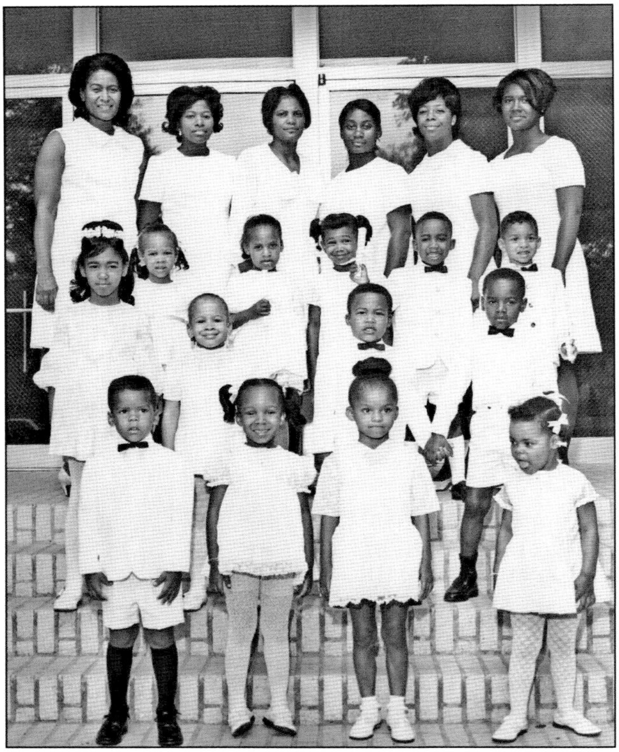

Students beginning their educational journey are pictured in the 1965 photograph at left of the Southern University nursery school. The university has played an important role in the lives of black residents in South Baton Rouge seeking an education at virtually every stage of life. Notable graduates of Southern University include *American Idol* judge Randy Jackson. Jackson attended Robert E. Lee High School in South Baton Rouge when the school's mascot was a Confederate general and black students were given Confederate flags as souvenirs during commencement ceremonies. (Both, courtesy of East Baton Rouge Parish Public Library Digital Archive.)

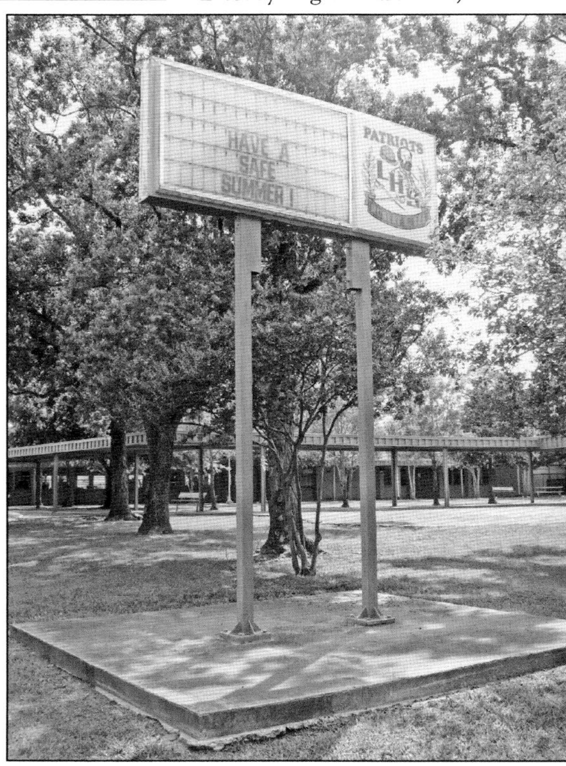

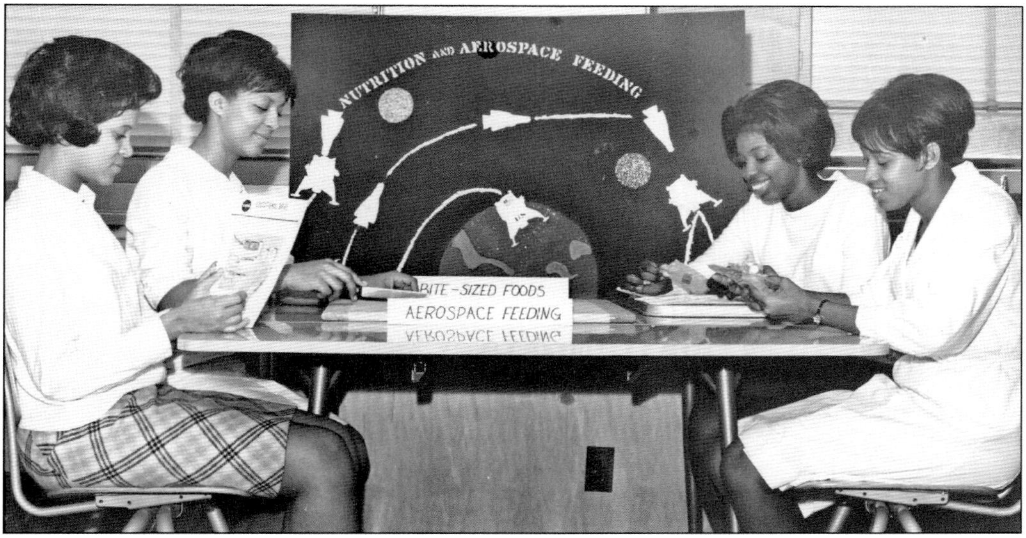

Nutrition programs were popular at HBCUs throughout the country for generations. Southern University's nutrition program attracted black students from South Baton Rouge and beyond. Two 1965 photographs of students in nutrition classes at Southern University are shown here. The nutrition program is still popular today. The mission of the program is "to advance the health and wellness of individuals through the education of professionals, provision of research-based programs, and generation and dissemination of knowledge. The program prepares graduates to enter dietetic internships, assume careers in food and nutrition and related areas, and engage in graduate study." The vision of the program is "to offer an educational environment that embraces excellence in instruction, research, and outreach." (Both, courtesy of East Baton Rouge Parish Public Library Digital Archive.)

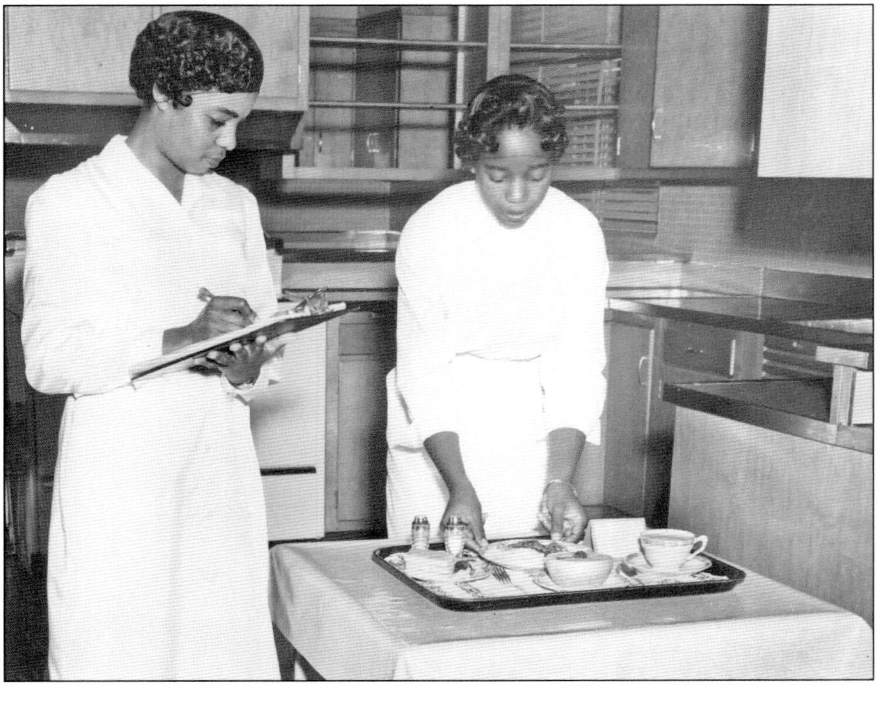

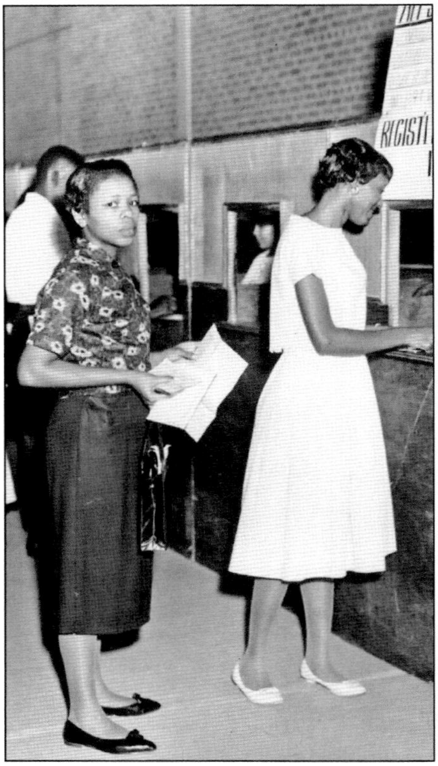

These two 1960 photographs depict unidentified students registering for courses at Southern University. According to the university's official web page, enrollment at Southern University is good and is on the rise in recent years: "Targeted recruitment campaigns, an innovative alumni enrollment initiative, and creative recruitment strategies helped boost Fall 2015 enrollment for the Southern University System. Overall enrollment for the SU System increased by 490 students (12,884), nearly four percent. Enrollment numbers show the overall enrollment for the SU System flagship campus in Baton Rouge increased by more than 200 students over the previous year. The freshman class enrollment increased by 31 percent. A breakdown of the Southern University Baton Rouge (SUBR) enrollment data indicates 6,389 students with 1,210 new freshmen. Recently, the Baton Rouge campus began a recruiting campaign, 'Pathway to Prominence,' that directly correlated to an influx of applications for admission. Campaign tour stops in Dallas, Houston, Atlanta, and Texas allowed students to hear from University administrators and student government leaders, as well as hear and see the SU Jaguar Marching Band and cheerleaders perform." (Both, courtesy of East Baton Rouge Parish Public Library Digital Archive.)

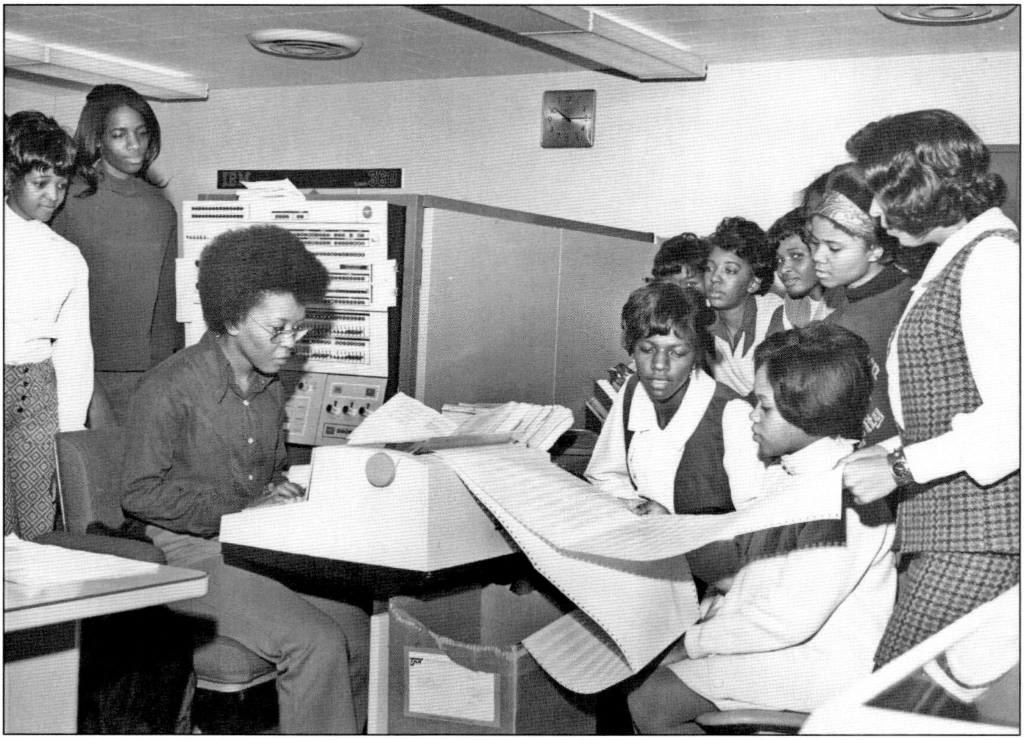

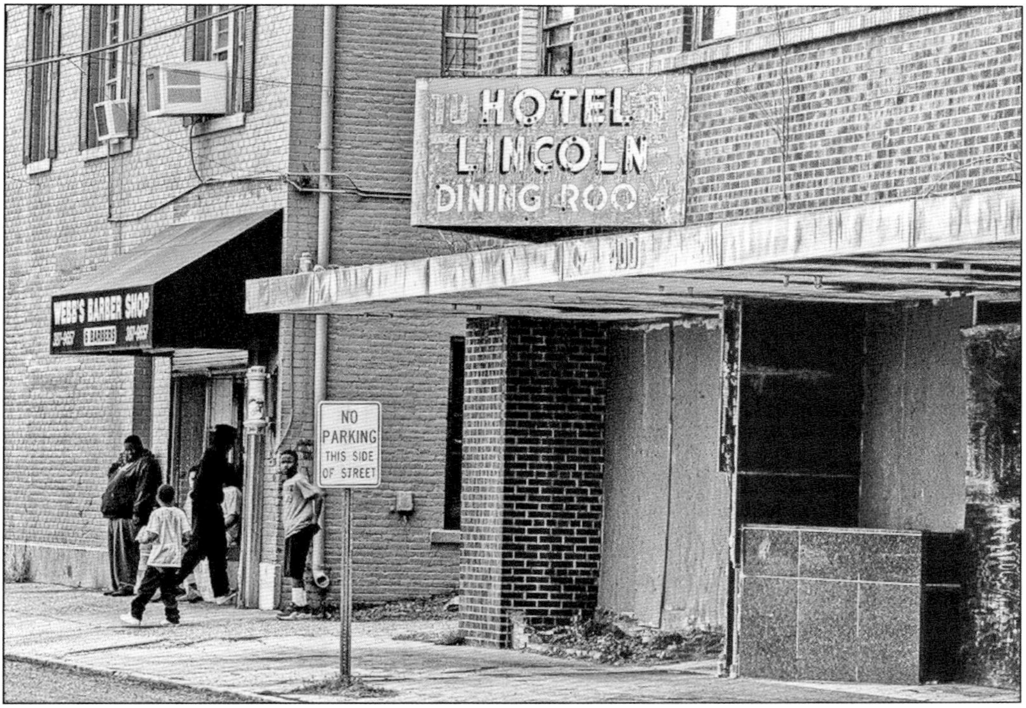

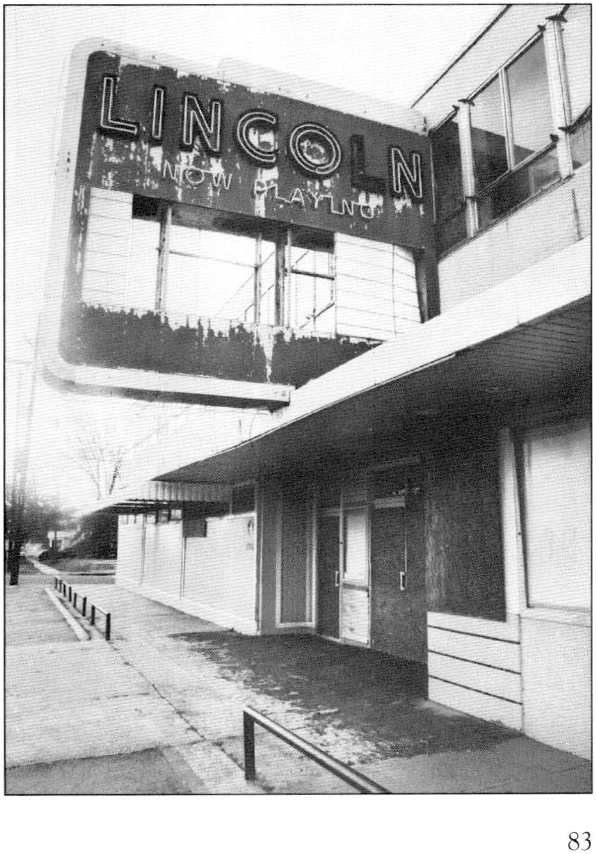

Schools, churches, and cemeteries were not the only places where racial groups were separated by law or by the racial norms of a given time period. Blacks were not permitted to attend the same theaters as whites during the Jim Crow era. Blacks in South Baton Rouge did not miss out on entertainment opportunities simply because whites refused them admission to facilities designated for whites only. Black residents throughout the city, but especially in South Baton Rouge, stayed at Hotel Lincoln and took in shows at the historic Lincoln Theater. The theater, located on the corner of Eddie Robinson and Myrtle Drives, opened in 1949. It was one of three major black theaters in Baton Rouge at the time. Movies were 75¢ then. The building also housed several black-owned businesses, including insurance companies, a Laundromat, and a barbershop. Efforts to restore the theater are continuing. (Both, courtesy of East Baton Rouge Parish Public Library Digital Archive.)

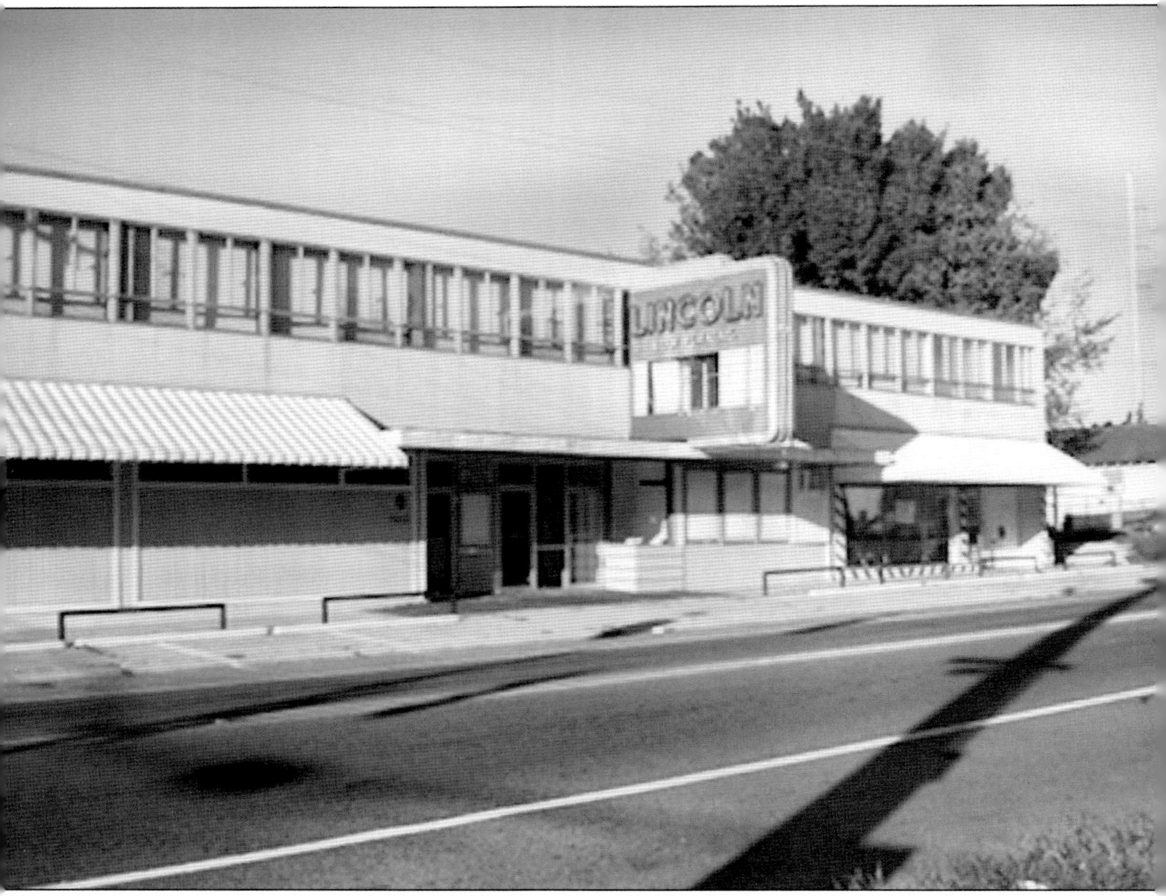

The historic Lincoln Theater, founded by Rev. Albert Chapman, was an important part of the South Baton Rouge community. According to a recent news report, upstairs rooms in the theater were used during the civil rights struggles in the 1950s. One longtime resident of South Baton Rouge reflected on the significance of the theater to the black community. With the end of legal segregation in the city, places like the Lincoln Theater soon disappeared or fell into disrepair. Efforts to restore and preserve the theater are ongoing. The Lincoln Theater Center Foundation Board is working to refurbish the building by trying to turn the structure into the Black History Hall of Fame. (Courtesy of East Baton Rouge Parish Public Library Digital Archive.)

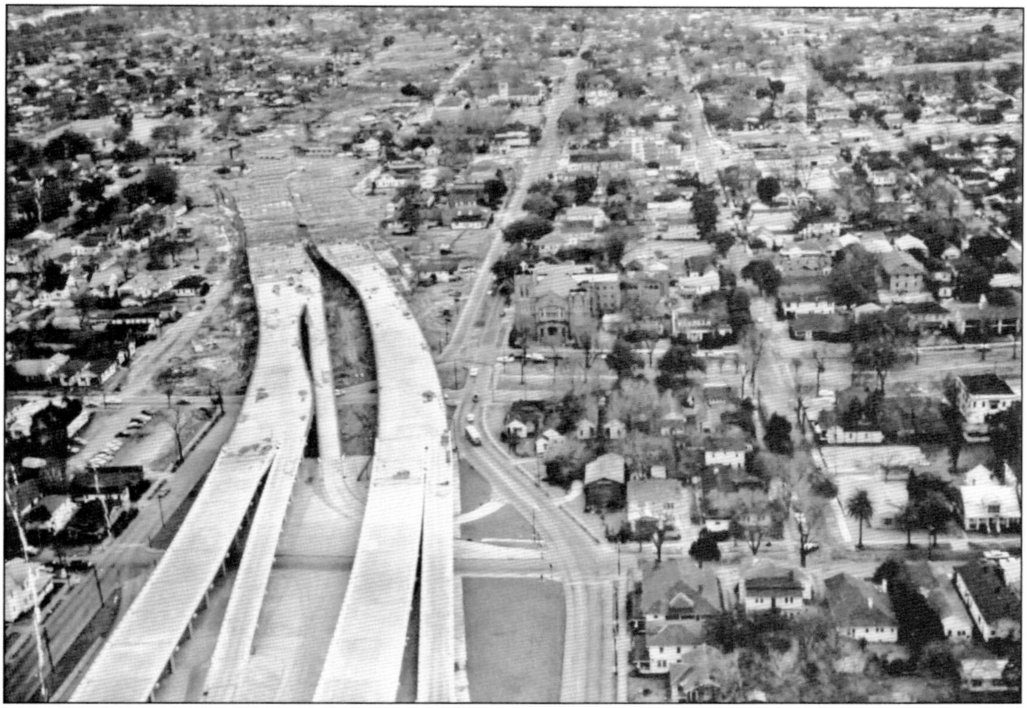

Segregation laws sought to keep blacks and whites separate. Black and white residents attended different schools, ate at different lunch counters, and sat separately on public buses and in other public settings. The construction of the interstate and the freeway further separated blacks and whites, facilitated white flight, and literally divided black neighborhoods in South Baton Rouge. Abrupt walls where streets suddenly end in predominately black neighborhoods are the direct result of the highway construction shown above. The homes surrounding Valley Park School on Bawell Street are a good example. This is where Sarah Coleman Jackson grew up and where her father owned Jackson Groceries. She was a graduate of McKinley High School and Southern University. Her son Wilbur Olinde (standing, second from left) was a member of the 1975 UCLA championship team and the first African American to play professional basketball in Germany. (Above, courtesy of East Baton Rouge Parish Public Library Digital Archive; below, courtesy of Wilbur Olinde.)

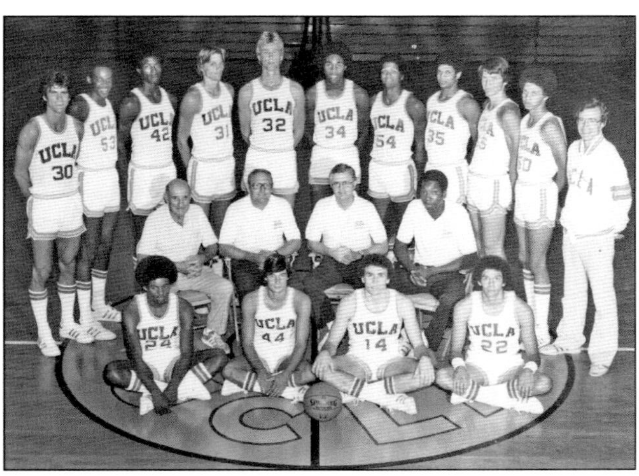

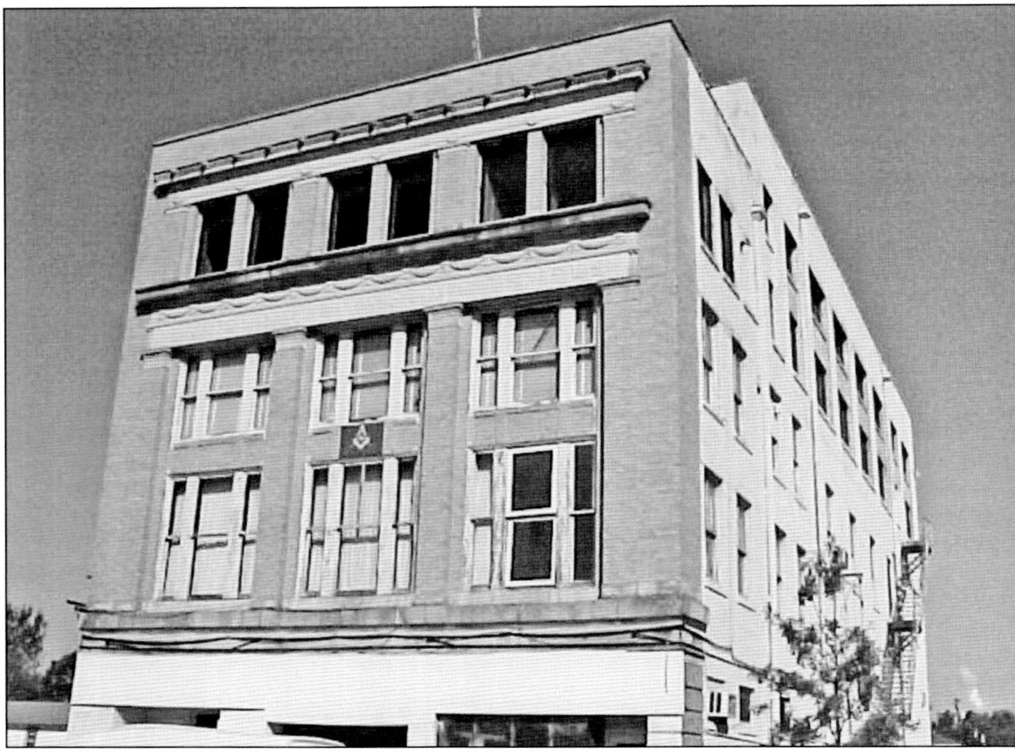

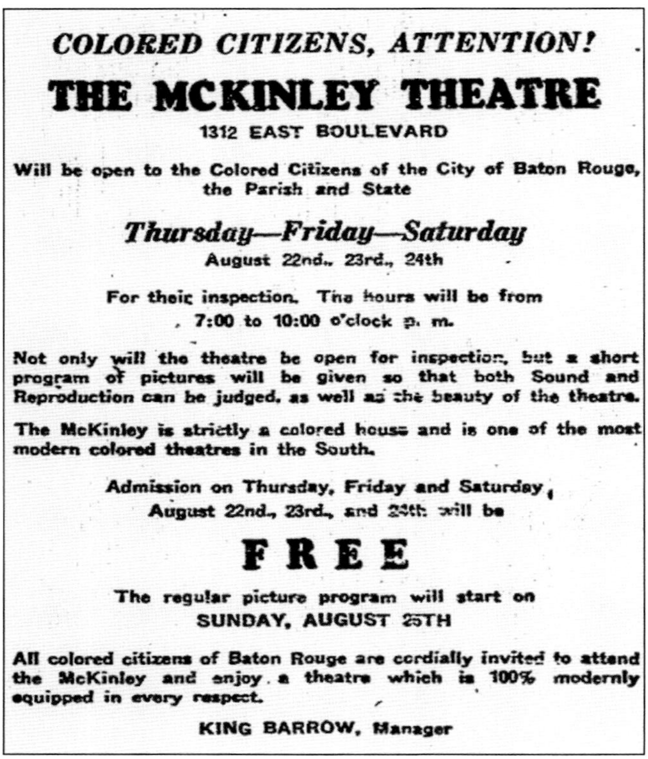

COLORED CITIZENS, ATTENTION!

THE MCKINLEY THEATRE

1312 EAST BOULEVARD

Will be open to the Colored Citizens of the City of Baton Rouge, the Parish and State

Thursday—Friday—Saturday

August 22nd., 23rd., 24th

For their inspection. The hours will be from 7:00 to 10:00 o'clock p. m.

Not only will the theatre be open for inspection, but a short program of pictures will be given so that both Sound and Reproduction can be judged, as well as the beauty of the theatre.

The McKinley is strictly a colored house and is one of the most modern colored theatres in the South.

Admission on Thursday, Friday and Saturday, August 22nd., 23rd., and 24th will be

FREE

The regular picture program will start on SUNDAY, AUGUST 25TH

All colored citizens of Baton Rouge are cordially invited to attend the McKinley and enjoy a theatre which is 100% modernly equipped in every respect.

KING BARROW, Manager

Blacks in South Baton Rouge belonged to many social groups created as parallel institutions to the whites-only institutions prohibiting black membership. Text on the website for Most Worshipful Master Prince Hall Grand Lodge states, "On March 6, 1775, Prince Hall and 14 men of color were made masons in Lodge #441 of the Irish Registry attached to the 38th British Foot Infantry at Castle William Island in Boston Harbor, Massachusetts. It marked the first time that Black men were made masons in America." The Masonic temple in Baton Rouge is a historic building. The McKinley Theatre in South Baton Rouge is described as "strictly a colored house" and one of the most modern in the South. (Both, courtesy of East Baton Rouge Parish Public Library Digital Archive.)

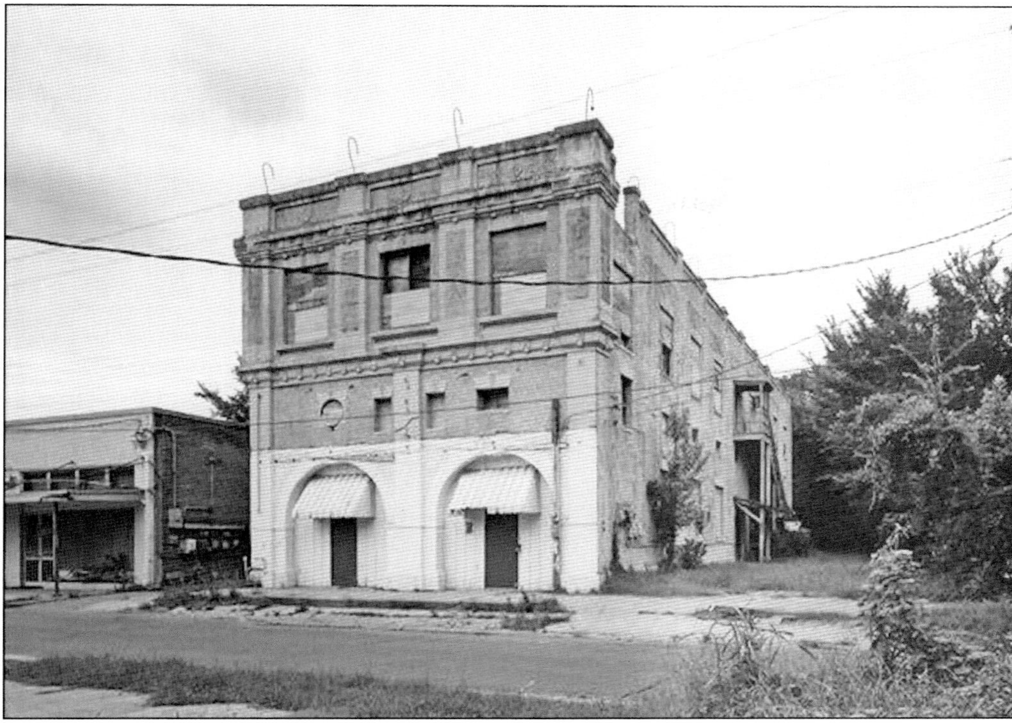

The Grand Theatre, which is located on Twelfth Street at North Boulevard in South Baton Rouge, is pictured above in the 1970s; below is Baton Rouge General Hospital in 1928. According to *Cinema Treasures*, Grand Theatre "was built in the late-1890's as an opera house and dance hall which was patronized by African Americans. The building was later converted into a movie theatre. The Grand Theatre is listed in the 1945 Film Daily Yearbook as closed with 475 seats. In the 1950's the theatre was converted into a night club." Not only were theaters segregated in Baton Rouge, so were hospitals, including Baton Rouge General Hospital. Black nurses had to treat patients in the basement of the hospital in segregated areas with limited resources but still provided a high quality of care. (Both, courtesy of East Baton Rouge Parish Public Library Digital Archive.)

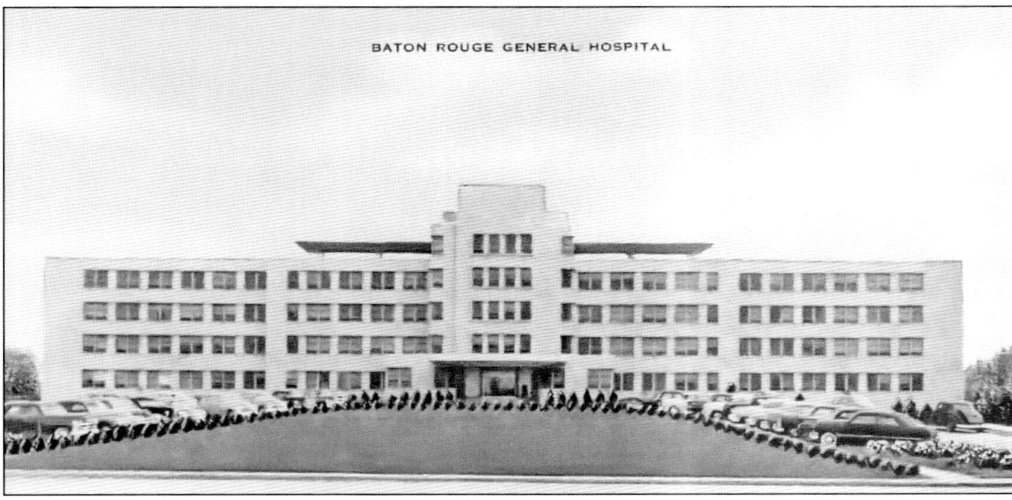

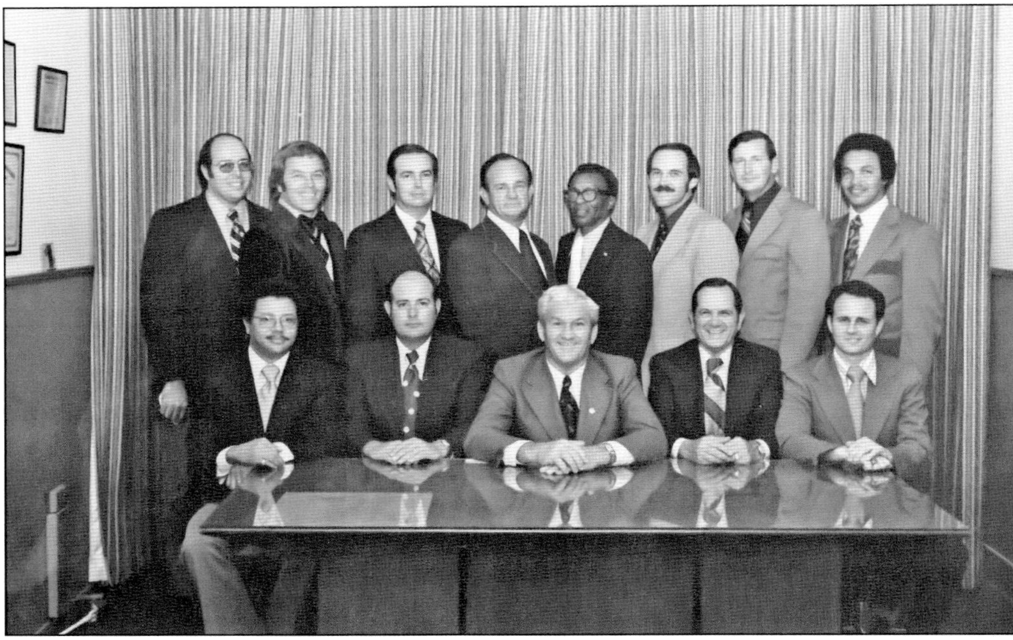

Black protests and persistence led to the integration of public institutions, such as schools, pools, hospitals, lunch counters, and theaters. Voting and civic engagement also led to breakthroughs in politics. Today, the mayor-president of Baton Rouge is Kip Holden, a black male graduate of Southern University, but it was Joseph A. Delpit who paved the way, becoming the first black elected official, to the city council in the 1960s. Delpit is standing in the center of these pictures. He attended several predominately black schools in South Baton Rouge, including St. Francis Xavier for elementary school and McKinley Senior High School. Since 1959, Delpit has owned and operated the Chicken Shack, a restaurant started by his father in 1935 with only 34¢ in capital. (Both, courtesy of East Baton Rouge Parish Public Library Digital Archive.)

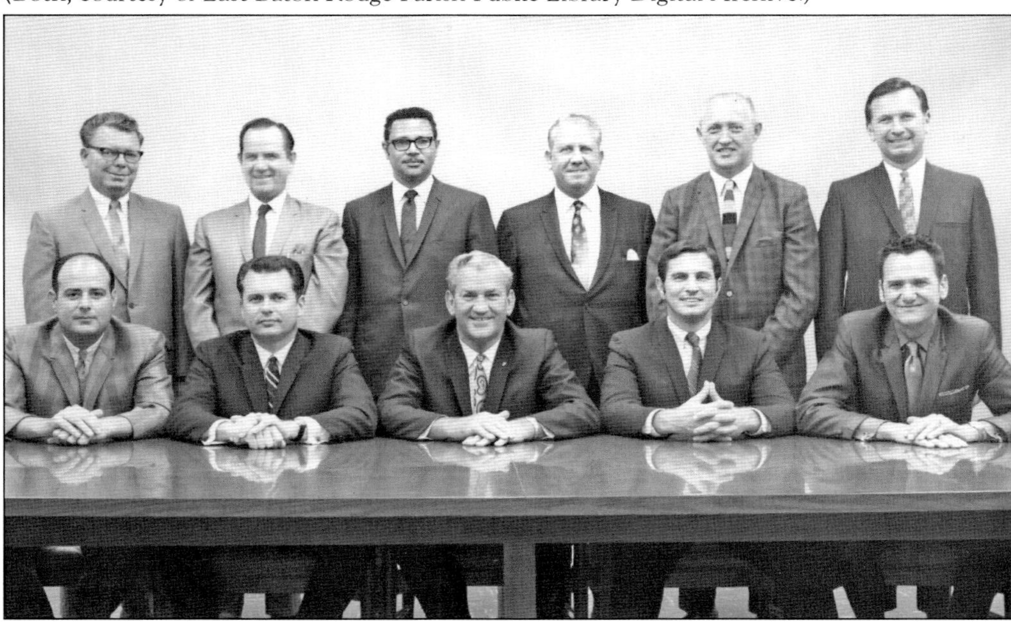

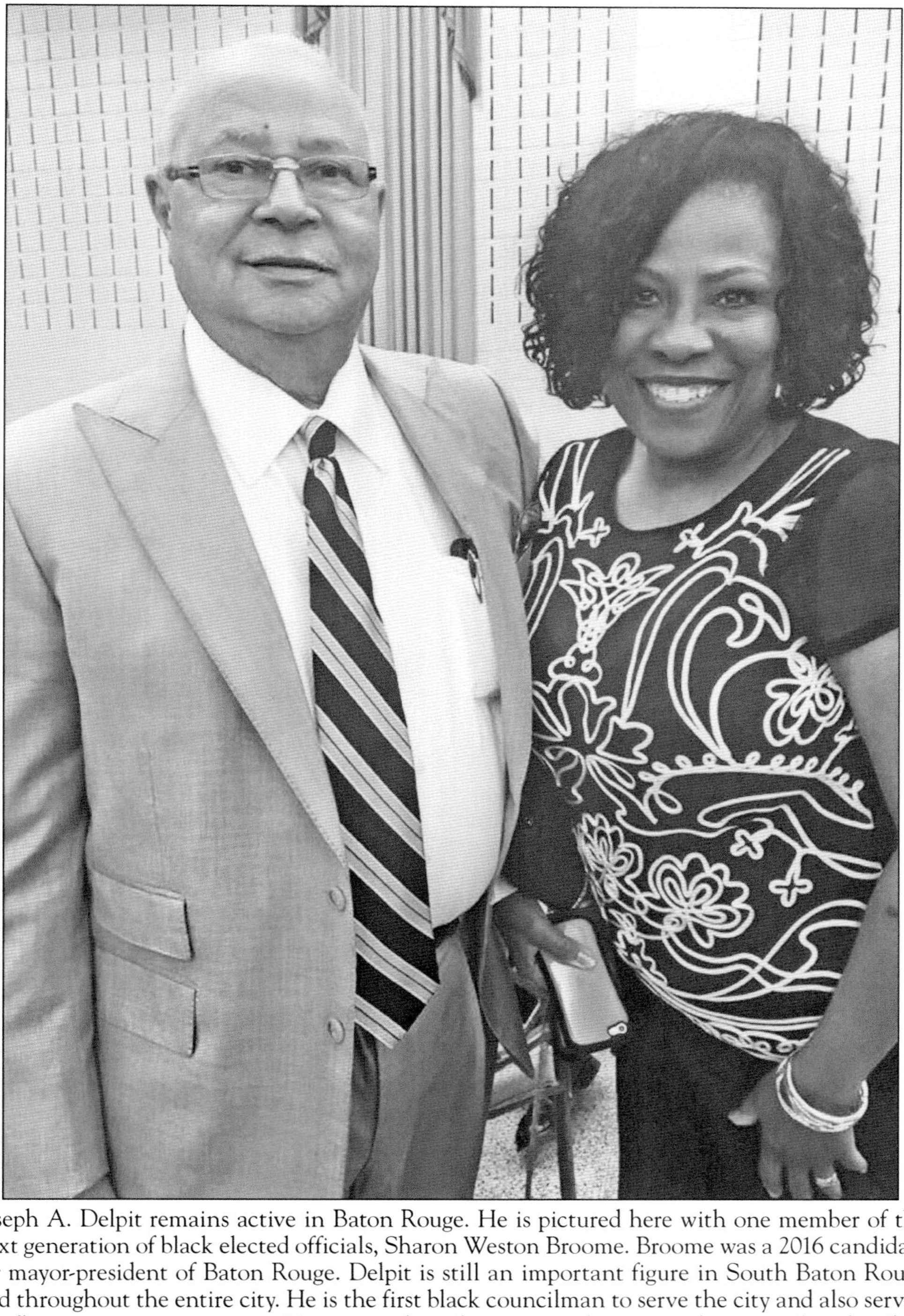

Joseph A. Delpit remains active in Baton Rouge. He is pictured here with one member of the next generation of black elected officials, Sharon Weston Broome. Broome was a 2016 candidate for mayor-president of Baton Rouge. Delpit is still an important figure in South Baton Rouge and throughout the entire city. He is the first black councilman to serve the city and also served briefly as mayor pro tempore. He was re-elected to a second term on the council with a first primary victory. While on the council, he was elected chairman of the executive committee and was appointed by the governor to the Greater Baton Rouge Port Commission. (Courtesy of Marvin Broome.)

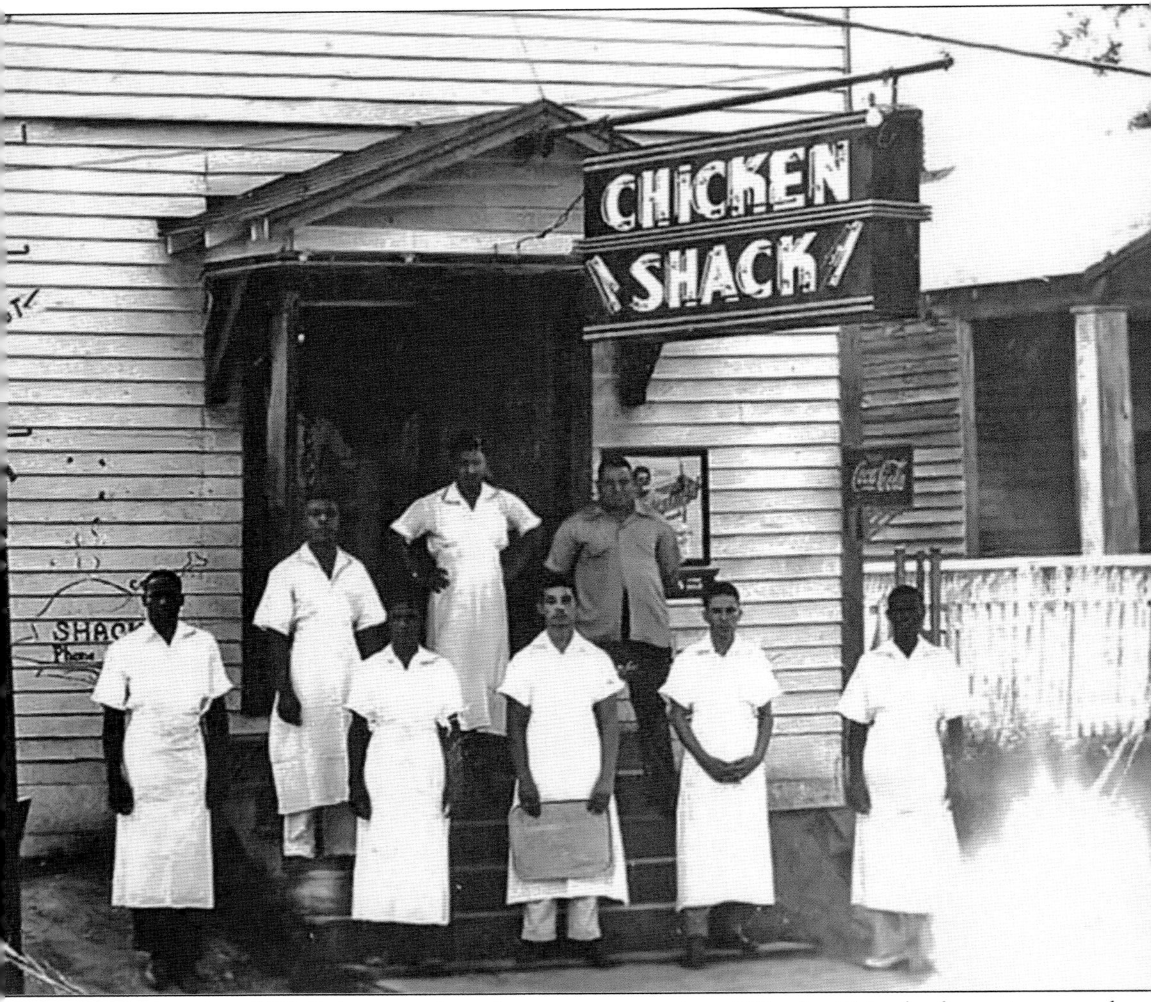

In November 1975, Delpit was elected state representative of District 67 in the first primary and served on the municipal and parochial affairs committee, the agriculture committee, and the appropriations committee. The Chicken Shack joins other staples in South Baton Rouge, including Webb Barber Shop, pictured here too. The barbershop, founded by Henry Webb, was established around 1916 and is still considered the go-to place for haircuts. (Courtesy of East Baton Rouge Parish Public Library Digital Archive.)

Three

The Fight for Social Justice

Blacks in Baton Rouge experienced unequal treatment for centuries but maintained the belief that change was possible. The fight for social justice in South Baton Rouge in many ways mirrors the fight for social justice in other parts of the Deep South and the nation. Among the most notable examples of fights for equal treatment are the establishment of Brooks Park, the 1953 Baton Rouge bus boycott, the Kress sit-ins, and efforts to desegregate schools. In the three-mile neighborhood of "old" South Baton Rouge, black residents endured exclusion from public places, including City Park, a municipal pool near the predominately black neighborhood in South Baton Rouge that was off-limits to black residents for many years. Although black tax dollars were collected for the maintenance of the pool, as were white tax dollars, fears about the mixing of the races in social settings kept blacks and whites from equal access to the facilities. Without a safe place to swim, black youths sought relief from the hot summer months wherever they could find water. Sadly, several drowned. In an interview with *Around the Bar* magazine, longtime South Baton Rouge resident Judge Trudy White describes her grandfather's role on the board of United Negro Recreational Association (UNRA). Other members of the board included Thelma Lois Cary Tacneau. Rev. Willie K. Brooks was the board president. The board led efforts to raise money to purchase a safe place for black children to swim and play in the 1940s, which resulted in Brooks Park. Judge White, a graduate of McKinley High School, observed that Brooks Park was later donated to BREC (the Recreation and Park Commission for the Parish of East Baton Rouge), the agency responsible for the operation of parks in East Baton Rouge Parish. Elvin "Tampoo" Dalcourt, also a longtime resident of South Baton Rouge and a youngster in the 1940s, was a first person in the new swimming pool in Brooks Park and a legendary swimmer in his neighborhood.

At the beginning of every year since the early 1980s, the nation pauses to remember and to reflect on the life and legacy of Rev. Dr. Martin Luther King Jr. A few weeks later, many Americans turn their attention to the contributions of people of African ancestry in America as part of Black History Month. Atlanta, Montgomery, and Selma are among the cities that come to mind when one thinks about black history in America. Baton Rouge was also a site of many significant events in the fight for social justice during the 20th century, including a bus boycott that inspired and motivated participants in the broader civil rights movement throughout the Deep South and beyond.

African American Registry describes the 1953 bus boycott, which originated in South Baton Rouge, as the first civil rights bus boycott. On June 15, 1953, black residents in South Baton Rouge took the first step towards dismantling segregation on public buses in the Deep South. A few months earlier, in March, black residents in South Baton Rouge had appealed to the city council for an ordinance permitting riders to sit on a first-come-first-served basis. The residents were successful in securing Ordinance 222. The ordinance stated blacks were required to sit from the rear to the front, while whites had to sit from the front to the rear. The bus drivers, all white, refused to comply with the ordinance, went on strike, and gained the support of the state attorney general, who said the ordinance was in conflict with the segregation laws of the state and therefore illegal.

Black residents in South Baton Rouge refused to ride the bus once the drivers returned to work after the attorney general's ruling. The residents instead established a free-ride system, a method that was used by Rev. Dr. Martin Luther King Jr. during the Montgomery bus boycott in Alabama in 1955.

The boycott in South Baton Rouge lasted about two weeks before a compromise was reached between the leadership of the boycott and those in decision-making positions. The compromise stated that the two side front seats of buses were reserved for whites and the long rear seats of buses were to be reserved for blacks.

Efforts to desegregate schools, ban discrimination in areas of public accommodation, and gain full voting rights were met with much resistance. Sit-ins at Kress and efforts to integrate local schools and universities left their tolls on the city, especially busing and one of the longest desegregation cases in the nation. Out of the continued struggle for social justice across the city emerged great civic and political leaders. South Baton Rouge was not only a significant city in the civil rights movement but also in the Black Power movement. H. Rap Brown was born and raised in South Baton Rouge. Baton Rouge was home to and hosted many Black Muslims, especially in the late 1960s and early 1970s. One of the most notorious and deadliest riots in the city's history involved Black Muslims and took place near the historic Temple Theater.

According to an article published in the January 11, 1972, *New Orleans Times-Picayune*, two sheriff's deputies and two black males were killed in South Baton Rouge in what is described as "a street shootout between law enforcement officers and a group identified by city officials as Black Muslims." According to the article, shots were fired around noon after black youths blocked a city street in South Baton Rouge. The cars reportedly belonged to out-of-state residents. Although all was quite by nightfall, "Louisiana National Guardsmen were posted at gun stores in the city and about 100 Guardsmen were on duty in front of the city hall." The article also states almost 30 people went to area hospitals for treatment of injuries related to the conflict. The injured included black residents of South Baton Rouge, police officers, and journalists. Of the 20 black men arrested in the deaths of the sheriff's deputies, eight were charged with murder. Officials claimed Black Muslims from Chicago arrived in the city weeks earlier with plans of taking over the city and "they were able to get some militants, like any other community has, to side with them." The official account of the so-called racial battle was not the same as accounts from black residents in South Baton Rouge who were eyewitnesses to the event. The following chapter includes images of people, places, and events related to civil rights struggles in Baton Rouge.

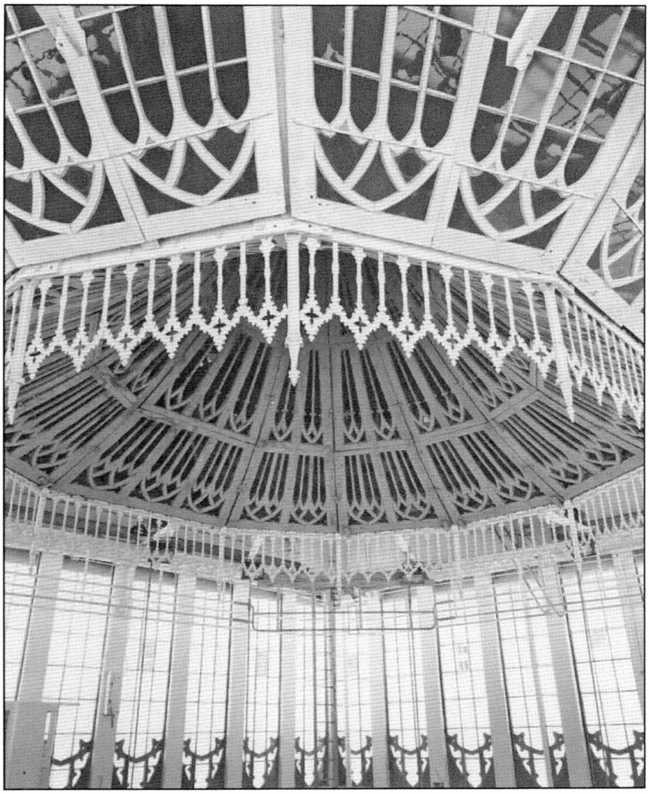

The Old State Capitol is a beautiful castle used as a museum and as a reception hall for weddings and special events. The interior of the building is shown at right. Outside the building is an important place in the history of blacks in South Baton Rouge and in the global struggle for human and civil rights. Protests calling for equal treatment of Baton Rouge residents regardless of race took place right in front of the Old State Capitol, which is located at 100 North Boulevard. The individuals pictured below in front of the Old State Capitol building are taking part in the 1953 bus boycott. (Both, courtesy of East Baton Rouge Parish Public Library Digital Archive.)

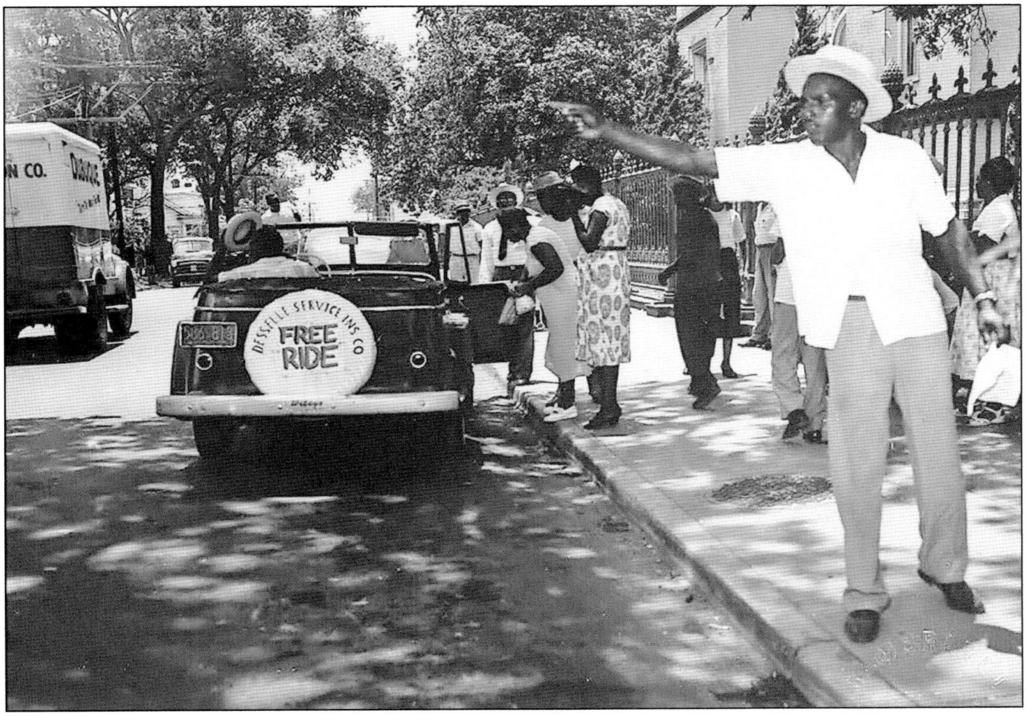

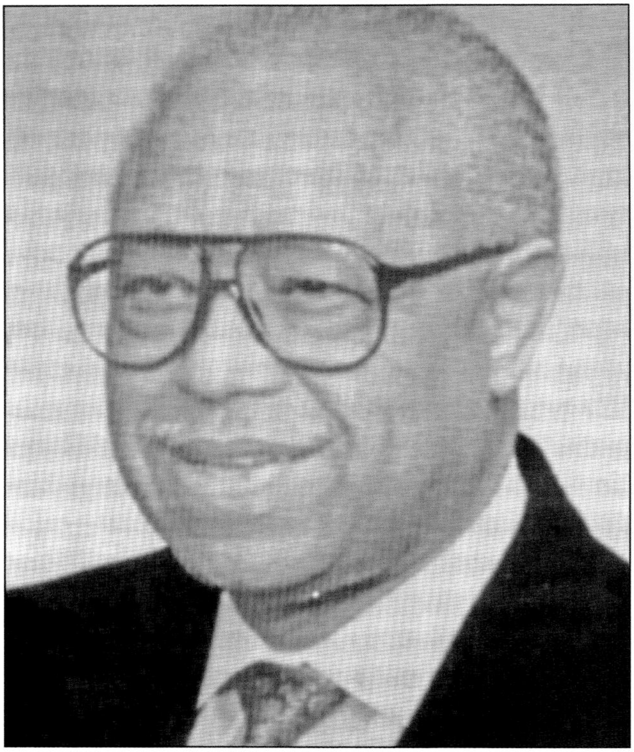

Many men and women played active roles during the civil rights era in Baton Rouge. Alex Pitcher Jr. (left), and Leo S. Butler (below) were two examples. Pitcher was a lawyer for the NAACP. He worked on the *Clifford Eugene Davis Jr. et al v. the East Baton Rouge Parish School Board et al.* desegregation case. The case originated with a student at McKinley High School dating back to 1956. Butler was the first male to graduate from the Baton Rouge Colored School in 1918 (the school later became McKinley High School). Dr. Butler dedicated much of his time to the Blundon Home, an orphanage in South Baton Rouge, and was a founder of the First Savings and Loan Association in October 1956. (Both, courtesy of East Baton Rouge Parish Public Library Digital Archive.)

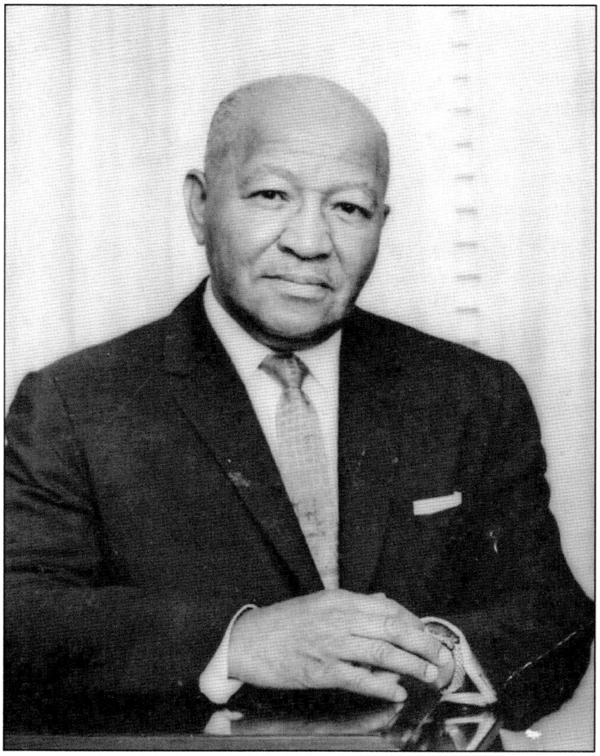

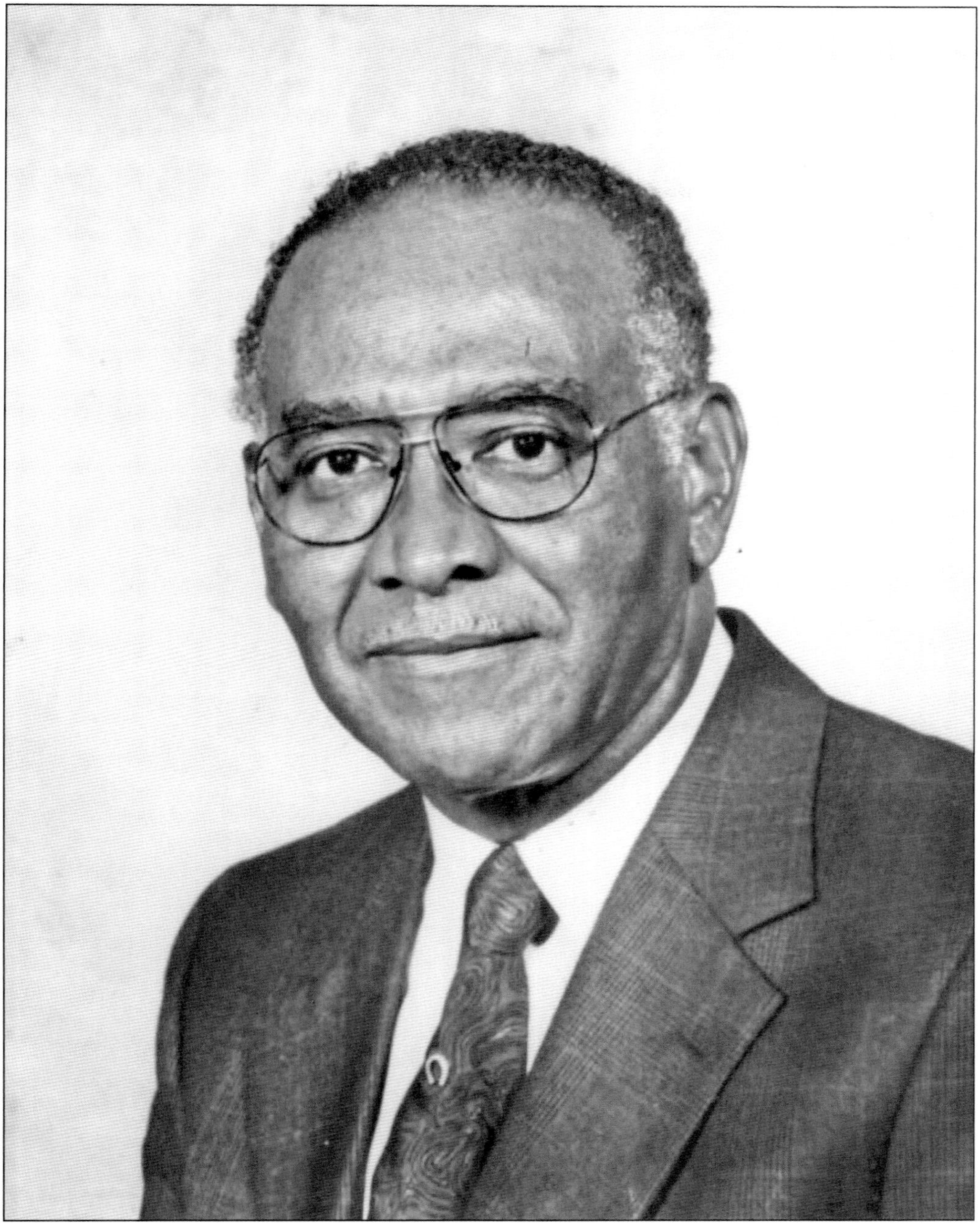

Dr. Louis James was one of the giants in the history of civil rights in South Baton Rouge. Dr. James graduated from McKinley High School. He earned a medical degree from Howard University after receiving a degree from Southern University. He served in the US Army and was a member of Mount Zion First Baptist Church. He was the first African American on the Executive Board of Baton Rouge General Hospital, among other firsts for blacks with ties to South Baton Rouge. Dr. James participated in the bus boycott and Kress lunch counter protests during the 1950s and 1960s. (Courtesy of East Baton Rouge Parish Public Library Digital Archive.)

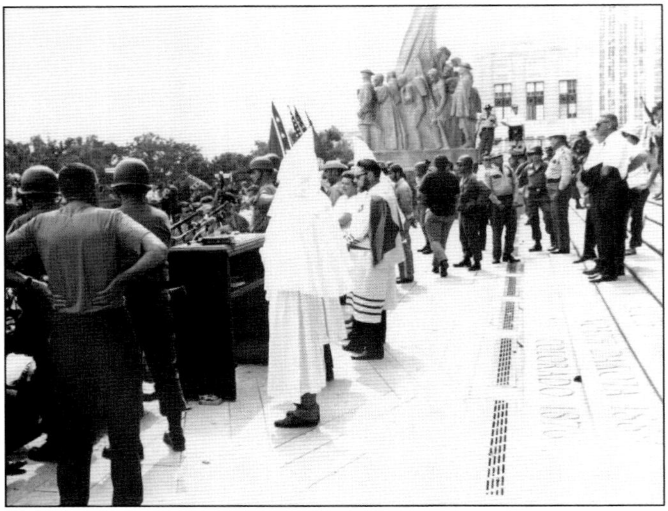

Members of the Ku Klux Klan are shown in the 1960s during a rally at the Louisiana State Capitol. The rally served as a counterdemonstration to those of blacks and other civil rights workers. (Courtesy of East Baton Rouge Parish Public Library Digital Archive.)

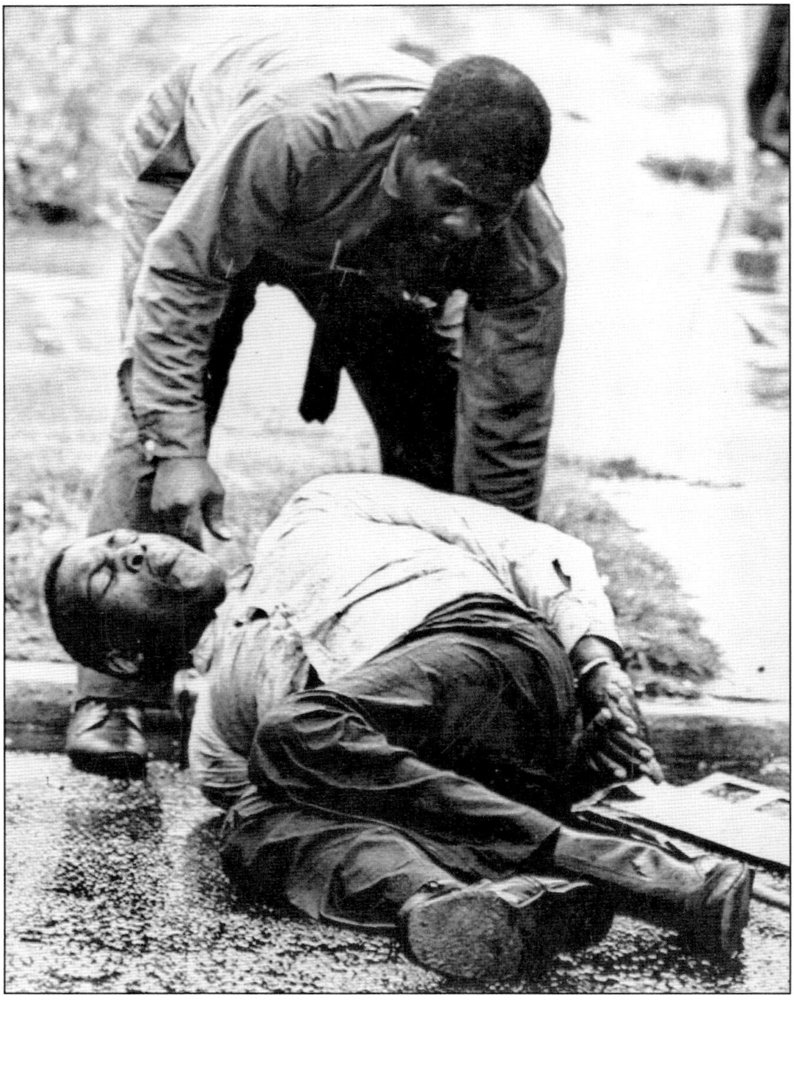

An officer reaches down to lift an injured man following a shooting incident on January 11, 1972, that left four dead. (Courtesy of East Baton Rouge Parish Public Library Digital Archive.)

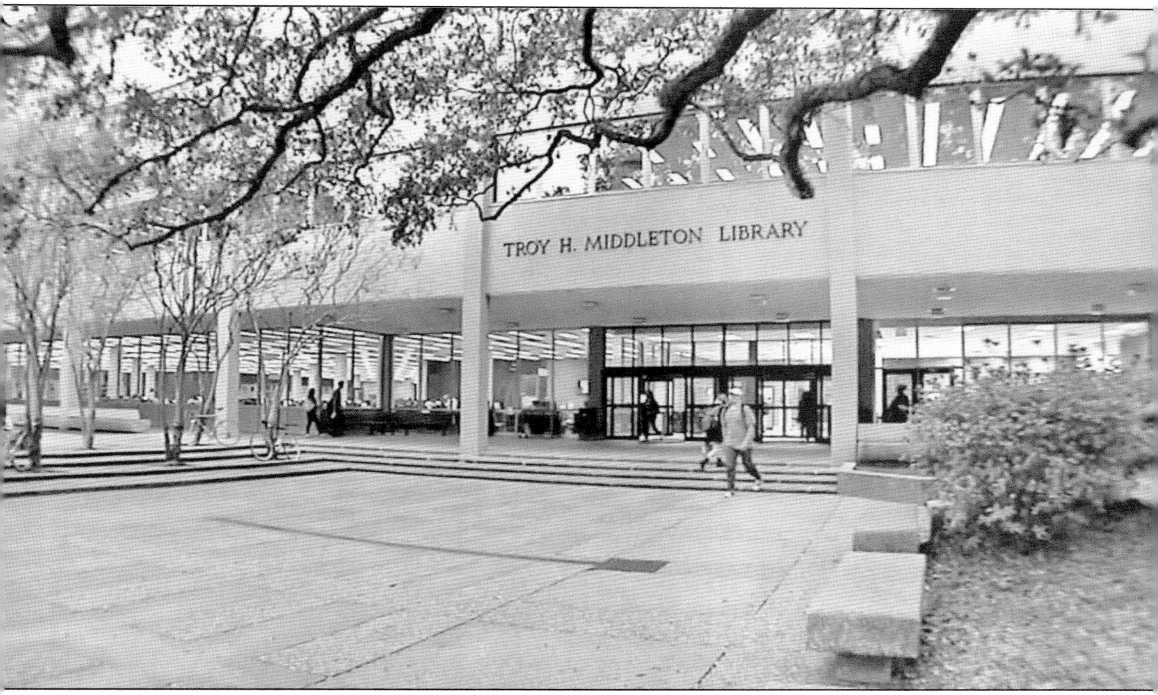

Schools across the country have the names of Confederate generals and segregationists, including Robert E. Lee High School in South Baton Rouge. Although the flagship university for the state of Louisiana freely admits and recruits students of color, many building on the campus wear the names of individuals who fought long and hard to keep blacks and whites separate. Troy H. Middleton is one example: the main library on the campus of Louisiana State University, adjacent to the historic black community of South Baton Rouge, is named in honor of a man who refused to allow black undergraduates to attend the university without a directive from the highest court in the land. (Courtesy of East Baton Rouge Parish Public Library Digital Archive.)

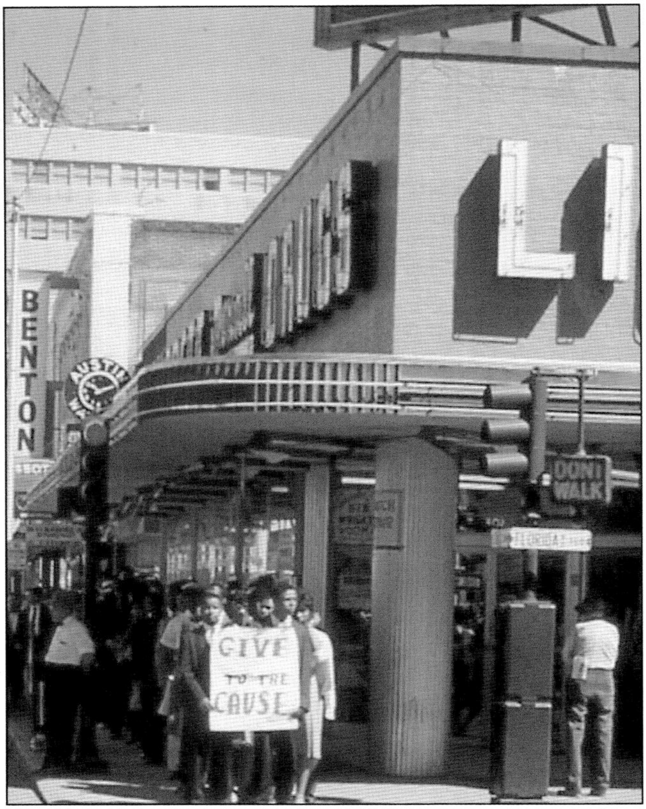

On December 15, 1961, about 2,000 people marched without incident through Baton Rouge to protest the arrest of almost two dozen Southern University students the previous day for picketing businesses that refused to serve blacks. The picture at left shows a protest in front of Liggett's Drug Store, which was located on the corner of Third and Florida Streets in South Baton Rouge. Another attempt to change the course of race relations during this time period involved efforts to integrate all-white Baton Rouge Junior High School. Rev. Arthur Jelks, former president of the local chapter of the NAACP, is pictured below leading a group of African American girls who were turned away. The girls pictured are, from left to right, Ellis Marie Lamotte, Olivia Sandiford, and Reverend Jelk's daughter Patricia. (Both, courtesy of East Baton Rouge Parish Public Library Digital Archive.)

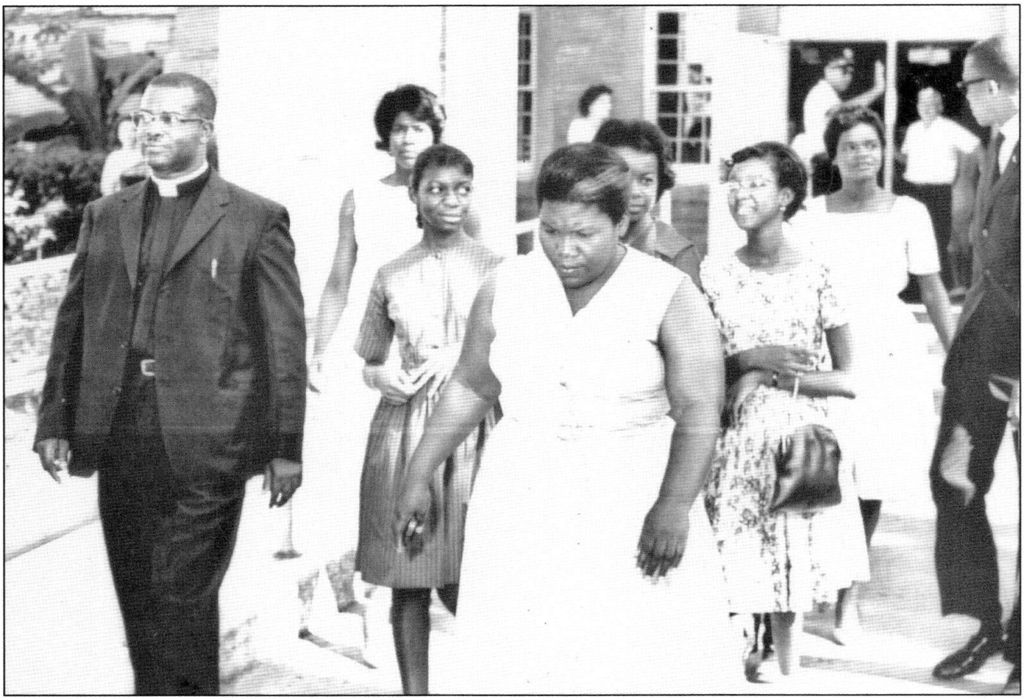

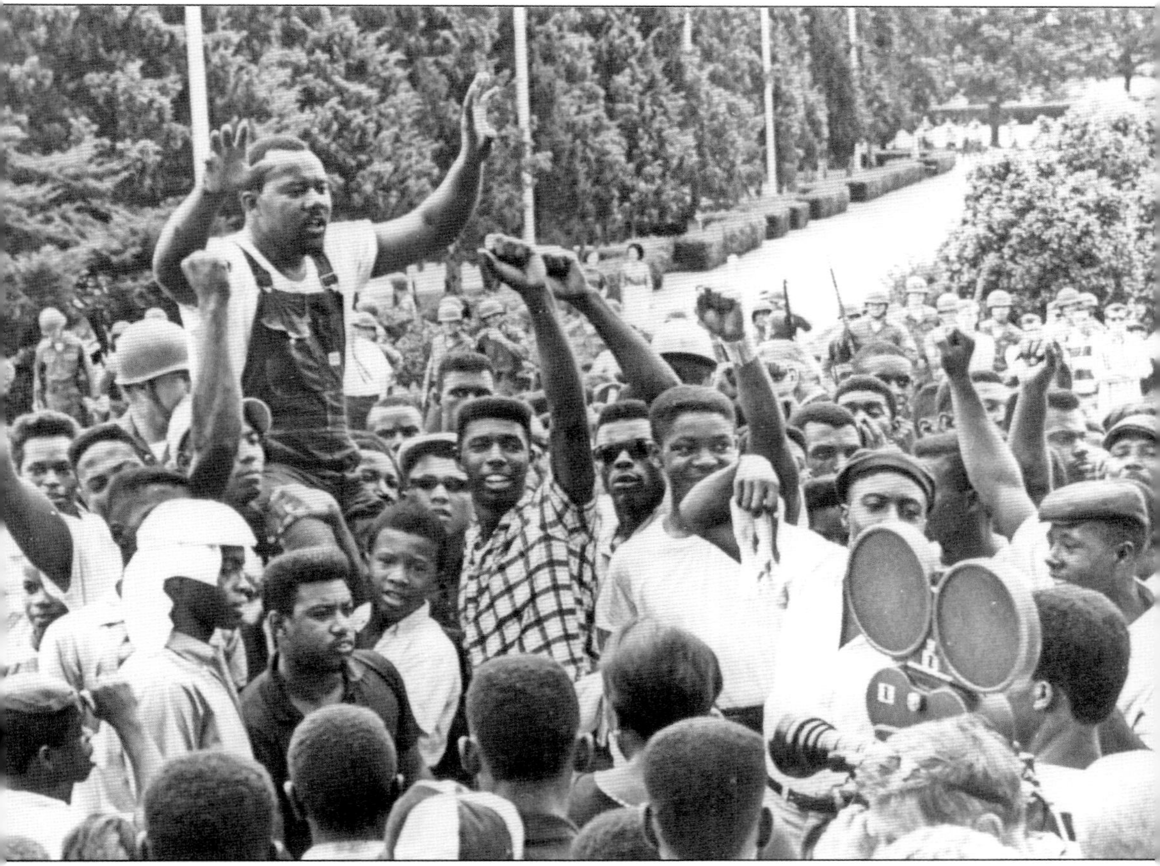

According to text in the East Baton Rouge Parish Public Library Digital Archive, "Billy Brooks, director of the Louisiana Black People Advancement Association, sits on the shoulders of some of his followers and leads a group in shouts of "Black Power." The group formed from a larger one that was holding a rally on the steps of the Louisiana State Capitol on August 20, 1967. The larger rally was the climax of the historic 11-day, 105-mile civil rights march from Bogalusa to Baton Rouge." (Courtesy of East Baton Rouge Parish Public Library Digital Archive.)

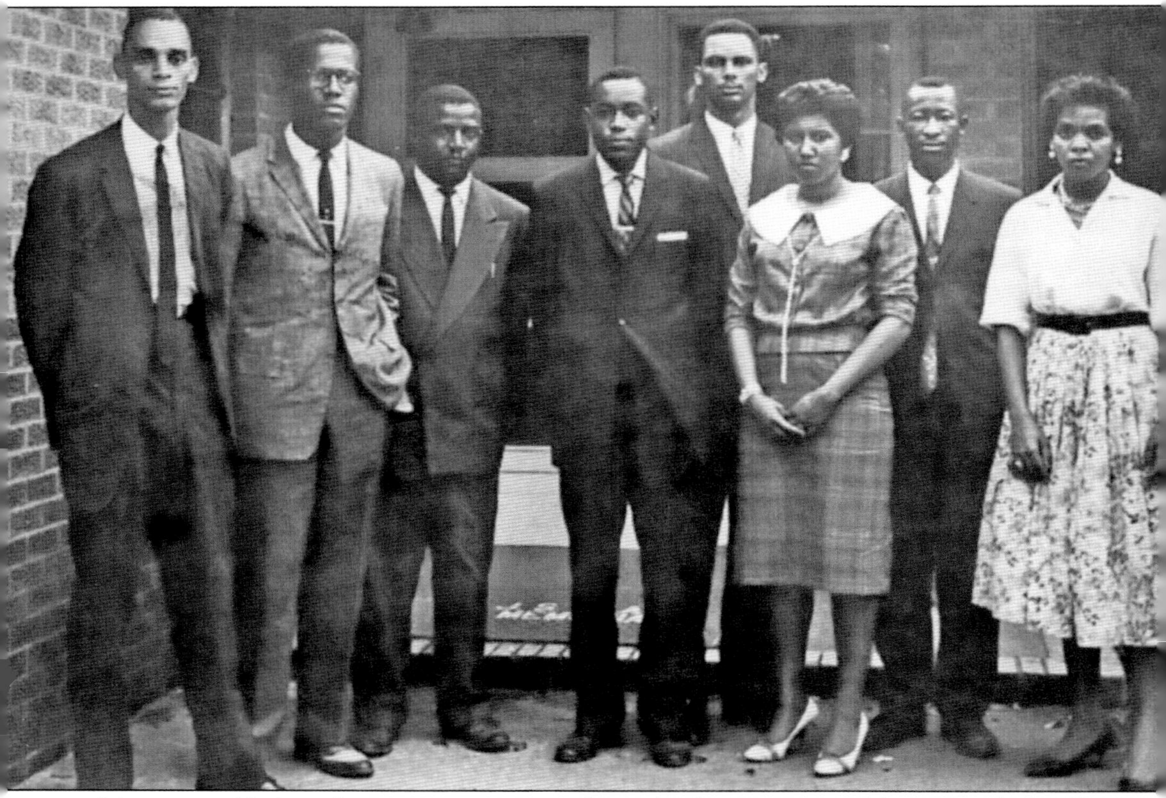

Many young black residents were eager to join the civil rights movement of the 1960s. Black college students in Baton Rouge participated in Louisiana's first sit-ins. The students pictured are, from left to right, Marvin Robinson, Felton Valdry, Major Johns, John Johnson, Donald Moss, Janette Houston Harris, Kenneth Johnson, and JoAnn Morris. Instead of applauding the students for their bravery, Southern University punished them. The students found refuge and comfort in the black community of South Baton Rouge, where they were welcomed into area churches to receive support and financial assistance with their legal defense. (Courtesy of East Baton Rouge Parish Public Library Digital Archive.)

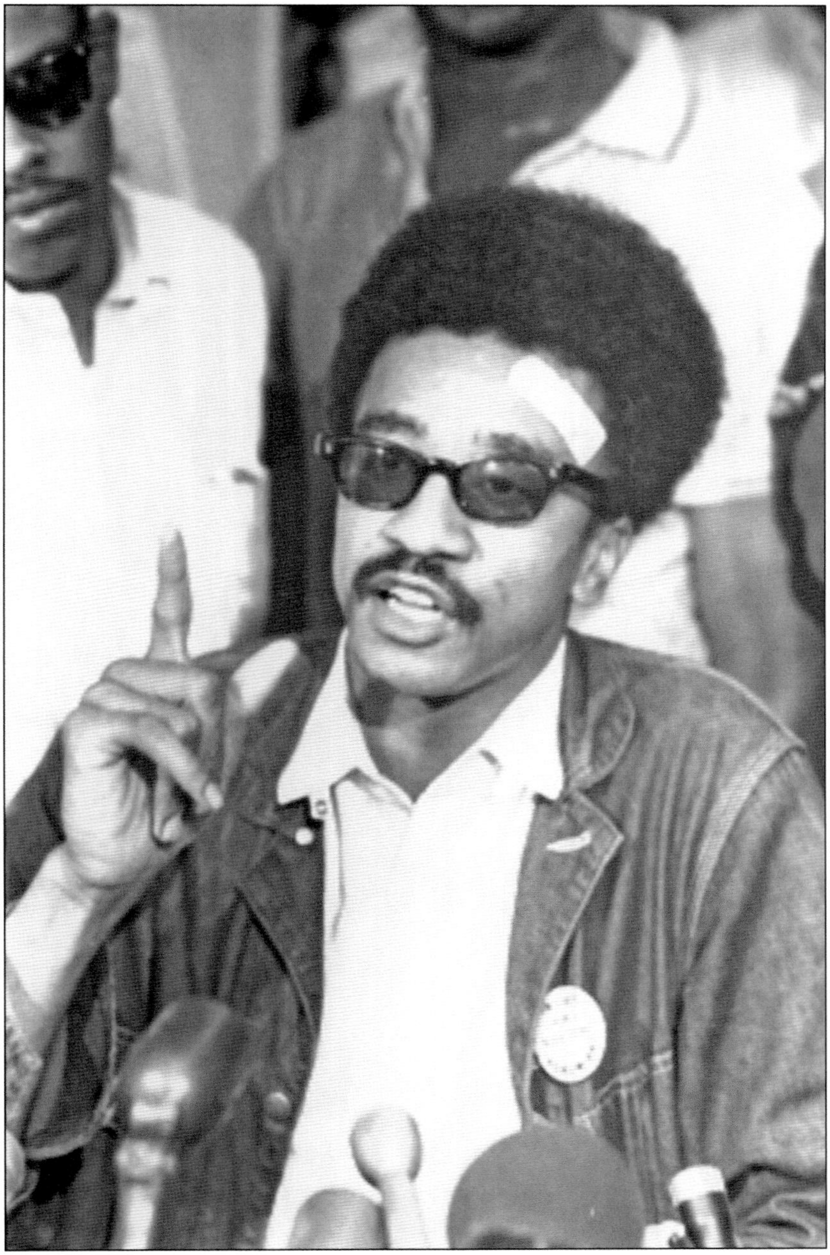

Much is written about the role that civil rights leaders played in addressing racial conflict and unequal treatment in South Baton Rouge. The leaders receiving the most attention are men with ties to area churches, especially churches affiliated with Baptist and Methodist Episcopal denominations. However, other faith traditions and other movements thrived in South Baton Rouge in the 1960s and 1970s. Black Panthers and Black Muslims were very visible. Jamil Abdullah Al-Amin, born H. Rapp Brown in 1943, was a member of the Black Panther Party from South Baton Rouge who attended McKinley High School. He even worked for a time at the historic Chicken Shack, according to owner Joseph Delpit. (Courtesy of East Baton Rouge Parish Public Library Digital Archive.)

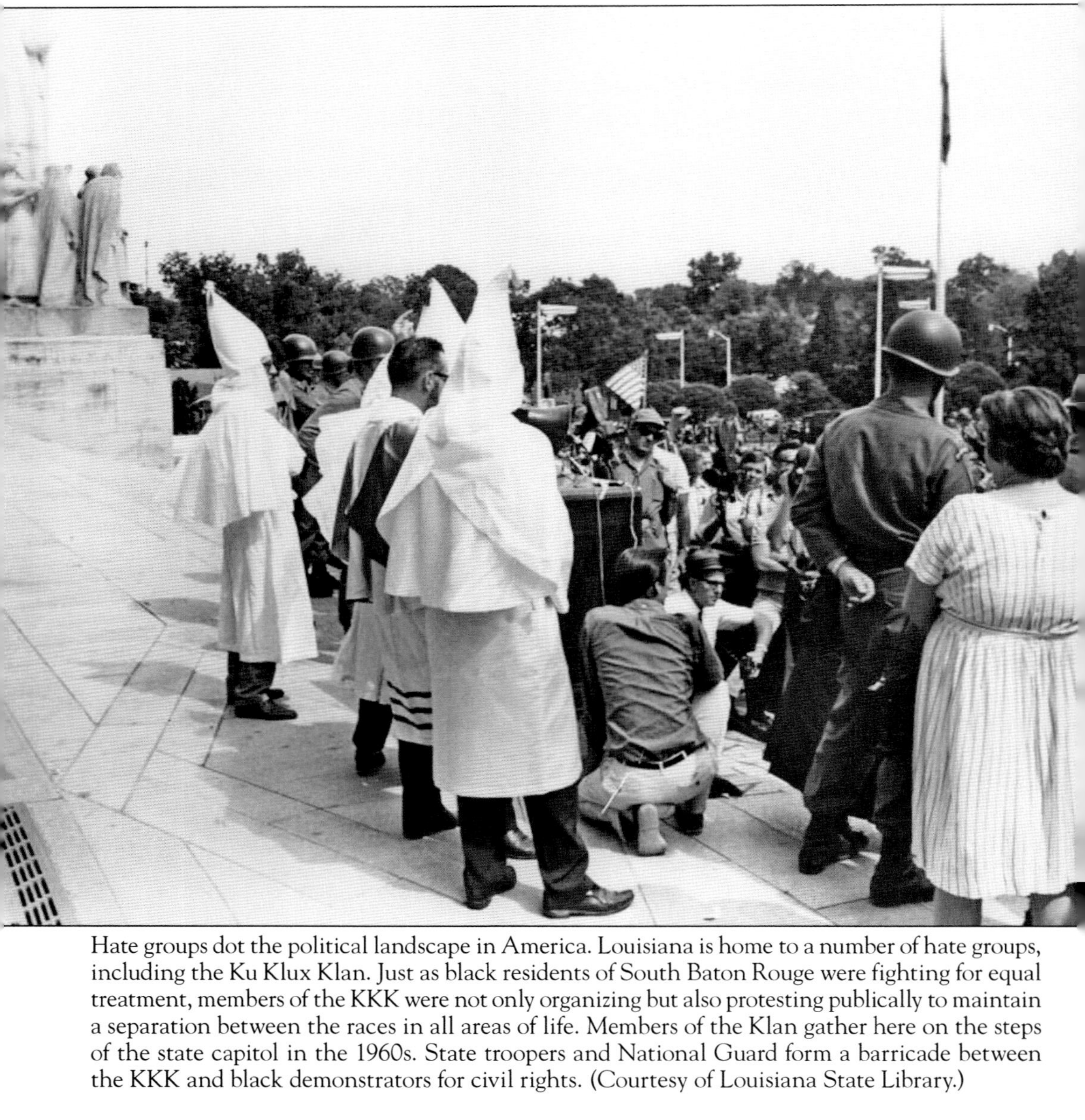

Hate groups dot the political landscape in America. Louisiana is home to a number of hate groups, including the Ku Klux Klan. Just as black residents of South Baton Rouge were fighting for equal treatment, members of the KKK were not only organizing but also protesting publically to maintain a separation between the races in all areas of life. Members of the Klan gather here on the steps of the state capitol in the 1960s. State troopers and National Guard form a barricade between the KKK and black demonstrators for civil rights. (Courtesy of Louisiana State Library.)

Alexander Pierre "A.P." Tureaud was the local attorney for the NAACP Legal Defense and Education Fund. For about two decades beginning in the 1940s, Tureaud handled most of the desegregation cases in Louisiana. He was also involved in efforts throughout the state, including in Baton Rouge, to desegregate city buses. (Courtesy of Special Collections, LSU Libraries.)

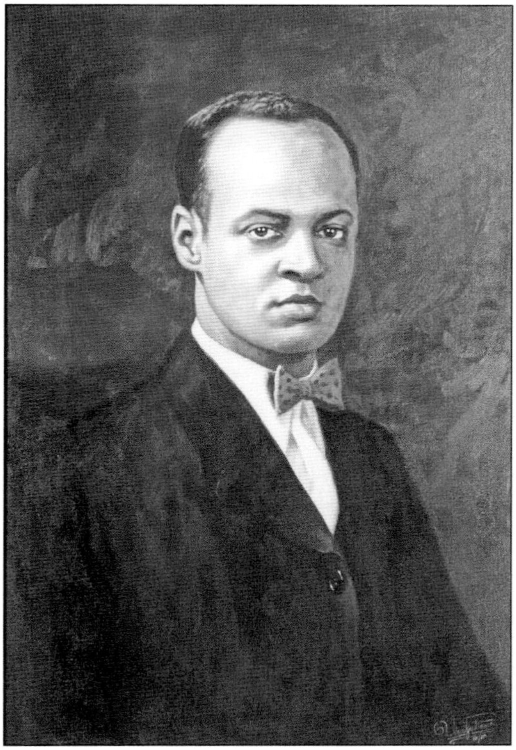

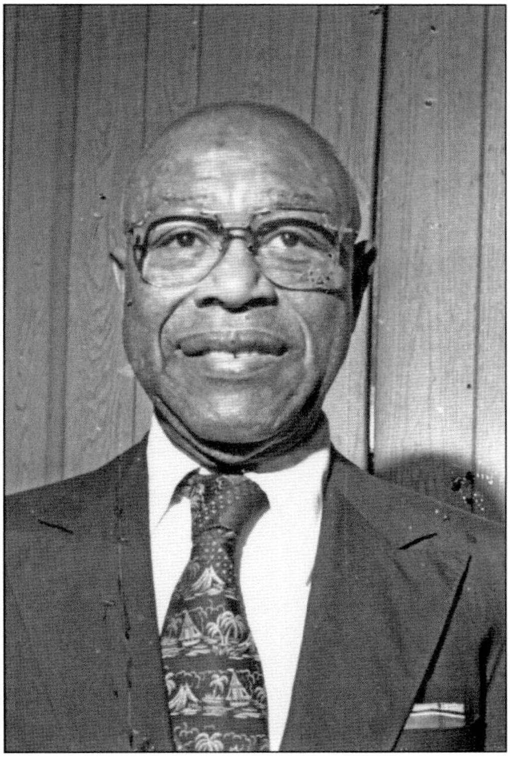

Dr. Curtis Gilliam was a longtime civil rights activist. He was also the first black optometrist in Baton Rouge and a president of the Baton Rouge chapter of the NAACP. He also has the distinction of being the first black person from Louisiana to join the US Marine Corps and served in World War II. Dr. Gilliam was an active participant in the bus boycott and efforts to desegregate the local school board. (Courtesy of East Baton Rouge Parish Public Library Digital Archive.)

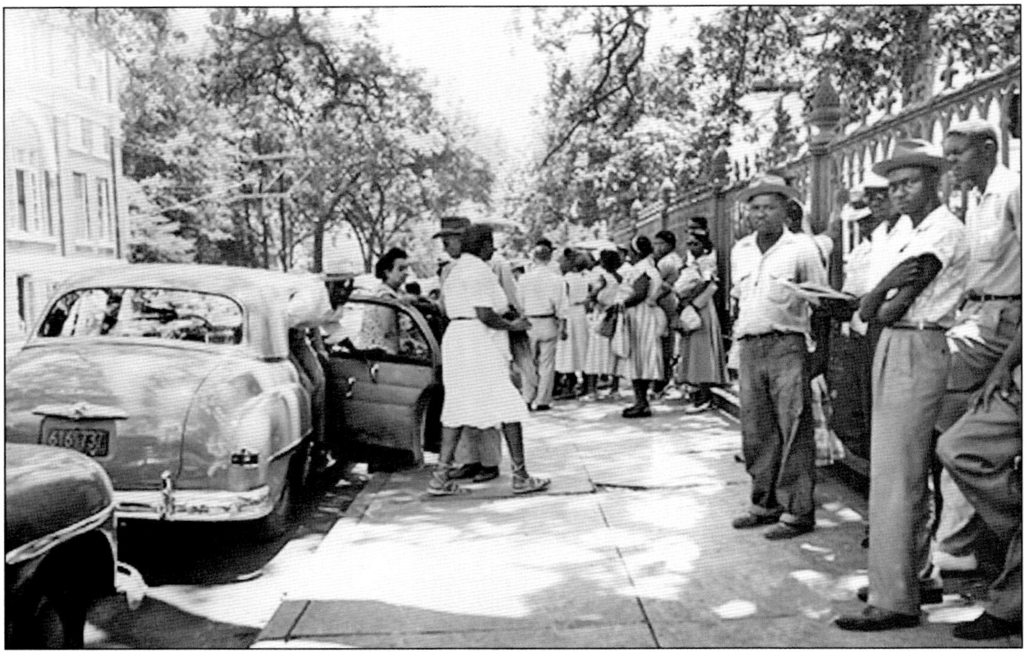

In 1953, residents of South Baton Rouge boycotted the city's public transportation system. A few months prior to the boycott, an ordinance was passed to allow for blacks to fill up the back of the buses first before entering the front reserved for whites. After the predominately white drivers refused to drive the public buses, the Louisiana attorney general overturned the ordinance. The boycott led to a compromise that mirrored the earlier ordinance but vowed to keep blacks and whites from sitting or standing next to one another. Dr. Martin Luther King Jr. used the boycott as a model for the 1955 bus boycott in Montgomery, Alabama. (Courtesy of East Baton Rouge Parish Public Library Digital Archive.)

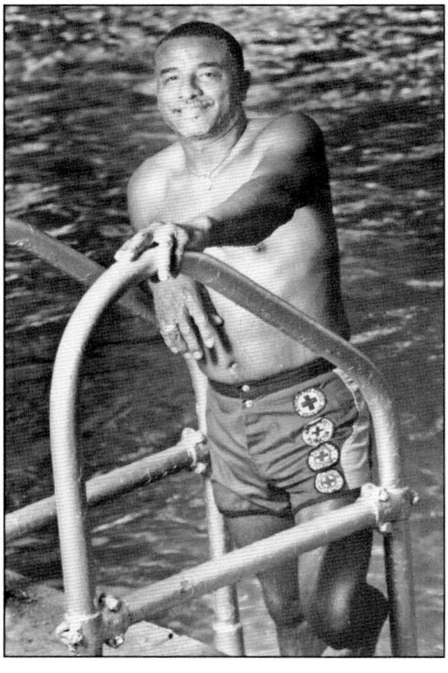

Elvin "Tampoo" Dalcourt is a lifelong resident of South Baton Rouge. He was involved in a number of efforts to integrate public places in Baton Rouge. After black residents built and paid for a swimming pool during the height of Jim Crow, Tampoo was the first child in the pool when it opened in the 1940s. (Courtesy of Elvin Dalcourt.)

Four

A Bench by the Road

While the American landscape is dotted with monuments and memorials to a host of historic events, places, and people, there are few such structures dedicated to the experiences of enslaved Africans or their descendants. The Toni Morrison Society's goal was to address the oversight in America's efforts to collectively remember and commemorate its past through the creation of the Bench by the Road Project.

According to the official website for the Toni Morrison Society, "The Bench by the Road Project is a memorial history and community outreach initiative of the Toni Morrison Society." Founded in 2006, the Bench by the Road Project was launched on February 18, 2006, and was named based upon Toni Morrison's remarks in a 1989 interview with *World* magazine. During the interview, Morrison addressed the lack of historical markers to honor and help people remember the lives of Africans who were enslaved. Morrison also remarked on how her acclaimed novel, *Beloved*, filled a tremendous void:

> There is no place you or I can go, to think about or not think about, to summon the presences of, or recollect the absences of slaves. . . . There is no suitable memorial, or plaque, or wreath, or wall, or park, or skyscraper lobby. There's no 300-foot tower, there's no small bench by the road. There is not even a tree scored, an initial that I can visit or you can visit in Charleston or Savannah or New York or Providence or better still on the banks of the Mississippi. And because such a place doesn't exist . . . the book had to.

One of the aims of the Toni Morrison Society is to be a place where scholars and general admirers of Morrison's body of work can remember slavery and "many of the forgotten moments in African American history." The society chose the phrase "a bench by the road" as its motto when it was founded. The Bench by the Road Project, as outlined on the society's official website, extends the society's commitment to never forgetting to remember important times in the history of Africans in America and beyond. While there have been several notable African American museums built in American cities since 1989, the goal of the Bench by the Road Project is to create an outdoor museum that will mark important locations in black history both in the United States and throughout the globe.

On February 6, 2016, South Baton Rouge joined an elite and highly selective group of communities where a commemorative bench would be placed. McKinley High School Alumni Center was chosen as the site for the bench because of its historic location in South Baton Rouge and because of its role as a meeting place for organizers and participants of the 1953 Baton Rouge bus boycott, for which the bench is named. The McKinley High School Alumni Center is the former site of McKinley High School, where the first class, which graduated in 1916, consisted of four black students. The alumni center also served as a meeting place for several events related to the civil rights movement. In many ways, the alumni center is the cultural epicenter of the historic African American community of South Baton Rouge. It houses many historical artifacts related to the long and plentiful history of African Americans in the surrounding community.

Among the places being considered by the Bench by the Road Project are those that have special significance in Morrison's novels—Fifth Avenue in New York City, where the Silent Parade, protesting the East St. Louis Riots, was held in 1917; the site of Emmett Till's death in Mississippi; train stations in Mississippi, Alabama, and Georgia where thousands began their journeys in the Great Migration; an all-black town in Oklahoma; University Hall in Providence, Rhode Island; the home of Fannie Lou Hamer in Mississippi; and other unmarked sites that have historical meaning for African Americans.

South Baton Rouge joins the following impressive list of placement sites for the prestigious benches: Sullivan's Island, South Carolina (July 26, 2008); Oberlin, Ohio (April 23, 2009); Hattiesburg, Mississippi (October 3, 2009); Paris, France (November 6, 2010); Concord, Massachusetts (May 21, 2011); George Washington University, Washington, DC (September 23, 2011); First Congregational Church, Atlanta, Georgia (May 27, 2012); Mitchelville (Hilton Head), South Carolina (April 16, 2013);Lincoln, Massachusetts (May 22, 2013); Fort-de-France, Martinique (June 26, 2013); Eden Cemetery, Collingdale, Pennsylvania (April 24, 2014); Nyack, New York (May 18, 2015); Morehouse College (March 8, 2016); the Cozard-Bates House in Cleveland, Ohio (April 24, 2016); and the Schomburg Center for Research in Black Culture, in Harlem, New York City (July 24, 2016).

The ceremony in South Baton Rouge featured keynote speaker Christopher Tyson. Tyson is a law professor, native son of Baton Rouge, and recent candidate for secretary of state of Louisiana. In his address to the hundreds gathered for the celebration, he commented on the special place South Baton Rouge holds for him personally, as one of his grandmothers graduated from McKinley High School. Tyson also reflected upon his fond memories of patronizing historic South Baton Rouge businesses, including the original Chicken Shack, operated by the Delpit family. Representatives from the Toni Morrison Society's Bench by the Road Project, Craig Stutman and Carolyn Durnard, also addressed the gathering. Current McKinley High School football players participated, as did many of the school's alumni and local elected officials. Robin Clark, an educator who grew up in South Baton Rouge, delivered a powerful and memorable poem in honor of the historic event. The event was widely covered by the *Baton Rouge Advocate* and *Baton Rouge Drum* newspapers. Features also appeared in *225 Magazine*, *Country Roads*, and on local television news stations, including WBRZ. The commemorative committee members included the authors of South Baton Rouge and individuals with personal, familial, and business ties to the area: Judge Trudy White, Kali Johnson, Kenneth Fasching-Varner, Sadie Roberts-Joseph, Sarah Corie, April Hawthorne, Stephen Finley, Joyce Marie Jackson, Lisa Freeman, Modrall Lathers, Cleveland Davis, Marc Garnier, and Lorri Burgess. Funding for the bench was made possible by contributions from Aetna Better Health of Louisiana. Selected images from the historic event are included in this chapter.

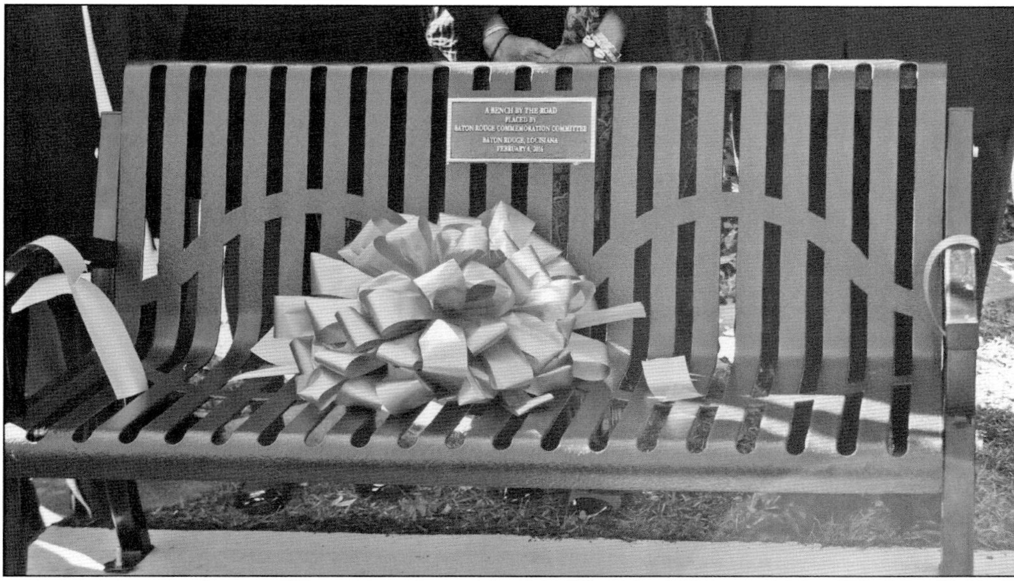

On February 6, 2016, Baton Rouge joined a very exclusive club when it became one of only 20 cities honored by the Toni Morrison Society for its commitment to social justice and to preserving the history and heritage of South Baton Rouge. In a ceremony held at McKinley High School Alumni Center, a bench was dedicated in honor of the 1953 bus boycott. The center is located in the old McKinley High School, near the current McKinley Middle and High Schools. Chris Tyson, a recent candidate for Louisiana secretary of state and a law professor at Louisiana State University, delivered the keynote address, and representatives from the Toni Morrison Society's Bench by the Road Project were in attendance. Here are two pictures of the bench as it appeared at the dedication and ribbon cutting. (Both, courtesy of Tat Yau.)

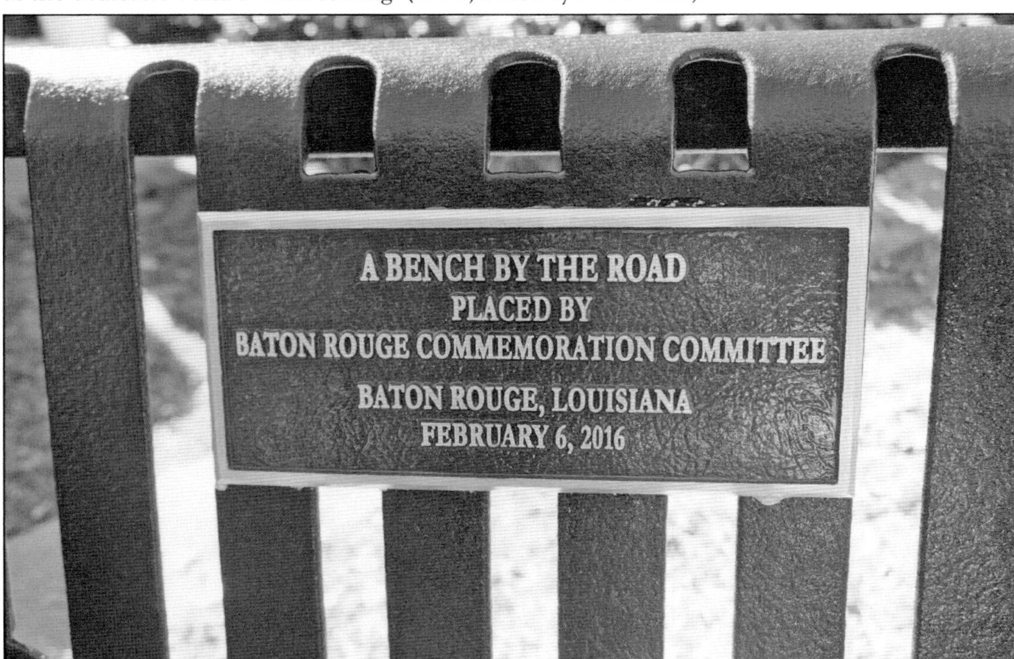

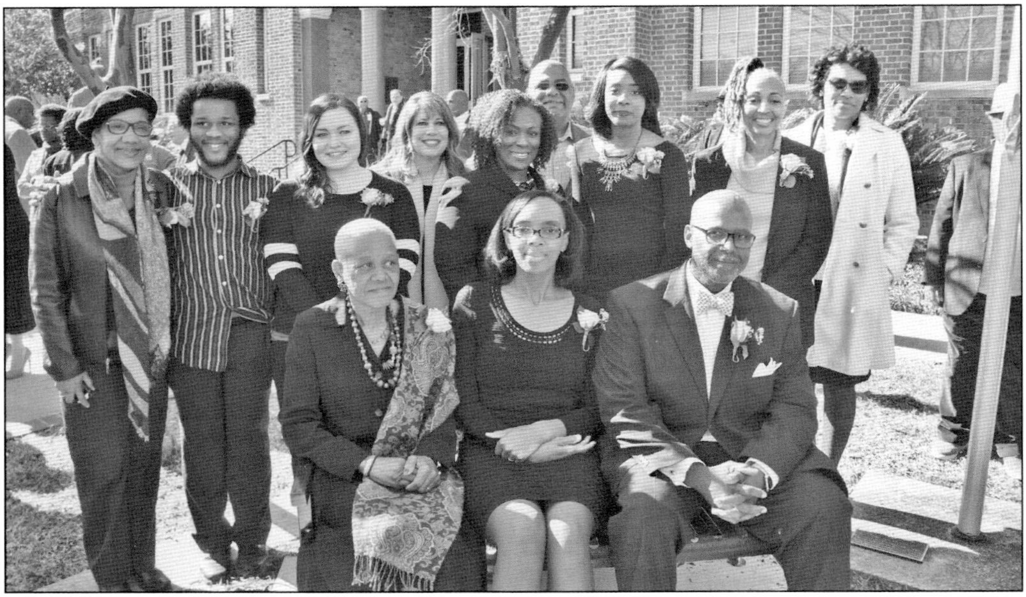

Members of the Baton Rouge Commemorative Committee are pictured above with the cochairs of the Toni Morrison Society's Bench by the Road Project. Committee members, from left to right, are (seated) Sadie Roberts Joseph, Dr. Lori Latrice Martin, and pastor Raymond A. Jetson; (standing) Dr. Joyce Jackson, Jeremiah Anthony Rogers, Sarah Corie, Lisa Freeman, Modrall Lathers, Marc Garnier, Kali Johnson, Judge Trudy White, and April Hawthorne. Joseph is the founder and curator of the Odell S. Williams Now and Then African American Museum, dedicated to preserving the history of blacks in South Baton Rouge. Dr. Martin and Pastor Jetson are the coauthors of this book and served as cochairs of the committee. Pictured below, from left to right, (seated) Sadie Roberts Joseph, Dr. Martin, and Dr. Carolyn Denard, cochair of the international commemorative project; (standing) Dr. Craig Stutman, cochair of the Bench by the Road Project, Russell Kelly, and Pastor Jetson. (Both, courtesy of Tat Yau.)

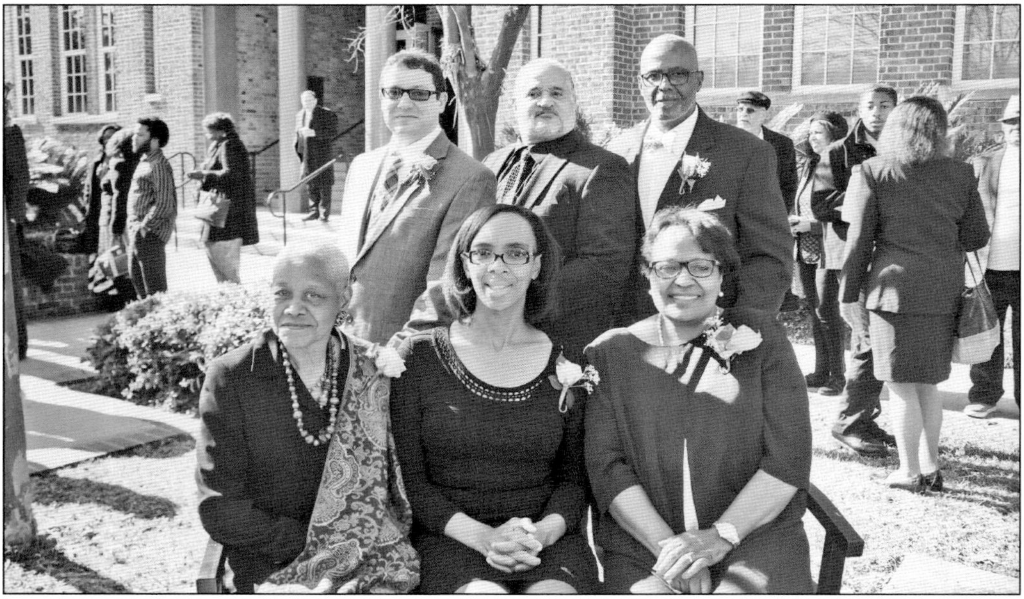

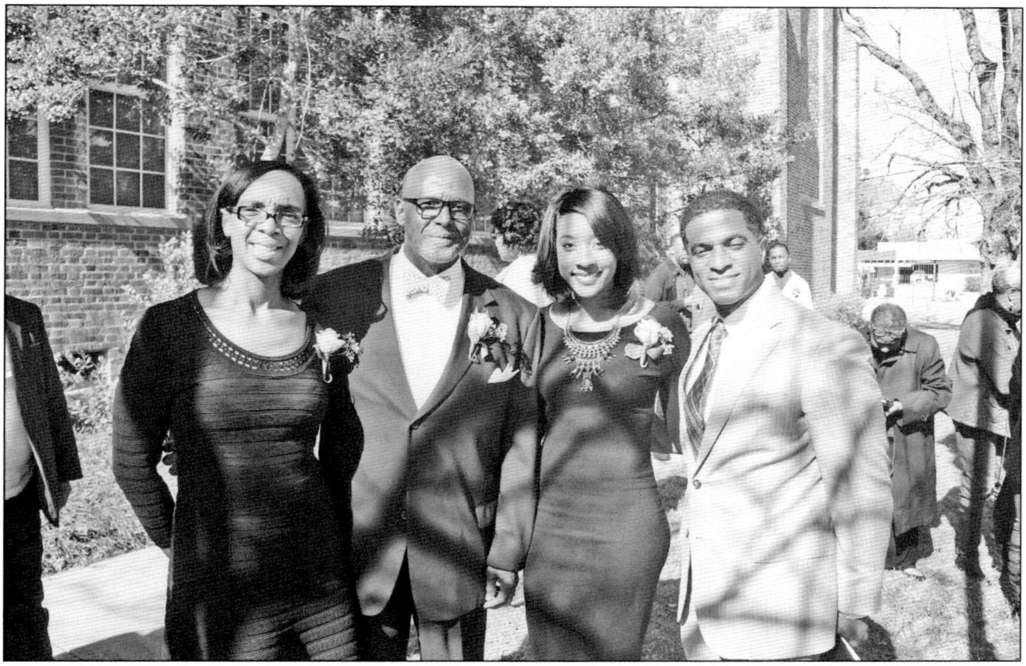

Key figures in the effort to remember the residents of South Baton Rouge and the historic bus boycott are pictured here. Above, from left to right, committee members Dr. Lori Martin, Rev. Raymond A. Jetson, and Kai Johnson are pictured with Chris Tyson (right), who delivered the keynote address. Tyson was born and raised in Baton Rouge. His grandmother is a graduate of McKinley High School, and he has fond memories of visiting relatives and patronizing businesses in the historic and predominately black community of South Baton Rouge. Below, LSU law professor Chris Tyson poses with Sadie Roberts. (Both, courtesy of Tat Yau.)

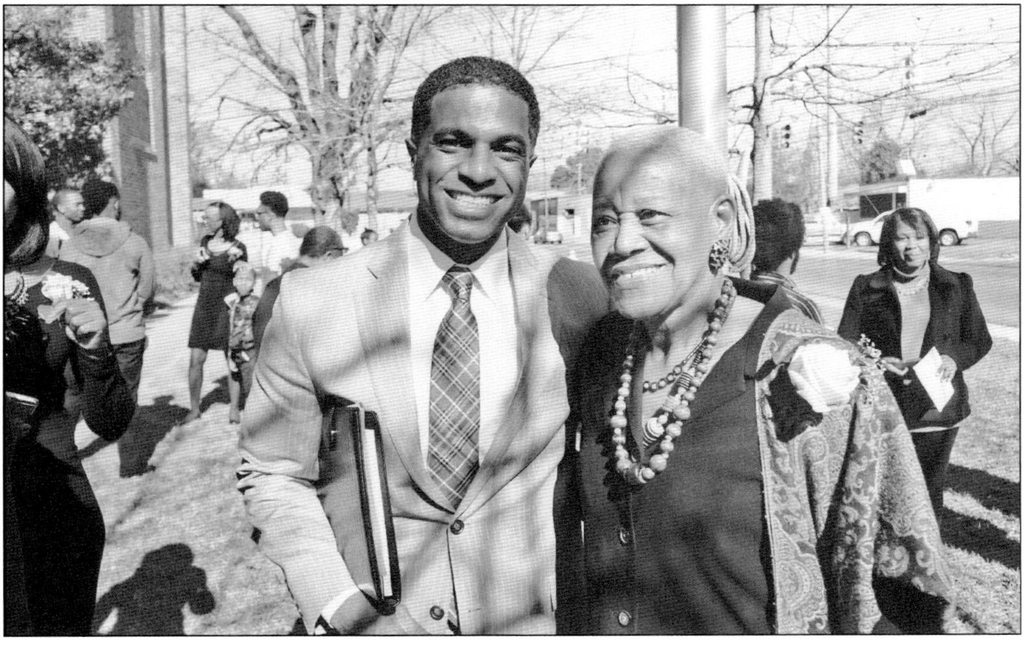

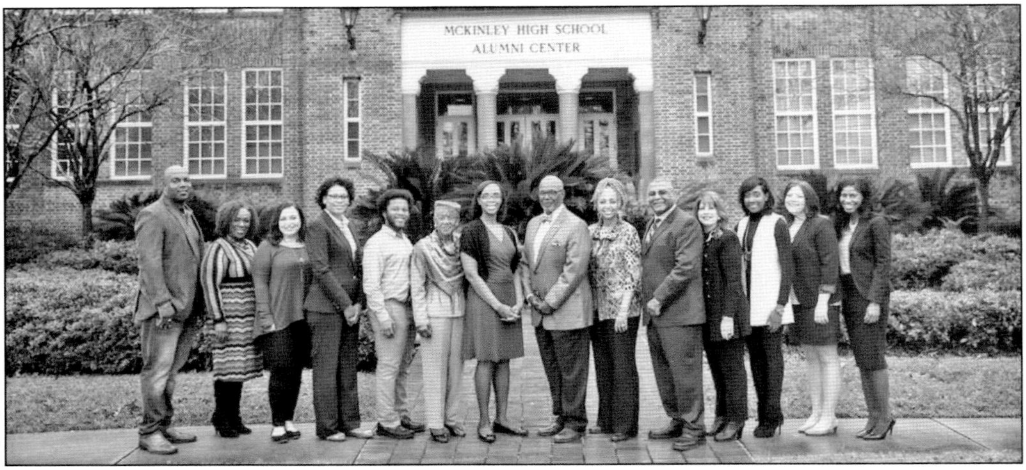

Each Bench by the Road is accompanied by a large plaque as well as a smaller plaque affixed directly to the bench. Many members of the planning committee are pictured above in front of the McKinley High School Alumni Center. From left to right are Garrick Mayweather, Modrall Lathers, Sara Corie, April Hawthorne, Jeremiah Anthony Rogers, Sadie Roberts Joseph, Lori Latrice Martin, Raymond A. Jetson, Judge Trudy White, Marc Garnier, Lisa Freeman, Kali Johnson, Melanie Henderson, and Ronnise Clark. The bench was made possible through generous donations from Aetna Better Health Louisiana and MetroMorphosis, Inc. It is located on the grounds of McKinley High School Alumni Center on Thomas H. Delpit Drive in South Baton Rouge, near the flagpole. The picture below shows the building when it was used as a high school. (Courtesy of Collin Ritchie.)

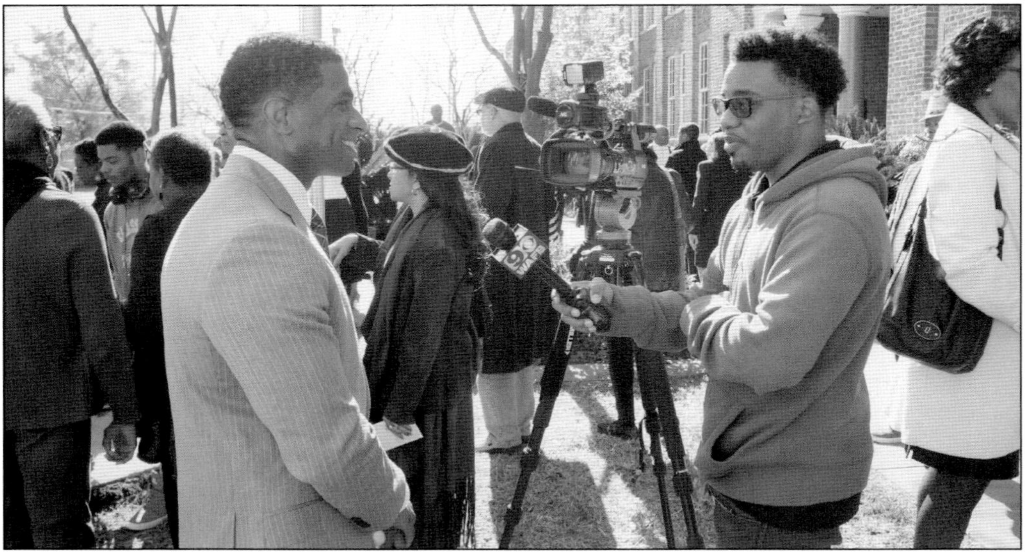

A reporter from local news station WAFB interviews Christopher Tyson (left) outside the former home of McKinley High School. Tyson is a former candidate for Louisiana secretary of state in 2015 and a Louisiana State law professor. For much of the 20th century, McKinley High Schools was the only place people of color could earn a high school diploma in East Baton Rouge Parish. The alumni center, which is located in the heart of South Baton Rouge, serves as a meeting place for residents and contains memorabilia from the original high school, including photographs of and artifacts from proud McKinley alumni. (Courtesy of Tat Yau.)

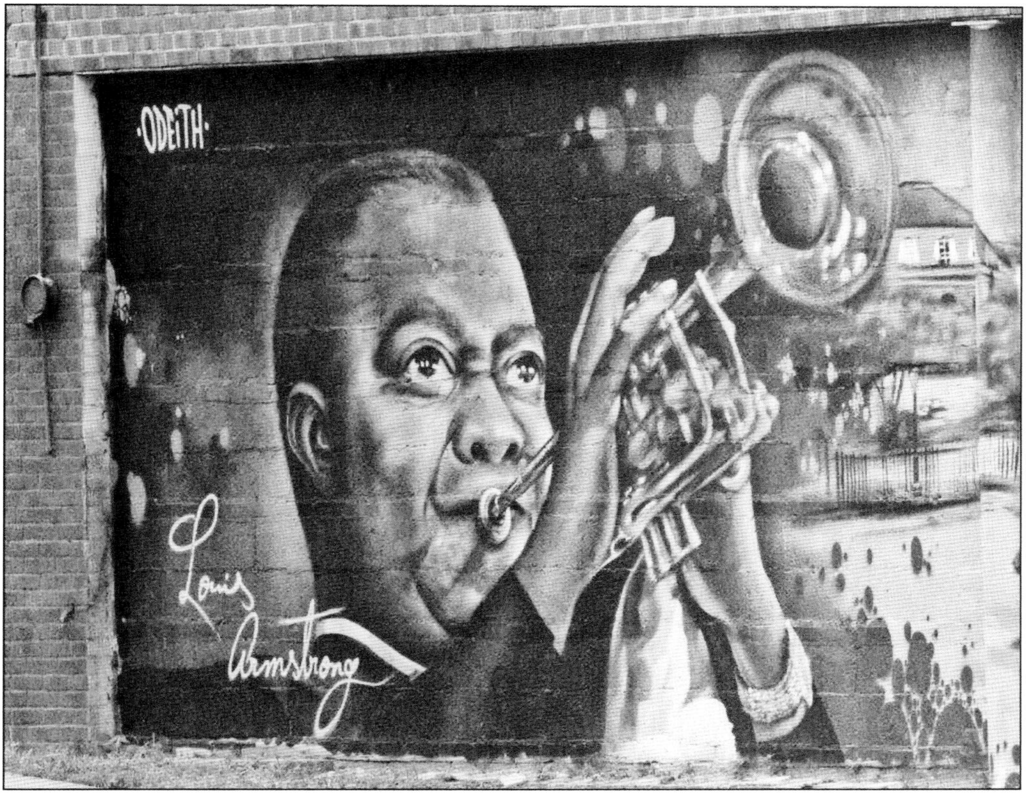

Other efforts to preserve the history of the African American experience in South Baton Rouge include a public arts project. Music is an important part of culture in America and in Louisiana. Jazz and the blues are especially influential. Louis Armstrong is memorialized in the public art project above, and black women are not forgotten. On a home in South Baton Rouge, the mural seen below features a black woman. (Both, courtesy of Marvin Broome.)

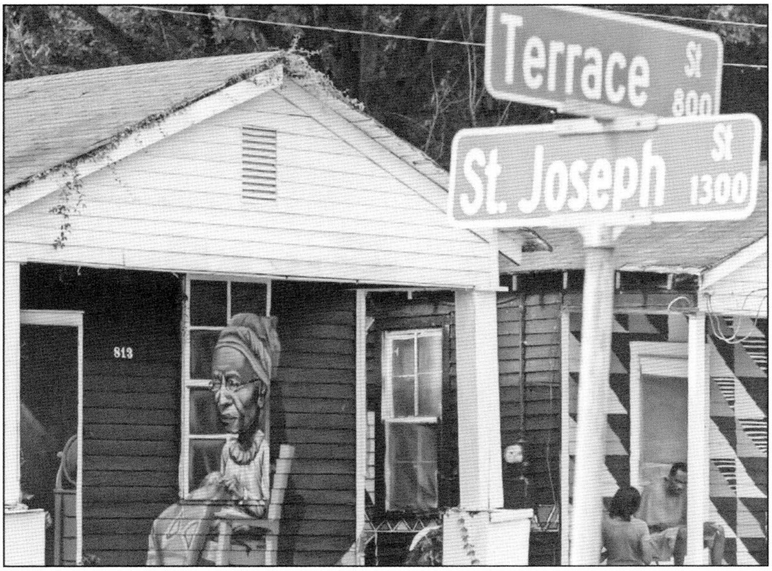

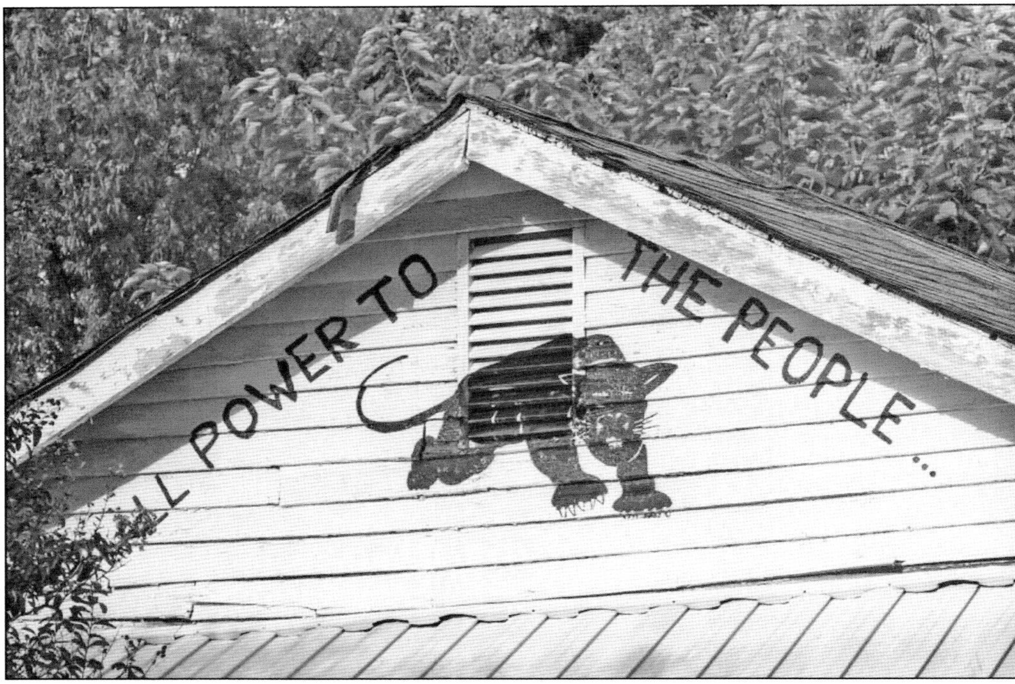

The mural above in South Baton Rouge pays tribute to the influence of the Black Power movement in Louisiana and in South Baton Rouge in particular. Black figures including Malcolm X (center) are also depicted in the image below. (Both, courtesy of Marvin Broome.)

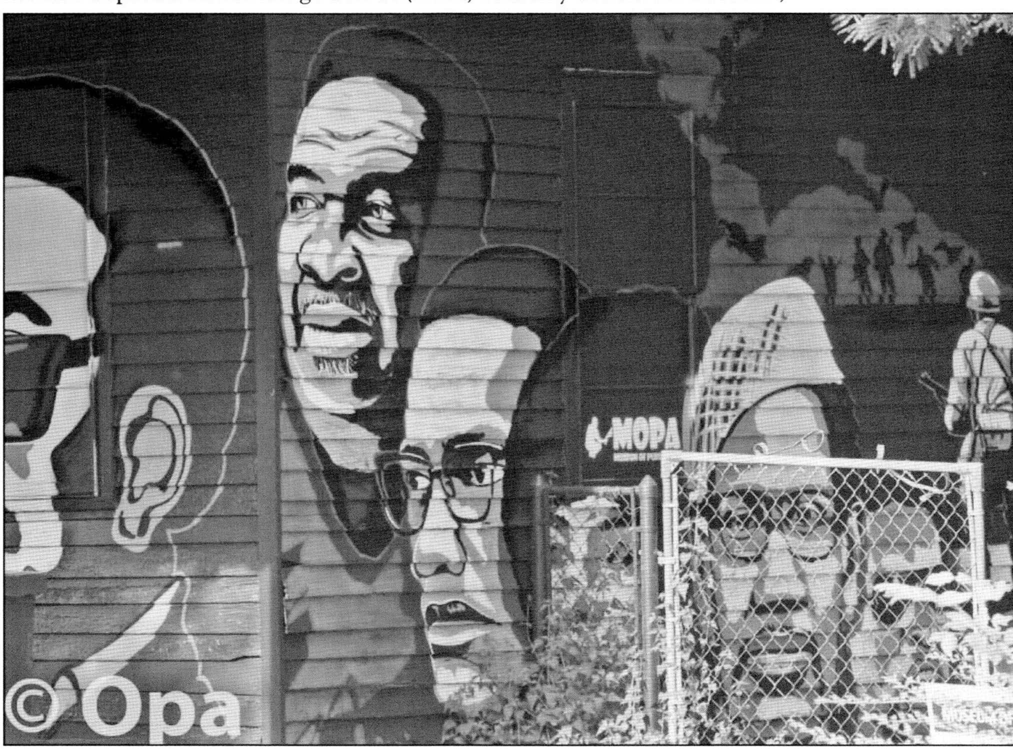

Joe Delpit, the first black city councilperson, is immortalized in a public mural with his image next to one dedicated to the 1953 bus boycott. The mural, photographed by Marvin Broome, also includes the names of other prominent figures associated with the boycott, including Willis Reed, attorney Johnnie Jones, and Martha White, known as the "Rosa Parks of the Baton Rouge bus boycott." Another view of the mural of a black woman on the house at the intersection of Terrace and St. Joseph Streets in South Baton Rouge is shown below. (Both, courtesy of Marvin Broome.)

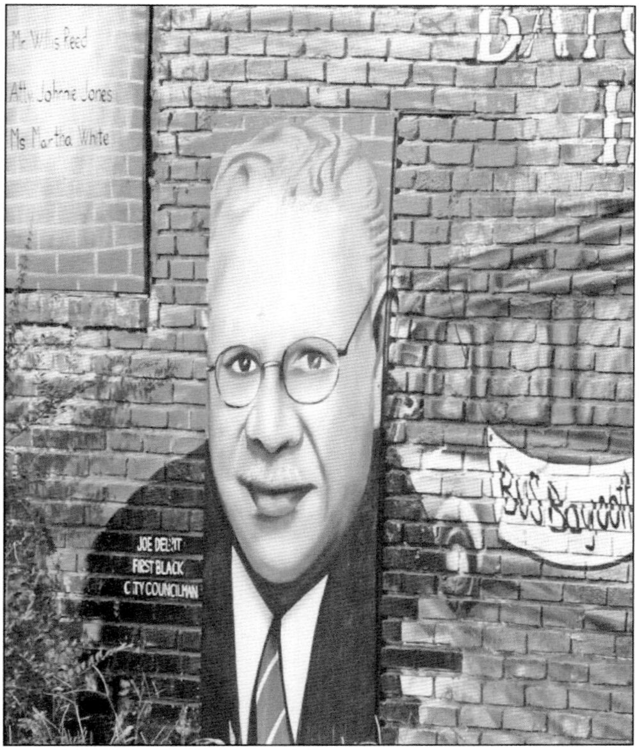

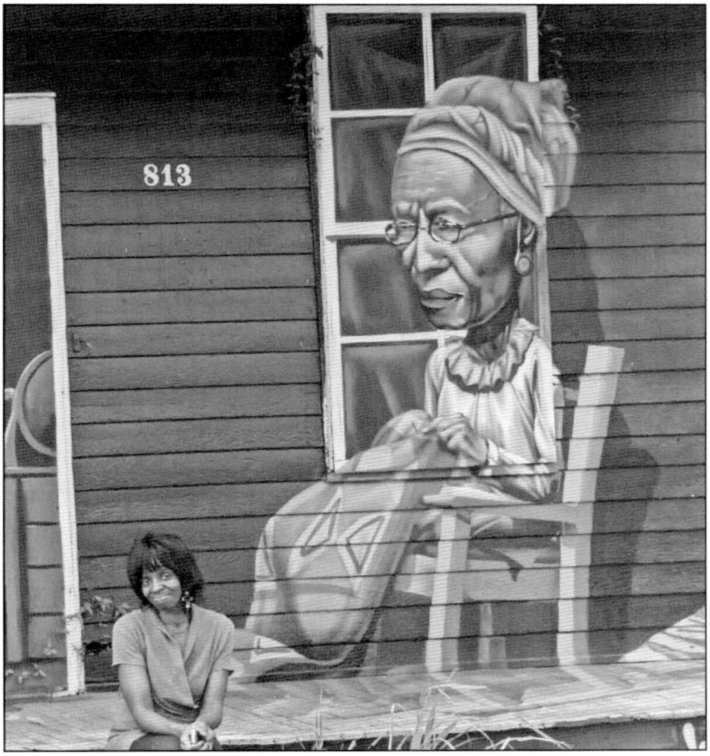

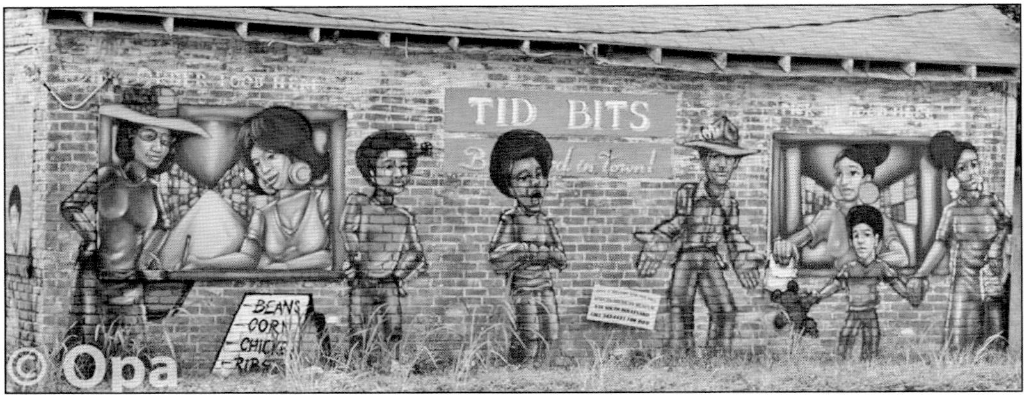

Images from the public arts project pay tribute to important businesses and families. The image below makes it clear that the purpose of the public arts project is to share Baton Rouge history and includes empowering messages about collective action, including black men, women, and children holding signs that read "Let's come together!," "Education is the Key!," and "Knowledge is Power!," with messages calling for unity and community. (Both, courtesy of Marvin Broome.)

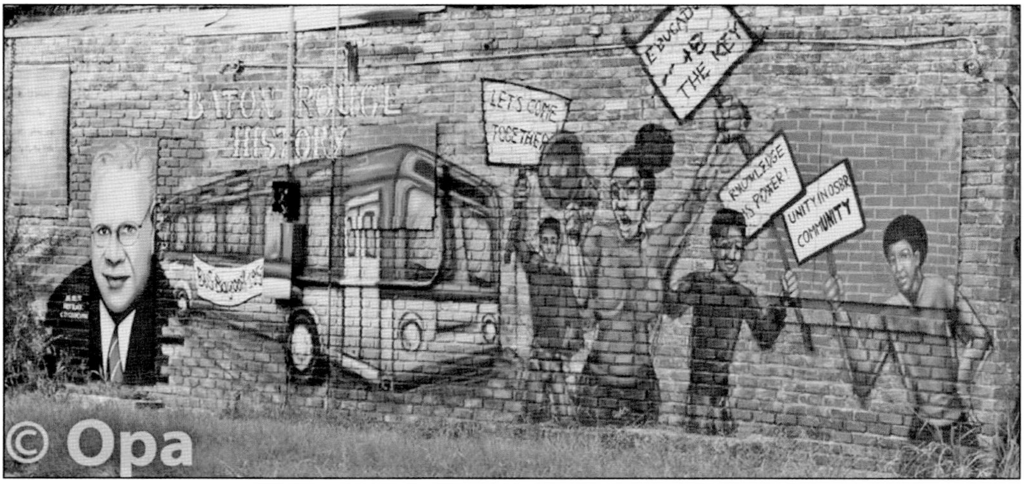

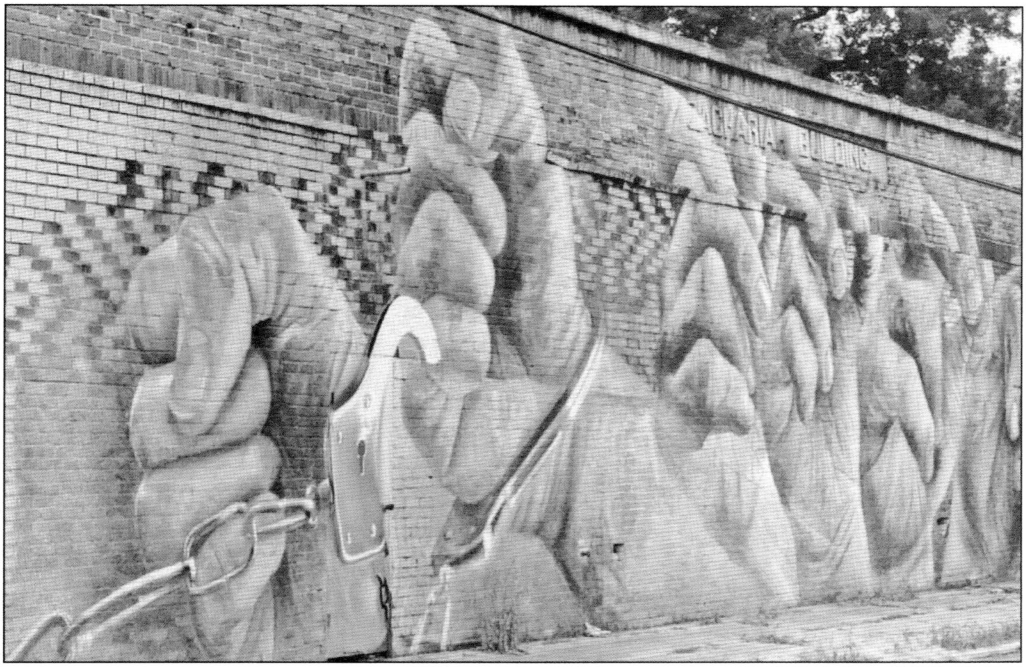

The mural above shows black hands with handcuffs. Some of the handcuffs are closed and some are open. One might interpret the mural as addressing the need to free oneself or the community from the challenges holding it back or more literally as a call to end the mass incarceration impacting so many communities of color, including black South Baton Rouge. People in several zip codes in the community are part of citywide efforts to reduce violent crime, which has resulted in the stigmatization of some neighborhoods. The mural below is a tribute to black women and girls and to the diversity, strength, and beauty therein. (Both, courtesy of Marvin Broome.)

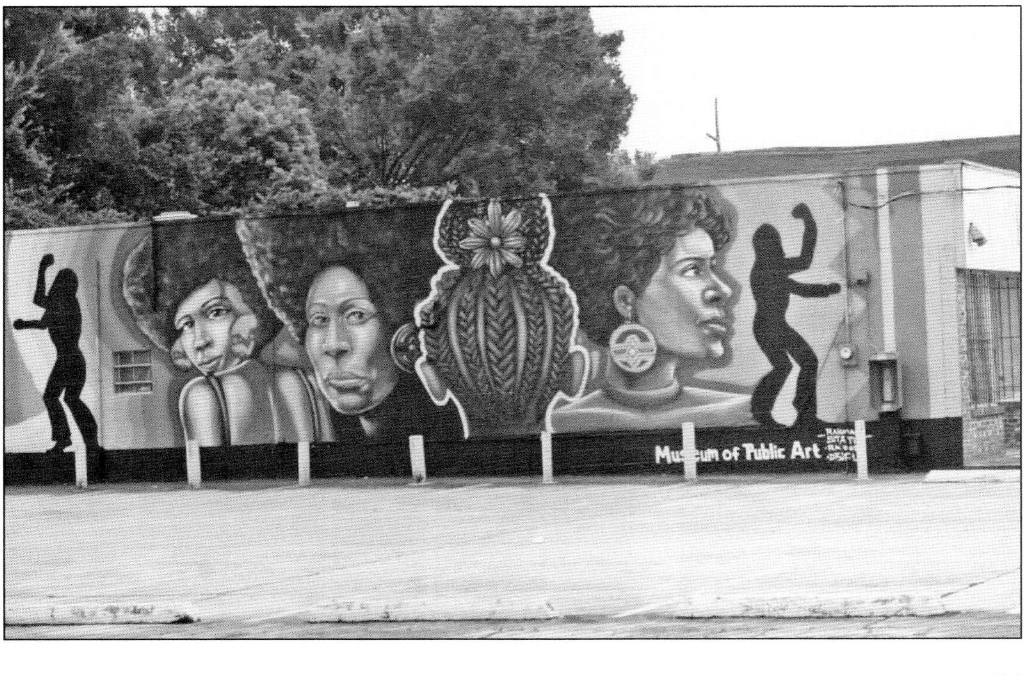

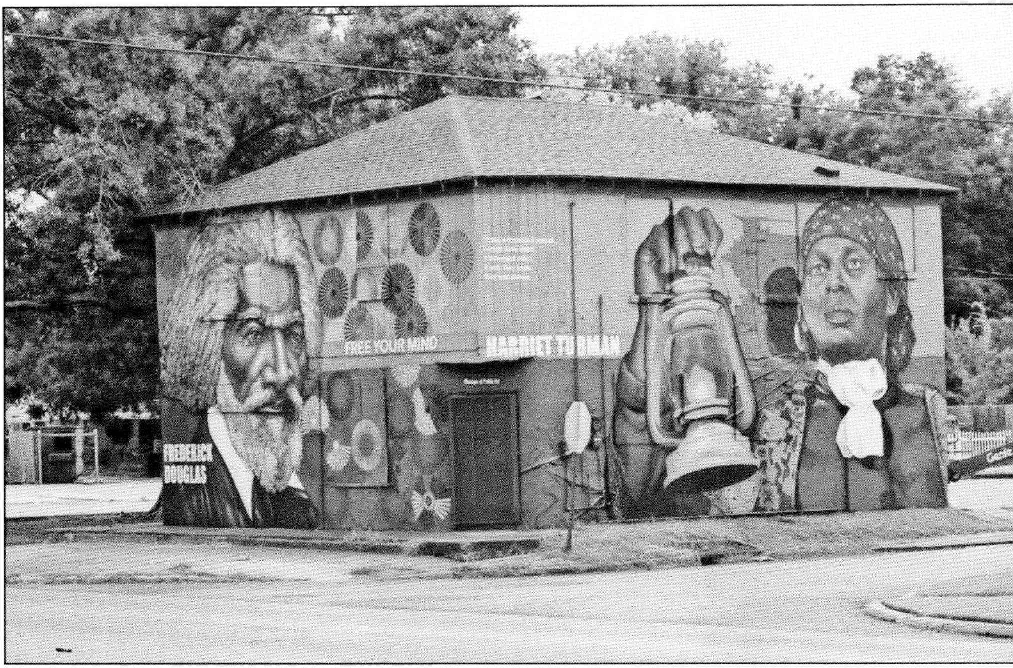

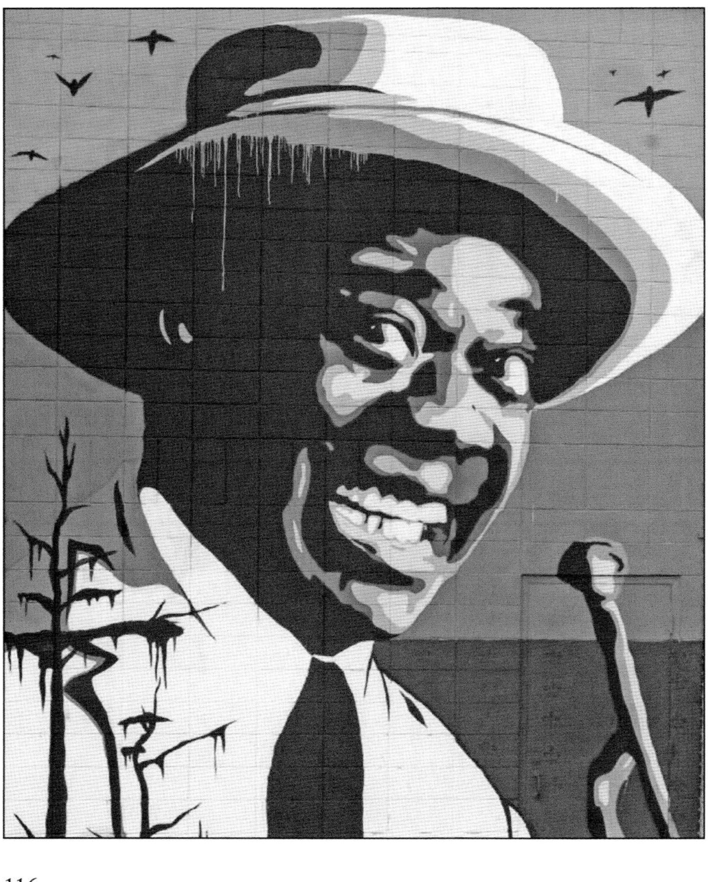

Tributes to Frederick Douglass and Harriet Tubman are featured in the above photograph by Marvin Broome. The photograph at left shows another tribute to Louis Armstrong, who was not only a giant in the music world but also spent time in Baton Rouge, including in segregated hotels that served black performers in South Baton Rouge when they could not get rooms in white hotels. (Both, courtesy of Marvin Broome.)

Five

Perfomers to Presidents

South Baton Rouge chronicles some of the important people, places, and events in the community from the 1800s through the 1970s. South Baton Rouge has hosted people of African ancestry seeking a refuge from slavery, served as a haven to black performers denied service in the city's hotels and restaurants when Jim Crow laws were still on the books, and welcomed the nation's first black president. Clearly, this is a significant place in the hearts and minds of residents but also in the city, state, nation, and the world.

The first chapter provides a general overview of South Baton Rouge. Chapter 2 highlights important families, churches, schools, and institutions. It shows social institutions that played important roles in the lives of African Americans in general and in South Baton Rouge in particular. It highlights social institutions created to meet the basic human needs of residents in South Baton Rouge.

Chapter 3 discusses how blacks in Baton Rouge experienced unequal treatment for centuries but maintained hope that change was on the horizon. The fight for social justice in South Baton Rouge mirrored the fight in other parts of the Deep South and in the nation. The chapter includes pictures from some of the most significant fights for equal treatment, such as the establishment of Brooks Park, the 1953 Baton Rouge bus boycott, the Kress sit-ins, and the integration of segregated schools.

Chapter 4 highlights South Baton Rouge's selection by an international society because of its historical significance in the lives of people of African ancestry. While America, including South Baton Rouge, is home to many monuments and memorials to a host of historic events, places, and people, prior to the installation of the Baton Rouge bench, there were no structures in this community dedicated to the experiences of enslaved Africans or their descendants. The Toni Morrison Society's goal of addressing the oversight in America's efforts to collectively remember and commemorate its past through the creation of the Bench by the Road Project was realized in South Baton Rouge. Images from the dedication capture the significance of the historic moment. The society plans to publish a book highlighting each of the first 20 bench locations, including South Baton Rouge

The authors are pleased the images in this important work show the important role South Baton Rouge has played in the lives of people of African ancestry. The area was a haven for fleeing slaves and a home to free people of color. South Baton Rouge was a place where black people were challenged, resisted, and thrived for many years. The residents upheld the tradition of self-help by establishing their own businesses and schools when Jim Crow laws forced the separation of blacks and whites in all areas of public and private life. South Baton Rouge provided a place to stay and play for entertainers traveling through nearby cities who could not stay in area hotels because of the color of their skin. Residents of South Baton Rouge showed what people could accomplish by simply refusing to accept the status quo. They fought for their children's lives, pooled their resources, and established Brooks Park. They declared their dignity and right to equal treatment by refusing to ride buses until their despair became the city's change. They succeeded in providing what Dr. Calvin Mackie cited as critical to bringing about transformative change during a talk to members of the all-male Urban Leadership Development Institute on Saturday, June 11, 2016, in Baton Rouge. The residents of South Baton Rouge provided the leadership and the people of Montgomery, Alabama, with the structure, standards, and strategy to achieve victory in what must have seemed like an improbable and very hostile racial climate.

Given the rich history of the people of South Baton Rouge, it is not surprising that the first black president chose the area as the site for his historic visit to the state in January 2016. Pres. Barack Obama picked South Baton Rouge to host a town hall meeting and spoke at McKinley High School. Hundreds of South Baton Rouge residents stood in line for hours for the chance to receive tickets to be in the same room as President Obama. The first black president addressed a crowd of predominately black residents in the first high school for blacks in Southeast Louisiana. The significance of his visit was not lost on these residents, especially those with deep roots in the immediate areas surrounding the historic high school.

Edward Pratt, columnist for the *Baton Rouge Advocate* and former president of the McKinley High School Alumni Association, penned a wonderful piece highlighting the significance of President Obama's visit in a section of the city regarded today by some as a distressed community. Pratt remarks how he felt watching the president of the United States walking into the gymnasium in the middle of a cheering audience. He remarks how many of the audience members never thought they would drive through "the Bottom" on purpose, park their cars on unfamiliar streets, and set foot on McKinley's campus. For Pratt and others, it was simply incredible what some people will do to see the most powerful man in the world, who happens to be black. Pratt goes on to defend his emphasis on the president's racial identity. He also states the president's racial identification is significant. He describes his column as anything but a typical column. Pratt says it is all about him, his blackness, and his feelings about seeing Obama at his school. It is about where Pratt and others grew up—South Baton Rouge, a place considered by some whites as undesirable and at the same time by African American residents as a very nurturing environment that provided the intellectual and spiritual foundation that produced many talented men and women of color.

Pratt adds that the president's visit was not just about politics. The visit was also about seeing a man who could have bought two-for-a-penny butter cookies from the corner store near Pratt's house. He could have been with Pratt and his friends at the Chicken Shack listening to music, talking stuff while gorging two-piece orders with two sides. The visit was also about Pratt's late grandmother, Annie Rose, and how he wished she could have been in the crowd to see the president. Pratt laments that, after explaining to her that this was really "*the* Obama," the black president everyone was talking about, she probably would have wept tears drawn from a lifetime of pain and racism. Images from the historic presidential visit follow and conclude this effort to document the rich and diverse experiences of black South Baton Rouge.

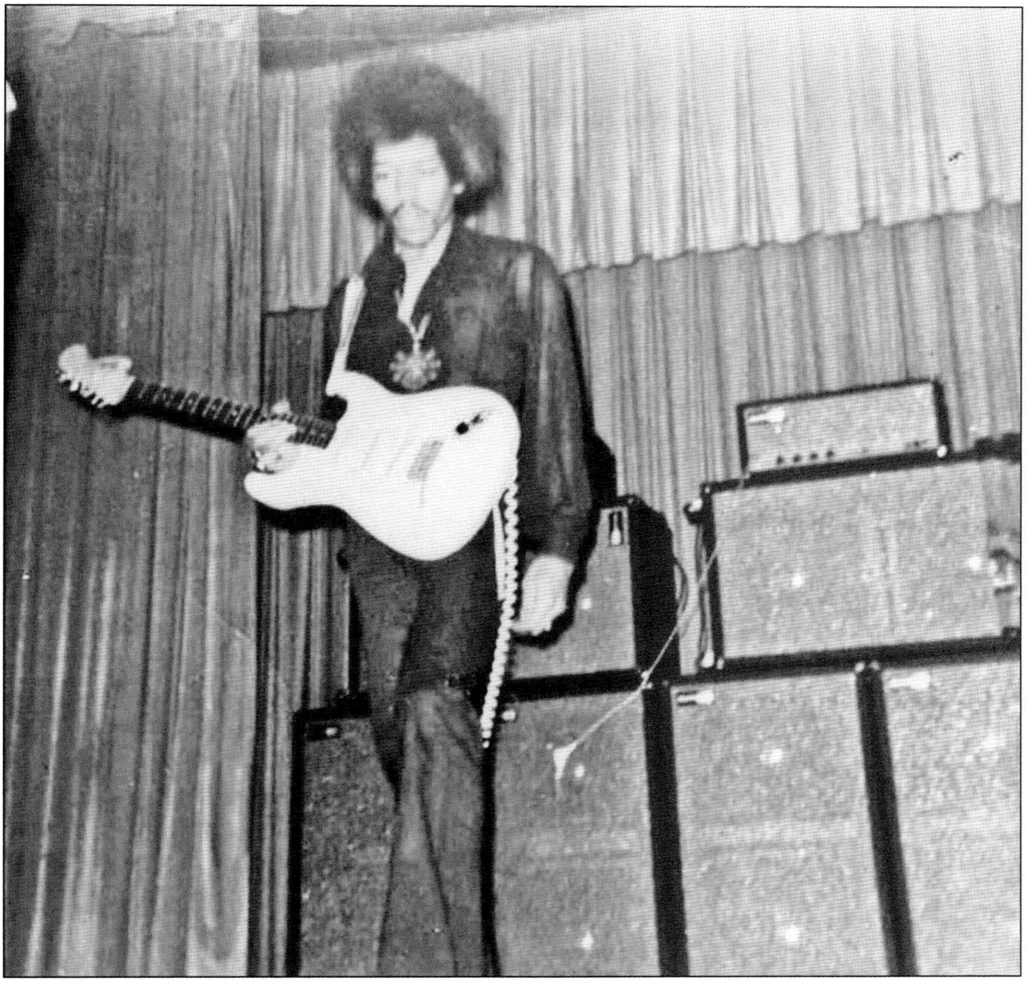

South Baton Rouge has opened its doors and welcomed with open arms people from all walks of life, from performers to the first black president. Famed guitarist Jimi Hendrix is pictured during a performance at Independence Hall in South Baton Rouge in August 1968. (Courtesy of Joe Richardson.)

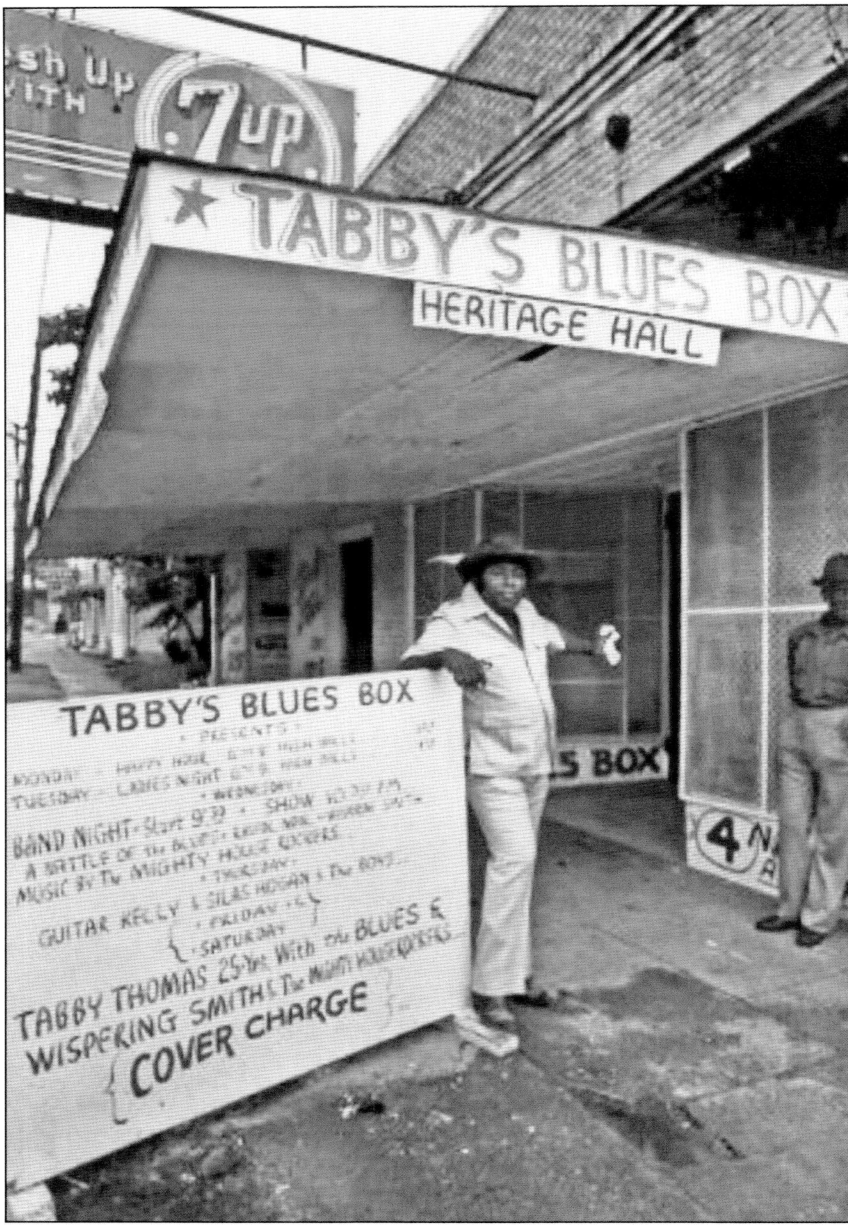

Tabby Thomas is pictured here in front of his establishment in South Baton Rouge, Tabby's Blues Box. The February 16, 2014, *New York Times* reports that there was a time, several decades ago, when Baton Rouge was not only the blues capital of Louisiana but also one of the busiest blues centers in the entire United States. From ramshackle juke joints in the countryside to rough blues bars scattered throughout the city came the raw sound of some of the greats of the genre—Slim Harpo, Raful Neal, and Buddy Guy. It was nothing short of a golden age. That was a while ago now, though. As the legends disappeared, so did the places they once played; there are few juke joints left anywhere, and most of the clubs have long since been torn down. For blues fans these days, Baton Rouge is an altogether much quieter affair. (Courtesy of East Baton Rouge Parish Public Library Digital Archive.)

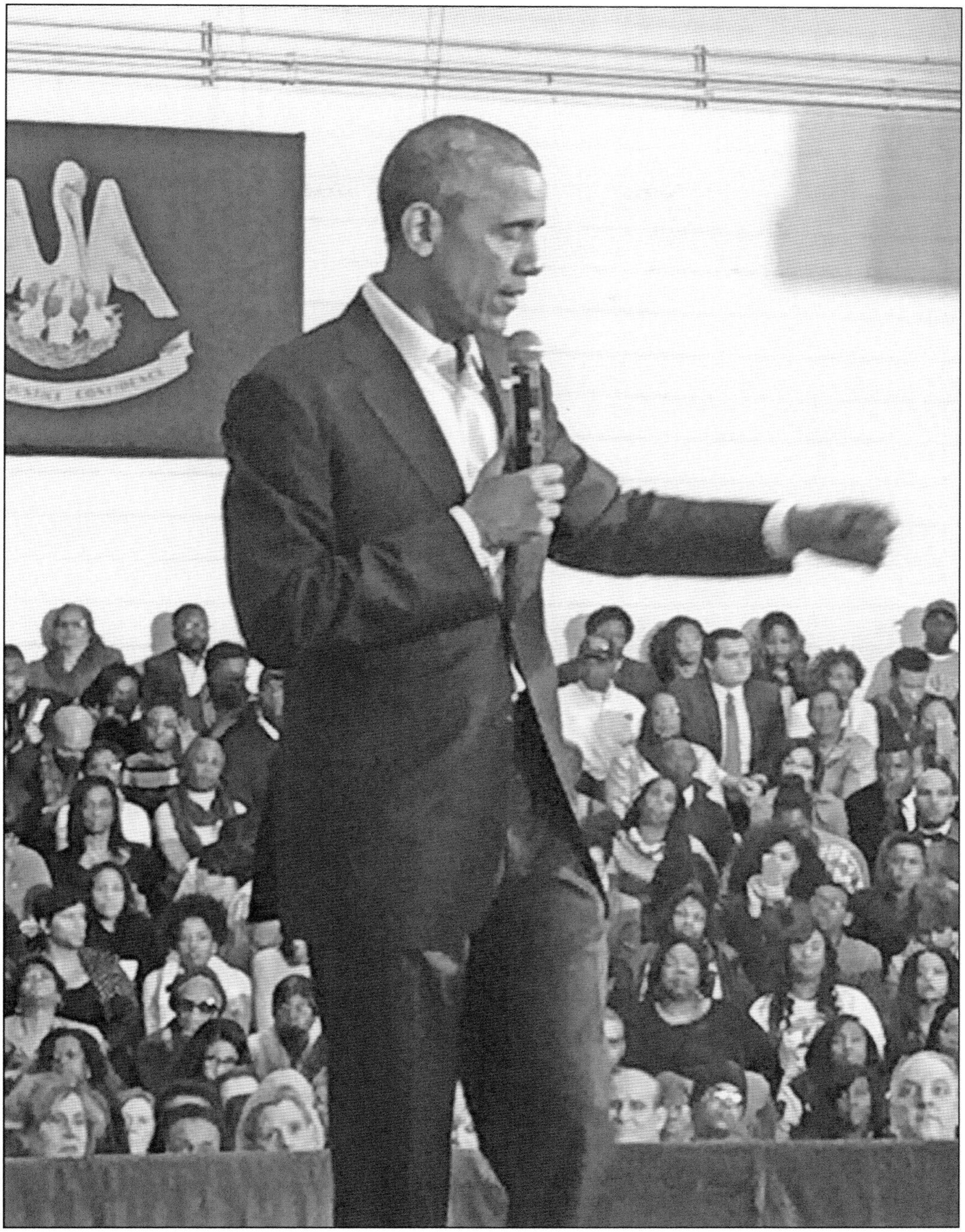

South Baton Rouge hosted the nation's first black president in January 2016. Of all the places in the world the president could have chosen, he chose to meet the predominately black residents of South Baton Rouge in one of the first places blacks could receive a high school education in all of southern Louisiana. He chose to visit the site of the nation's first bus boycott. A place many residents of the region only drive through on their way from home in the suburbs to work and back was chosen by the president for a town hall meeting during his last year in office. Photographs from the historic town hall meeting are presented here. (Courtesy of Kendra Wisham.)

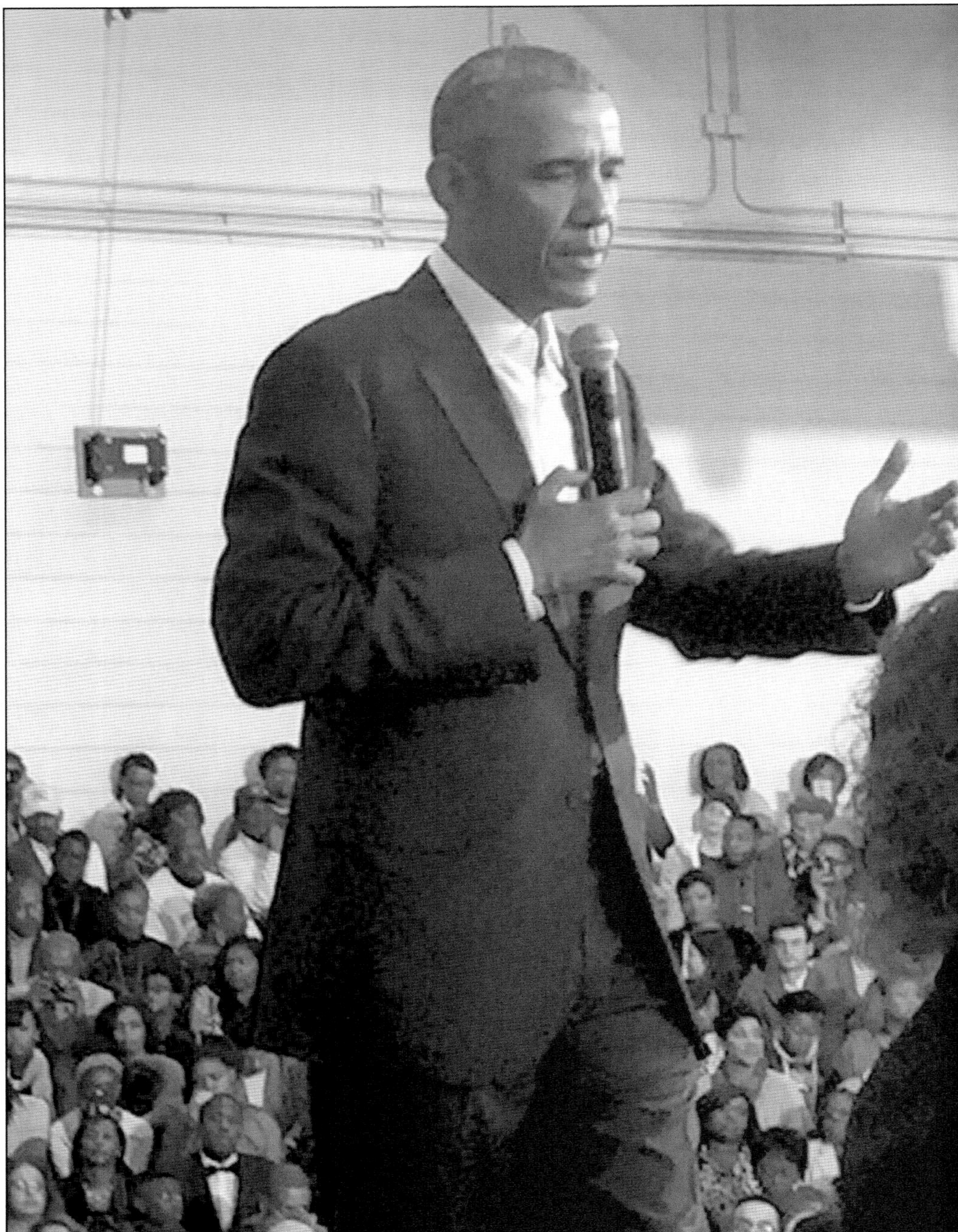

Louisiana has hosted many presidents and presidential hopefuls. South Baton Rouge made history when it hosted America's first black president in January 2016. Residents of South Baton Rouge braved cold temperatures, waiting in long lines at McKinley High School Alumni Center for a limited number of free tickets to hear Pres. Barack Obama speak in the gymnasium of the current McKinley Senior High School. President Obama is pictured speaking to the crowd. (Courtesy of Kendra Wisham.)

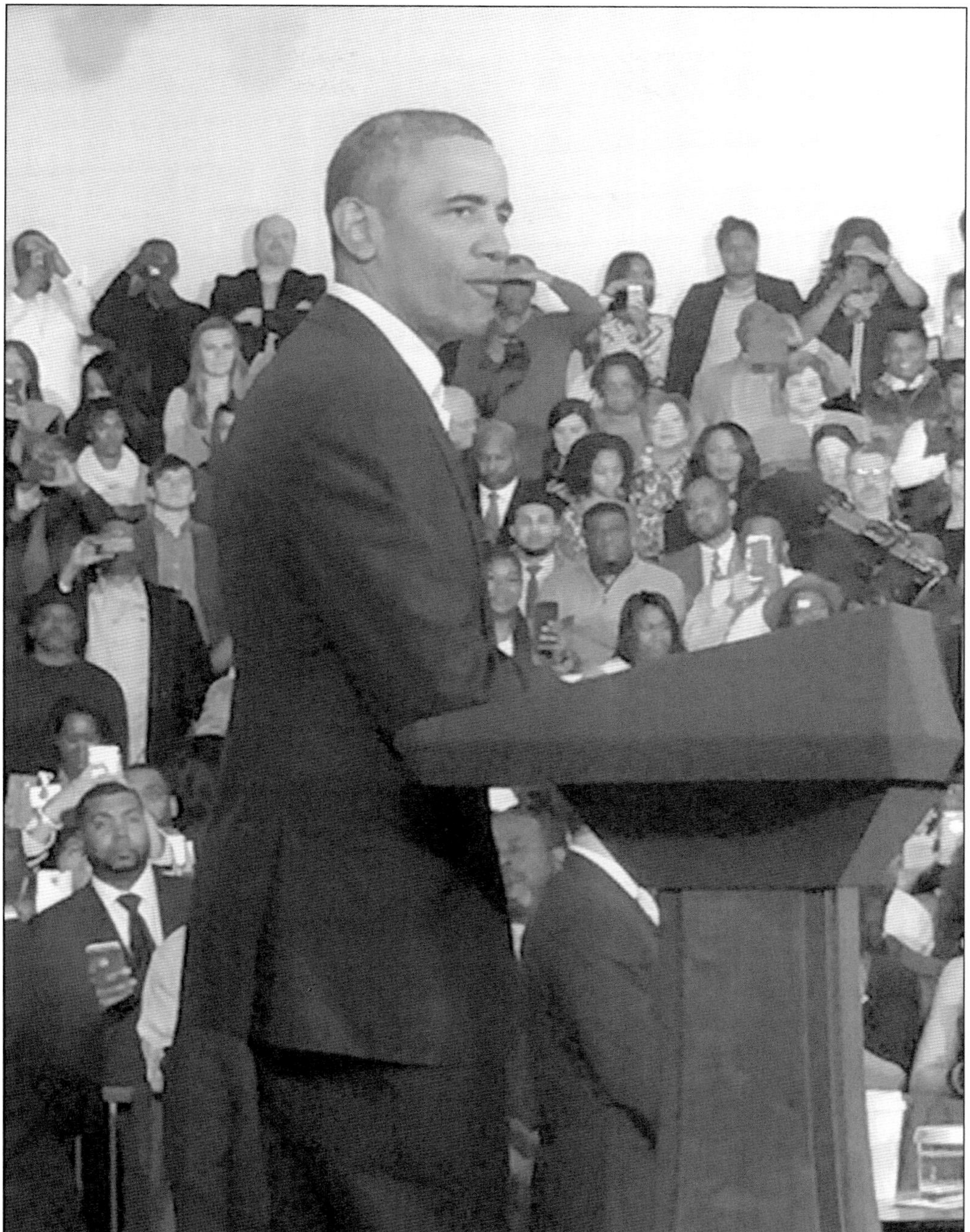

President Obama fielded a number of questions from the individuals in attendance. He was asked to comment on his regrets and future plans. The president was asked about a number of public policies, including his administration's plans to assist ex-offenders as they transition from jails and prisons to mainstream society. The future of historically black colleges and universities was also a topic of discussion, which was especially important to the many people in attendance who were proud graduates of Southern University. (Courtesy of Kendra Wisham.)

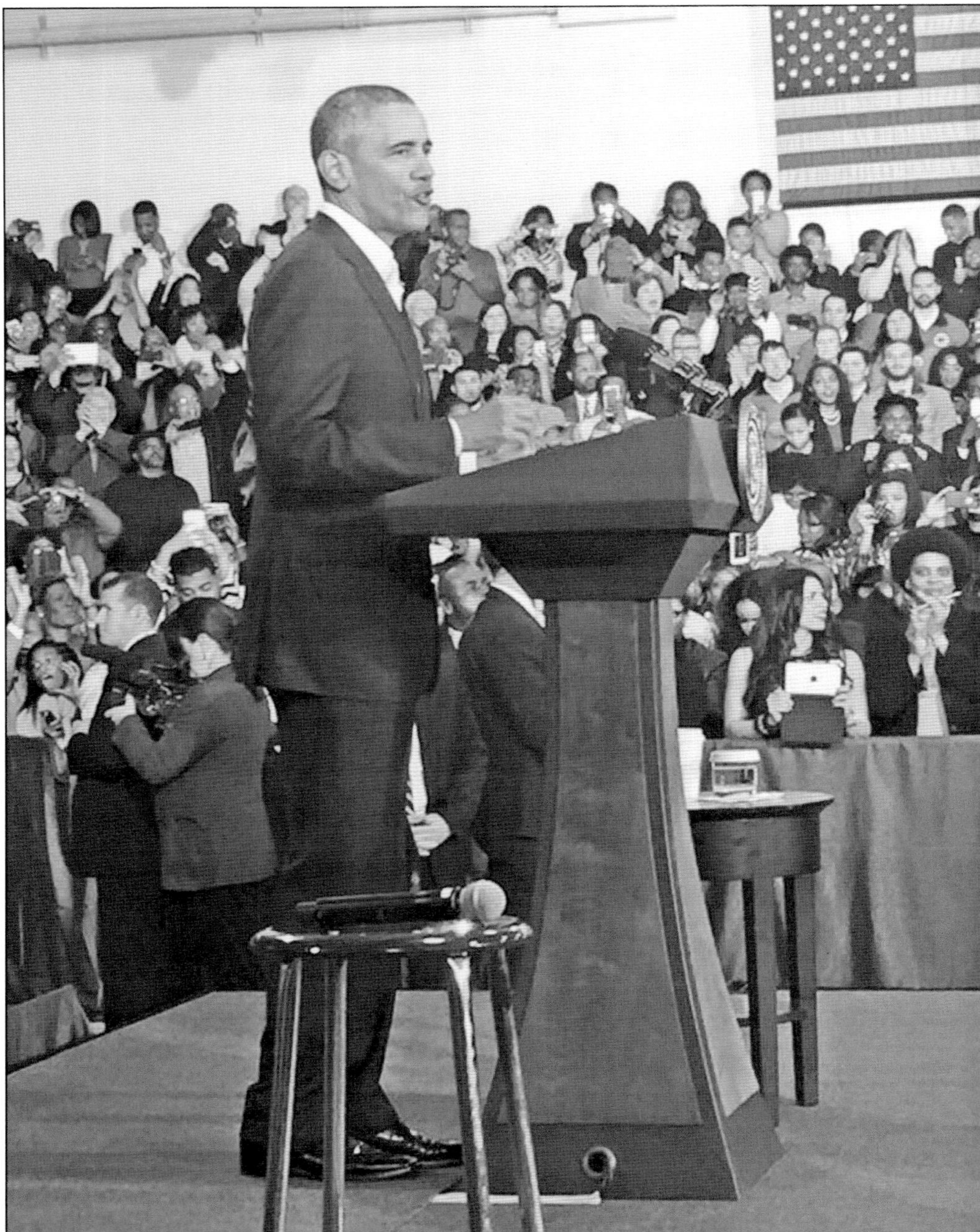

President Obama speaks at McKinley High School. Many in the audience had long familial ties to South Baton Rouge. Garrick Mayweather, executive director of the McKinley High School Alumni Center, is the grandson of a graduate of McKinley High School, and his second child is a recent graduate. Twenty current students were granted tickets to the town hall meeting. Five students from each grade were chosen through a lottery. The school district provided live streaming of President Obama's address and interaction with residents of South Baton Rouge. (Courtesy of Kendra Wisham.)

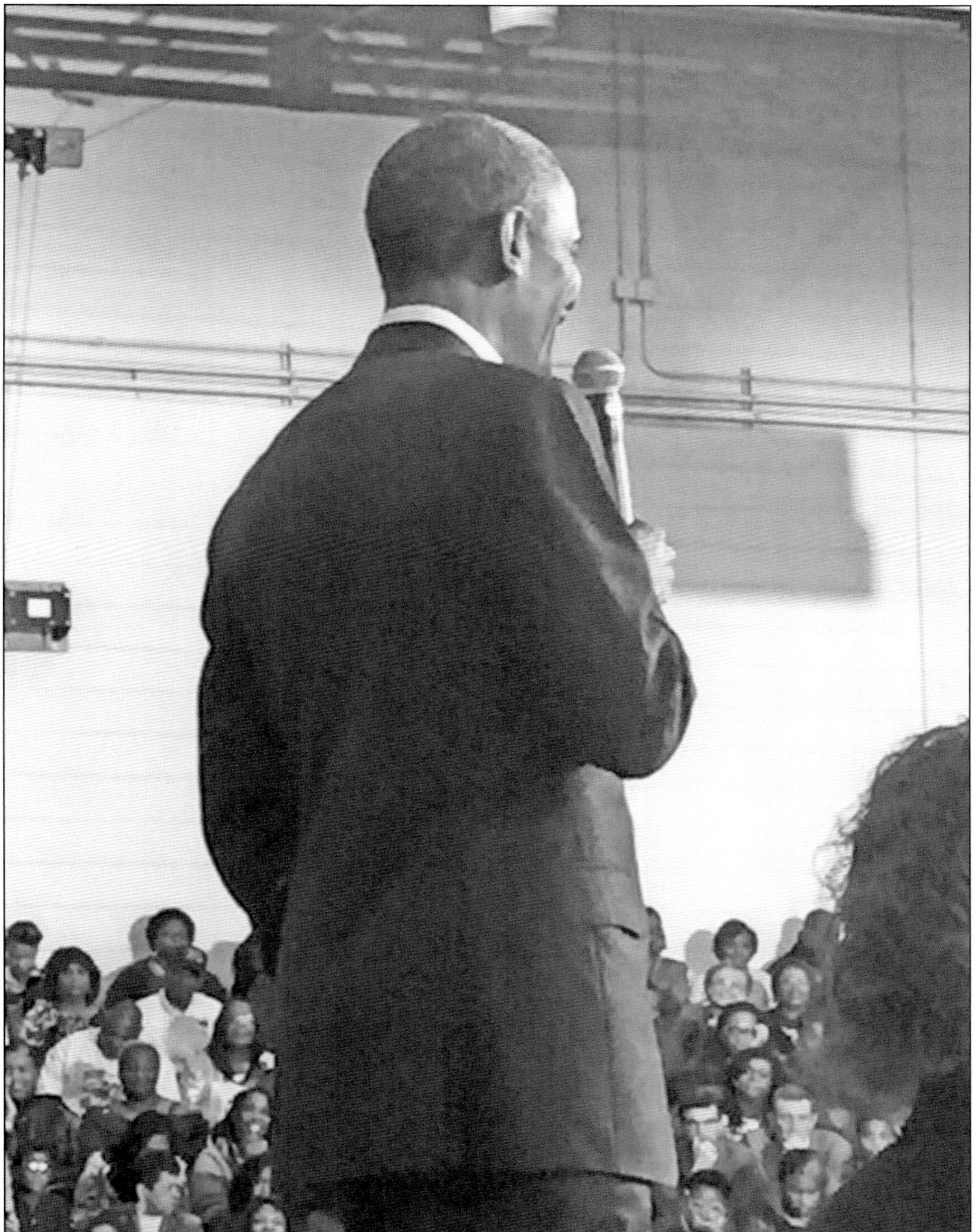

Pres. Barack Obama responds to questions. The visit from President Obama will not soon be forgotten by the hundreds of people in the venue or by the thousands of other residents watching as the president addressed South Baton Rouge and the nation. President Obama was introduced by McKinley High School's Student of the Year, Che'dra Joseph. Joseph delivered a memorable speech in which she thanked President Obama for giving the nation a nontraditional model of success. (Courtesy of Kendra Wisham.)

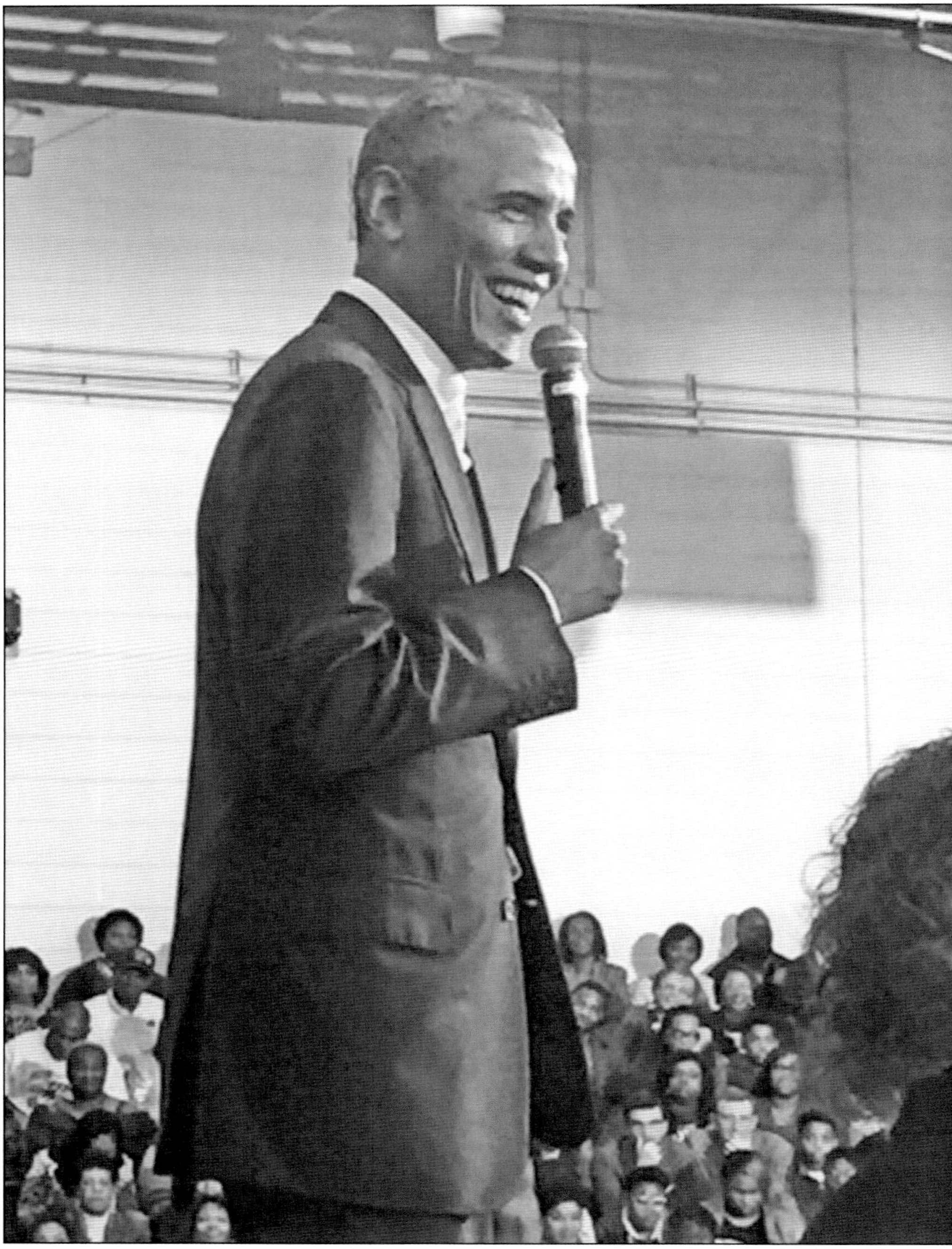

President Obama speaks about his plans after he leaves the White House. He told the hundreds gathered at the historic high school that he and his wife, First Lady Michelle Obama, plan to continue to focus on issues near and dear to their hearts, including political participation for young people, education, and international development. Before leaving Baton Rouge, President Obama dined on food from historic area businesses and answered questions live on social media. (Courtesy of Kendra Wisham.)

About the Authors

Lori Latrice Martin is associate professor of sociology and African and African American studies at Louisiana State University. Dr. Martin earned a bachelor's degree from Fordham University and a master's degree from University at Buffalo, State University of New York. Dr. Martin completed her doctoral studies from University at Albany, State University of New York. Her recent publications include *The Ex-Slave's Fortune: The Story of Cynthia D. Hestra* and *White Sports Black Sports*. Dr. Martin lives in Baton Rouge with her husband, Derrick, and two sons, Emir and Derrick Jr.

Raymond A. Jetson is a lifelong resident of Baton Rouge. He is president and chief executive officer of MetroMorphosis, Inc., and pastor of Star Hill Church. Jetson served as the state representative for District 61 in the Louisiana House of Representatives for more than 15 years. His many years of public service and experience have led Jetson to earn bachelor's and master's degrees at the New Orleans Theological Seminary. He and his wife, Tammy, are the proud parents of J'Erica Nicole and Jeremy Louis.